THE *HIGH SCHOOL*

PROBABILITY TUTOR®

D1403034

Staff of Research and Education Association
Dr. M. Fogiel, Chief Editor

Research and Education Association
61 Ethel Road West
Piscataway, New Jersey 08854

THE HIGH SCHOOL PROBABILITY TUTOR®

Printed in the United States of America

Library of Congress Catalog Card Number 95-67790

International Standard Book Number 0-87891-958-9

THE HIGH SCHOOL TUTOR is a registered trademark of Research & Education Association, Piscataway, New Jersey 08854

WHAT THIS BOOK IS FOR

For as long as probability has been taught in high schools, many students have found this subject difficult to understand and learn. Despite the publication of hundreds of textbooks in this field, each one intending to provide an improved approach to the subject over previous textbooks, students continue to be perplexed by these principles. As a result, probability often becomes a course taken only to meet school or departmental curriculum requirements.

In a study of the problem, REA found the following basic reasons underlying the difficulties that students experience with probability as it is taught in schools:

(a) No systematic rules of analysis have been developed which students may follow in a step-by-step manner to solve the usual problems encountered. This results from the fact that the numerous different conditions and principles which may be involved in a probability problem, lead to many possible different methods of solution. To prescribe a set of rules to be followed for each of the possible variations, would involve an enormous number of rules and steps to be searched through by students, and this task would perhaps be more burdensome than solving the problem directly with some accompanying trial and error to find the correct solution route.

(b) Probability textbooks currently available will usually explain a given principle in a few pages written by a professional who has an insight of the subject matter that is not shared by high school students. The explanations are often written in an abstract manner which leaves the students confused as to the application of the principle. The explanations given are not sufficiently detailed and extensive to make students aware of the wide range of applications and different aspects of the principle being studied. The numerous possible variations of principles and their applications are usually not discussed, and it is left for the students to discover these for themselves while doing exercises. Accordingly, the average student is expected to rediscover that which has been long known and practiced, but not published or explained extensively.

(c) The examples usually following the explanation of a topic are too few and too simple to enable the student to obtain a thorough grasp of the principles involved. The explanations do not provide sufficient basis to enable students to solve problems that may be subsequently assigned for homework or given on examinations.

The examples are presented in abbreviated form which leaves out much material between steps, and requires that students derive the omitted material themselves. As a result, students find the examples difficult to understand—contrary to the purpose of the examples.

Examples are, furthermore, often worded in a confusing manner. They do not state the problem and then present the solution. Instead, they pass through a general discussion, never revealing what is being sought.

Examples, also, do not always include diagrams/tables wherever appropriate, and students do not obtain the training to draw diagrams or tables to simplify and organize their thinking.

(d) Students can learn the subject only by doing the exercises themselves and reviewing them in class, to obtain experience in applying the principles with their different ramifications.

In doing the exercises by themselves, students find that they are required to devote considerably more time to probabilty than to other subjects of comparable credits, because they are uncertain with regard to the selection and application of the principles involved.

(e) When reviewing the exercises in classrooms, instructors usually request students to take turns in writing solutions on the boards and explaining them to the class. Students often find it difficult to explain in a manner that holds the interest of the class, and enables the remaining students to follow the material written on the boards. The remaining students seated in the class are, furthermore, too occupied with copying the material from the boards, to listen to the oral explanations and concentrate on the methods of solution.

This book is intended to aid high school students taking probability in overcoming the difficulties described, by supplying detailed illustrations of the solution methods which are usually not apparent to students. The solution methods are illustrated by problems selected from those that are most often assigned for class work and given on examinations. The problems are arranged in order of complexity to enable students to learn and understand a particular topic by reviewing the problems in sequence. The problems are illustrated with detailed step-by-step explanations, to save the students the large amount of time that is often needed to fill in the gaps that are usually found between steps of illustrations in textbooks or review/outline books.

The staff of REA considers that probability is best learned by viewing the methods of analysis and solution techniques. This approach to learning the subject matter is similar to that practiced in various scientific laboratories, particularly in the medical fields.

In using this book, students may review and study the illustrated problems at their own pace; they are not limited to the time allowed for explaining problems on the board in class.

When students want to look up a particular type of problem and solution, they can readily locate it in the book by referring to the index which has been extensively prepared. It is also possible to locate a particular type of problem by glancing at just the material within the boxed portions. To facilitate rapid scanning of the problems, each problem has a heavy border around it. Furthermore, each problem is identified with a number immediately above the problem at the right-hand margin.

To obtain maximum benefit from the book, students should familiarize themselves with the section, "How To Use This Book," located in the front pages.

To meet the objectives of this book, staff members of REA have selected problems usually encountered in assignments and examinations, and have solved each problem meticulously to illustrate the steps which are difficult for students to comprehend. REA would like to acknowledge Vance Berger, Ph.D., Adjunct Professor, Graduate School of Management, Rutgers University, for his writing and compiling of the manuscript. We would also like to acknowledge William Keller, Ph.D., Lufti Luftiyya, Ph.D., and Michael Wagner, B.S., for their editorial contributions to this book.

Max Fogiel, Ph.D.
Program Director

HOW TO USE THIS BOOK

This book can be an invaluable aid to probability students as a supplement to their textbooks. The book is subdivided into 10 chapters, each dealing with a separate topic. The subject matter is developed beginning with chapters which focus on basic concepts of probability, followd by chapters which discuss distributions, conditional probability, expectations, functions, and sampling theory.

TO LEARN AND UNDERSTAND A TOPIC THOROUGHLY

1. Refer to your class text and read the section pertaining to the topic. You should become acquainted with the principles discussed there. These principles, however, may not be clear to you at that time.

2. Then locate the topic you are looking for by referring to the "Table of Contents" in the front of this book.

3. Turn to the page where the topic begins and review the problems under each topic, in the order given. For each topic, the problems are arranged in order of complexity, from the simplest to the most difficult. Some problems may appear similar to others, but each problem has been selected to illustrate a different point or solution method.

To learn and understand a topic thoroughly and retain its contents, it will be generally necessary for students to review the problems several times. Repeated review is essential in order to gain experience in recognizing the principles that should be applied and in selecting the best solution technique.

TO FIND A PARTICULAR PROBLEM

To locate one or more problems related to a particular subject matter, refer to the index. In using the index, be certain to note that the numbers given there refer to problem numbers, not to page numbers. This arrangement of the index is intended to facilitate finding a problem more rapidly, since two or more problems may appear on a page.

If a particular type of problem cannot be found readily, it is recommended that the student refer to the "Table of Contents" in the front pages, and then turn to the chapter which is applicable to the problem being sought. By scanning or glancing at the material that is boxed, it will generally be possible to find problems related to the one being sought, without consuming considerable time. After the problems have been located, the solutions can be reviewed and studied in detail. For this purpose of locating problems rapidly, students should acquaint themselves with the organization of the book as found in the "Table of Contents."

In preparing for an exam, it is useful to find the topics to be covered on the exam in the "Table of Contents," and then review the problems under those topics several times. This should equip the student with what might be needed for the exam.

KEY TO TERMINOLOGY

Symbol	Explanation
$P\{A\}$	The probability of event A
Σ	Summation
$\sum_{i=1}^{4} i = 1 + 2 + 3 + 4 = 10$	On the bottom, "$i=1$" indicates to start at 1. On the top, "4" means to increment by 1 up to 4. "Σ" indicates to sum. The "i" indicates that what is being summed is "i," and "i" is the variable which is 1, 2, 3, and 4.

Contents

CHAPTER 1

BASIC CONCEPTS

VENN DIAGRAMS

In a survey carried out in a school snack shop, the following results were obtained. Of 100 boys questioned, 78 liked sweets, 74 liked ice cream, 53 liked cake, 57 liked both sweets and ice cream, 46 liked both sweets and cake, and only 31 boys liked all three. If all the boys interviewed liked at least one item, draw a Venn diagram to illustrate the results. How many boys like both ice cream and cake?

SOLUTION:

A Venn diagram is a pictorial representation of the relationship between sets. A set is a collection of objects. The number of objects in a particular set is the cardinality of a set.

To draw a Venn diagram, we start with the following picture:

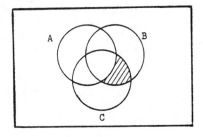

Each circle represents set *A*, *B*, or *C*, respectively. Let

A = set of boys who like ice cream,

B = set of boys who like cake,

C = set of boys who like sweets.

The sections of overlap between circles represents the members of one set who are also members of another set. For example, the shaded region in the picture indicates the set of boys who are in sets B and C but not A. This is the set of boys who like both cake and sweets but not ice cream. The inner section common to all three circles indicates the set of boys who belong to all three sets simultaneously.

We wish to find the number of boys who liked both ice cream and cake. Let us label the sections of the diagram with the cardinality of these sections. The cardinality of the region common to all three sets is the number of boys who liked all three items, or 31.

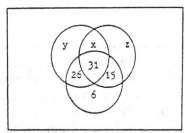

The number of boys who like ice cream and sweets was 57. Of these 57, 31 like all three, leaving 26 boys in set *A* and set *C* but not set *B*. Similarly, there are 15 boys in *B* and *C*, but not in *A*. There are 78 − 26 − 31 − 15 = 6 boys in *C* but not in *A* or *B*.

Let x = number of boys who are in A and B but not C

y = number of boys who are in A but not B or C

z = number of boys who are in B but not A or C

We know that the sum of all the labeled areas is 100 or

$$26 + 31 + 15 + 6 + x + y + z = 100$$
$$78 + x + y + z = 100$$

Also, there are 74 boys total in set A, or

$$x + y + 31 + 26 = 74 ,$$

2

and 53 total in set B, or
$$x + z + 46 = 53.$$
Combining: $\qquad x + y + z = 100 - 78 = 22$
$$x + y = 74 - 57 = 17$$
$$x + z = 53 - 46 = 7$$

Subtracting the second equation from the first gives $z = 5$, implying $x = 2$ and $y = 15$. Our answer is the number of boys in sets A and $B = x + 31 = 33$.

Of 37 men and 33 women, 36 are teetotalers. Nine of the women are non-smokers and 18 of the men smoke but do not drink. Seven of the women and 13 of the men drink but do not smoke. How many, at most, both drink and smoke?

SOLUTION:

A = set of all smokers
B = set of all drinkers
C = set of all women
D = set of all men

We construct two Venn diagrams and label them in the following way:

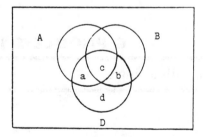 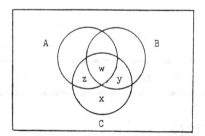

Each section on the graph indicates a subset of the group of men and women. For example, the section labeled "z" is the subset including all women who smoke but do not drink. The section labeled "b" is the subset including all men who drink but do not smoke.

In addition to labels, these letters also will indicate the cardinality — the number of objects — in the subset. We are told there are 37 men; thus, $a + b + c + d = 37$. There are 33 women; thus, $x + y + z + w = 33$. There are 9

3

women non-smokers which includes $x + y$. The number of non-drinking, smoking men is $d = 18$.

Similarly, $\qquad x + z + a + d = 36$, the non-drinkers

$\qquad\qquad\qquad\qquad b = 13$, the drinking, non-smoking men

$\qquad\qquad\qquad\qquad y = 7$, the drinking, non-smoking women.

Collecting all these equations, we wish to find the maximum value of $c + w$, the number of drinkers and smokers.

$$x + z + a + d = 36, \quad a + b + c + d = 37$$
$$b = 13, \ d = 18, \quad x + y + z + w = 33$$
$$y = 7, \quad x + y = 9 \ .$$

Substituting we see that

$$x + y = x + 7 = 9 \text{ or } x = 2.$$

From this we have

$$2 + z + a + 18 = 36 \quad a + 13 + c + 18 = 37$$
$$a + z = 16 \quad a + c = 6$$
$$2 + 7 + z + w = 33$$
$$z + w = 24$$

We now solve for $c + w$.

$$a = 6 - c \text{ and thus } z + 6 - c = 16 \text{ or } z - c = 10$$
$$c = z - 10 \text{ and } w = 24 - z$$

thus, $\qquad\qquad c + w = z - 10 + 24 - z = 14.$

The maximum number of drinkers and smokers is 14.

CLASSICAL MODEL OF PROBABILITY

● PROBLEM 1-3

What is the probability of throwing a six with a single die?

SOLUTION:

The die may land in any of six ways:

1, 2, 3, 4, 5, or 6.

The probability of throwing a six is

$$P \{6\} = \frac{\text{number of ways to get a six}}{\text{number of ways the die may land}}$$

Thus, $\qquad\qquad P \{6\} = \frac{1}{6} \ .$

A deck of playing cards is thoroughly shuffled and a card is drawn at random from the deck. What is the probability that the card drawn is the ace of diamonds?

SOLUTION:

The probability of this event occurring is

$$\frac{\text{number of ways this event can occur}}{\text{number of possible outcomes}} \cdot$$

In our case there is only one way this event can occur, for there is only one ace of diamonds and there are 52 possible outcomes (for there are 52 cards in the deck). Hence, the probability that the card drawn is the ace of

diamonds is $\frac{1}{52}$.

● **PROBLEM 1-5**

A box contains seven red, five white, and four black balls. One ball is drawn at random. What is the probability of drawing a red ball? A black ball?

SOLUTION:

There are $7 + 5 + 4 = 16$ balls in the box. The probability of drawing a red ball is

$$P\{R\} = \frac{\text{number of possible ways of drawing a red ball}}{\text{the number of ways of drawing any ball}}$$

$$P\{R\} = \frac{7}{16} \cdot$$

Similarly, the probability of drawing a black ball is

$$P\{B\} = \frac{\text{number of possible ways of drawing a black ball}}{\text{number of ways of drawing any ball}}$$

Thus, $\qquad P\{B\} = \frac{4}{16} = \frac{1}{4} \cdot$

Find the probability of drawing a black card in a single random draw from a well-shuffled deck of ordinary playing cards.

SOLUTION:

There are 52 cards and since the cards are well-shuffled, each card is assumed to be equally likely to be drawn. There are 26 black cards in the deck, and thus the number of outcomes leading to a black card being drawn is 26. Therefore,

$$P \{\text{drawing a black card}\} = \frac{26}{52} = \frac{1}{2} \ .$$

● **PROBLEM 1–7**

Find the probability of drawing a spade on a single random draw from a well-shuffled deck of cards.

SOLUTION:

There are 52 possible outcomes to the experiment of drawing a card. There are 13 spades in a deck and hence 13 possible outcomes to the experiment which lead to drawing a spade.

Thus, $\qquad P \{\text{drawing a spade}\} = \frac{13}{52} = \frac{1}{4} \ .$

● **PROBLEM 1–8**

What is the probability of obtaining a sum of seven in a single throw of a pair of dice?

SOLUTION:

There are $6 \times 6 = 36$ outcomes which could result from two dice being thrown, as shown in the accompanying figure.

1,1	1,2	1,3	1,4	1,5	1,6
2,1	2,2	2,3	2,4	2,5	2,6
3,1	3,2	3,3	3,4	3,5	3,6
4,1	4,2	4,3	4,4	4,5	4,6
5,1	5,2	5,3	5,4	5,5	5,6
6,1	6,2	6,3	6,4	6,5	6,6

The number of possible ways that a seven will appear are circled in the figure. Let us call this set B. Thus, B = { (1, 6), (2, 5), (3, 4), (4, 3), (5, 2), (6, 1) }.

There are six elements in B, so $P\{7\} = P\{B\} = \dfrac{6}{36} = \dfrac{1}{6}$.

● PROBLEM 1-9

In a single throw of a single die, find the probability of obtaining either a two or a five.

SOLUTION:

In a single throw, the die may land in any of six ways:
$$\{1, 2, 3, 4, 5, 6\} .$$
The probability of obtaining a two is

$$P\{2\} = \frac{\text{number of ways of obtaining a two}}{\text{number of ways the die may land}} , \quad P\{2\} = \frac{1}{6} .$$

Similarly, the probability of obtaining a five is

$$P\{5\} = \frac{\text{number of ways of obtaining a five}}{\text{number of ways the die may land}} , \quad P\{5\} = \frac{1}{6} .$$

As it is impossible for the single throw to result in a two and a five simultaneously, the two events are mutually exclusive. The probability that either one of two mutually exclusive events will occur is the sum of the probabilities of the separate events. Thus, the probability of obtaining either a two or a five, $P\{2 \text{ or } 5\}$, is

$$P\{2\} + P\{5\} = \frac{1}{6} + \frac{1}{6} = \frac{2}{6} = \frac{1}{3} .$$

If a card is drawn from a deck of playing cards, what is the probability that it will be a jack or a ten?

SOLUTION:

The probability of the union of two mutually exclusive events is $P\{A \cup B\} = P\{A\} + P\{B\}$. Here the symbol "$\cup$" stands for "or."

In this particular example, we only select one card at a time. Thus, we either choose a jack "or" a ten. Since no single selection can simultaneously be a jack and a ten, the two events are mutually exclusive.

$$P\{\text{jack or ten}\} = P\{\text{jack}\} + P\{\text{ten}\}.$$

$$P\{\text{jack}\} = \frac{\text{number of ways to select a jack}}{\text{number of ways to choose a card}} = \frac{4}{52} = \frac{1}{13}.$$

$$P\{\text{ten}\} = \frac{\text{number of ways to select a ten}}{\text{number of ways to choose a card}} = \frac{4}{52} = \frac{1}{13}.$$

$$P\{\text{jack or a ten}\} = P\{\text{jack}\} + P\{\text{ten}\} = \frac{1}{13} + \frac{1}{13} = \frac{2}{13}.$$

Suppose that we have a bag containing two red balls, three white balls, and six blue balls. What is the probability of obtaining a red or a white ball on one draw?

SOLUTION:

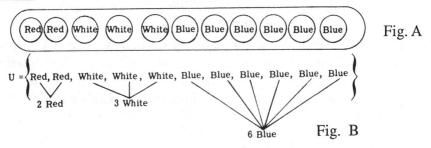

Fig. A

Fig. B

The bag is shown in figure A.

The probability of drawing a red ball is $\frac{2}{11}$, and the probability of drawing a white ball is $\frac{3}{11}$. Since drawing a red and drawing a white ball are mutually exclusive events, the probability of drawing a red or a white ball is the probability of drawing a red ball plus the probability of drawing a white ball, so

$$P \{\text{red or white}\} = \frac{2}{11} + \frac{3}{11} = \frac{5}{11} .$$

Note: In the above example the probability of drawing a blue ball would be $\frac{6}{11}$. Therefore, the sum of the probability of a red ball, the probability of a white ball, and the probability of a blue ball is $\frac{2}{11} + \frac{3}{11} + \frac{6}{11} = 1$.

If there are no possible results that are considered favorable, then the probability $P \{F\}$ is obviously 0. If every result is considered favorable, then $P \{F\} = 1$. Hence, the probability $P \{F\}$ of a favorable result F always satisfies the inequality

$$0 \leq P \{F\} \leq 1 .$$

● **PROBLEM 1–12**

A bag contains four white balls, six black balls, three red balls, and eight green balls. If one ball is drawn from the bag, find the probability that it will be either white or green.

SOLUTION:

The probability that it will be either white or green is

$$P \{\text{white or green}\} = P \{\text{white}\} + P \{\text{green}\} .$$

This is true because if we are given two mutually exclusive events A and B, then $P \{A \text{ or } B\} = P \{A\} + P \{B\}$. Note that two events, A and B, are mutually exclusive events if their intersection is the null or empty set. In this case the intersection of choosing a white ball and of choosing a green ball is the empty set. There are no elements in common. Now

$$P \{\text{white}\} = \frac{\text{number of ways to choose a white ball}}{\text{number of ways to select a ball}}$$

$$= \frac{4}{21} \text{ , and}$$

$$P \{\text{green}\} = \frac{\text{number of ways to choose a green ball}}{\text{number of ways to select a ball}}$$

$$= \frac{8}{21} \text{ .}$$

Thus,

$$P \{\text{white or green}\} = \frac{4}{21} + \frac{8}{21} = \frac{12}{21} = \frac{4}{7} \text{ .}$$

Find the probability of obtaining a sum of either six or seven in a single toss of two dice.

SOLUTION:

Let $A =$ the event that a sum of six is obtained in a toss of two dice

$B =$ the event that a sum of seven is obtained in a toss of two dice.

Then the probability of obtaining either a six or a seven in a single toss of two dice is

$$P \{A \text{ or } B\} = P \{A \cup B\} \text{ .}$$

The union symbol "∪" means that A and/or B can occur. Now $P \{A \cup B\} = P \{A\} + \{B\}$ if A and B are mutually exclusive. Two or more events are said to be mutually exclusive if the occurrence of any one of them excludes the occurrence of the others. In this case, we cannot obtain a six and a seven in a single toss of two dice. Thus, A and B are mutually exclusive.

Note: There are 36 different tosses of two dice.

$A = $ a six is obtained in a toss of two dice
$= \{ (1, 5), (2, 4), (3, 3), (4, 2), (5, 1) \}$
$B = $ a seven is obtained in a toss of two dice
$= \{ (1, 6), (2, 5), (3, 4), (4, 3), (5, 2), (6, 1) \}$.

$$P\{A\} = \frac{\text{number of ways to obtain a six in a toss of two dice}}{\text{number of ways to toss two dice}}$$

$$= \frac{5}{36}$$

$$P\{B\} = \frac{\text{number of ways to obtain a seven in a toss of two dice}}{\text{number of ways to toss two dice}}$$

$$= \frac{6}{36} = \frac{1}{6}$$

Therefore, $P\{A \cup B\} = P\{A\} + \{B\} = \frac{5}{36} + \frac{6}{36} = \frac{11}{36}$.

● **PROBLEM 1–14**

A coin is tossed nine times. What is the total number of possible outcomes of the nine–toss experiment? How many elements are in the subset "six heads and three tails"? What is the probability of getting exactly six heads and three tails in nine tosses of this unbiased coin?

SOLUTION:

There are two possible outcomes for each toss, and thus $\underbrace{2 \times 2 \times \ldots \times}_{\text{nine terms}} = 2^9$ possible outcomes in nine tosses, or 512 outcomes.

To count the number of elements in the subset "six heads and three tails" is equivalent to counting the number of ways six objects can be selected from nine. These objects will then be labeled "heads" and the remaining three objects will be labeled "tails." There are

$$\binom{9}{6} = \frac{9!}{6! \ 3!} = 84$$

ways to do this and hence the probability of observing this configuration is

$$\frac{\text{number of ways six heads and three tails can occur}}{\text{total possible outcomes}}$$

$$= \frac{\binom{9}{6}}{2^9} = \frac{84}{512} = 0.164$$

Suppose a die has been loaded so that the ⚀ face lands uppermost three times as often as any other face while all the other faces occur equally often. What is the probability of a ⚁ on a single toss? What is the probability of a ⚀?

SOLUTION:

Let p equal the probability of the ⚀ face landing uppermost. We know that $P\{⚀\} = 3\ P$ {any other face}. We also know that faces with j dots, j = 2, 3, 4, 5, 6 occur equally often. Thus,

$$\sum_{j=1}^{6} P\{j \text{ dots}\} = 1,$$

and P {one dot} +

$$\sum_{j=2}^{6} P\{j \text{ dots}\} = 1$$

or $p + 5\left(\frac{1}{3}\,P\right) = 1$.

Thus, $p = \frac{3}{8}$ and P {two dots} $= \frac{1}{3}\,P = \frac{1}{8}$.

The probability of a ⚀ is $\frac{3}{8}$.

In a single throw of a pair of dice, find the probability of obtaining a total sum of four or less.

SOLUTION:

Each die may land in six ways. By the Fundamental Principle of Counting the pair of dice may thus land in 6 × 6 = 36 ways:

1,1	1,2	1,3	1,4	1,5	1,6
2,1	2,2	2,3	2,4	2,5	2,6
3,1	3,2	3,3	3,4	3,5	3,6
4,1	4,2	4,3	4,4	4,5	4,6
5,1	5,2	5,3	5,4	5,5	5,6
6,1	6,2	6,3	6,4	6,5	6,6

Let us call the possible outcomes which are circled above set A. Then the elements of set A, $A = \{ (1, 1), (1, 2), (1, 3), (2, 1), (2, 2), (3, 1) \}$, are all the possible ways of obtaining a total sum of four or less.

The probability of obtaining four or less is

$$P \{(x + y) \leq 4\} = \frac{\text{no. of ways of obtaining four or less } \left(\text{no. of elements in set } A\right)}{\text{no. of ways the dice may land}}$$

$$= \frac{6}{36} = \frac{1}{6}$$

A card is drawn at random from a deck of cards. Find the probability that at least one of the following three events will occur:

Event A: a heart is drawn.
Event B: a card which is not a face card is drawn.
Event C: the number of spots (if any) on the drawn card is evenly divisible by three.

SOLUTION:

Let $A \cup B \cup C$ = the event that at least one of the three events above will occur. We wish to find P $\{A \cup B \cup C\}$, the probability of the event $A \cup B \cup C$. Let us count the number of ways that at least A, B, or C will occur. There are 13 hearts, 40 non-face cards, and 12 cards such that the number of spots is divisible by three (cards numbered 3, 6, or 9 are all divisible by three and there are four suits each with three such cards, $3 \times 4 = 12$). If we add $40 + 13 + 12$ we will have counted too many times. There are 10 cards which are hearts and non-face cards, three cards divisible by three and hearts, and 12 cards which are non-face cards and divisible by three. We must subtract each of these from our total of $40 + 13 + 12$ giving $40 + 13 + 12 - 10 - 3 - 12$. But we have subtracted too much; we have subtracted the three cards which are hearts and non-face cards and divisible by three. We must add these cards to our total, making

$$P\{A \cup B \cup C\} = \frac{40 + 13 + 12 - 10 - 3 - 12 + 3}{52} = \frac{43}{52}.$$

This counting technique used is called the Principle of Inclusion/Exclusion and is useful for problems of this sort. Notice that

$$P\{A \cup B \cup C\} = \frac{40 + 13 + 12 - 10 - 3 - 12 + 3}{52}$$

$$= \frac{13}{52} + \frac{40}{52} + \frac{12}{52} - \frac{10}{52} - \frac{3}{52} - \frac{12}{52} + \frac{3}{52}.$$

$$= P\{A\} + P\{B\} + P\{C\} - P\{AB\} - P\{AC\} - P\{BC\} + P(ABC), \text{ since}$$

$$P\{A\} = \frac{\text{number of hearts}}{\text{number of cards}} = \frac{13}{52},$$

$$P\{B\} = \frac{\text{number of non-face cards}}{\text{number of cards}} = \frac{40}{52},$$

$$P\{C\} = \frac{\text{number of cards divisible by three}}{\text{number of cards}} = \frac{12}{52},$$

$$P\{AB\} = \frac{\text{number of hearts and non -face cards}}{\text{number of cards}} = \frac{10}{52},$$

$$P\{AC\} = \frac{\text{number of hearts and cards divisible by three}}{\text{number of cards}} = \frac{3}{52},$$

$$P\{BC\} = \frac{\text{number of number cards divisible by three}}{\text{number of cards}} = \frac{12}{52}, \text{ and}$$

$$P\{ABC\} = \frac{3}{52} .$$

● **PROBLEM 1–18**

Find the probability of obtaining on a single throw of a pair of dice a sum total of five, six, or seven.

Define the events A, B, and C as follows:
Event A: a sum total of five is thrown,
Event B: a sum total of six is thrown, and
Event C: a sum total of seven is thrown.

SOLUTION:

Only one of these three events can occur at one time. The occurrence of any one excludes the occurrence of any of the others. Such events are called mutually exclusive. Let $A \cup B \cup C$ = the event that a sum total of five, six, or seven is observed. Then $P\{A \cup B \cup C\} = P\{A\} + P\{B\} + P\{C\}$, because the events are mutually exclusive. Referring to a previous table, we see that

$$P\{A\} = \frac{4}{36}, P\{B\} = \frac{5}{36}, \text{ and } P\{C\} = \frac{6}{36}. \text{ Therefore,}$$

$$P\{A \cup B \cup C\} = \frac{4}{36} + \frac{5}{36} + \frac{6}{36} = \frac{15}{36} = \frac{5}{12} .$$

● **PROBLEM 1–19**

What is the probability of obtaining a five on each of two successive rolls of a balanced die?

SOLUTION:

We are dealing with separate rolls of a balanced die. The two rolls are independent, and therefore we invoke the following multiplication rule: the probability of obtaining any particular combination in two or more independent trials will be the product of their individual probabilities. The probability of obtaining a five on any single toss is $\frac{1}{6}$, and by the multiplication rule

$$P \{5 \text{ and } 5\} = \frac{1}{6} \times \frac{1}{6} = \frac{1}{36}.$$

● PROBLEM 1–20

If a pair of dice is tossed twice, find the probability of obtaining a sum total of five on both tosses.

SOLUTION:

The ways to obtain five in one toss of the two dice are
(1, 4), (4, 1), (3, 2), and (2, 3) .

Hence, we can throw five in one toss in four ways. Each die has six faces and there are six ways for a die to fall. Then the pair of dice can fall in 6 × 6 = 36 ways. The probability of throwing five in one toss is

$$\frac{\text{number of ways to throw a five in one toss}}{\text{number of ways that a pair of dice can fall}} = \frac{4}{36} = \frac{1}{9} .$$

Now the probability of throwing a five on both tosses is
P {throwing five on first toss and throwing five on second toss} .
"And" implies multiplication if events are independent, thus
P {throwing five on first toss and throwing five on second toss}
= P {throwing five on first toss} × P {throwing five on second toss},
since the results of the two tosses are independent. Consequently, the probability of obtaining five on both tosses is

$$\left(\frac{1}{9}\right) \times \left(\frac{1}{9}\right) = \frac{1}{81} .$$

A penny is to be tossed three times. What is the probability that there will be two heads and one tail?

SOLUTION:

We start this problem by constructing a set of all possible outcomes:

We can have heads on all three tosses:	(HHH)
heads on the first two tosses, a tail on the third:	(HHT) (1)
a head on the first toss, and tails on the next two:	(HTT)
	(HTH) (2)
	(THH) (3)
	(THT)
	(TTH)
	(TTT)

Hence, there are eight possible outcomes (two possibilities on the first toss × two on the second, and × two on the third = 2 × 2 × 2 = 8).

If the coin is fair, then these outcomes are all equally likely and we assign the probability $\frac{1}{8}$ to each. Now we look for the set of outcomes that produce two heads and one tail. We see there are three such outcomes out of the eight possibilities (numbered (1), (2), (3) in our listing). Hence, the probability of two heads and one tail is $\frac{3}{8}$.

Of the approximately 635,000,000,000 different bridge hands, how many contain a ten–card suit?

SOLUTION:

As before, the number of ways a hand could be dealt can be thought of as the number of ways one can select such a hand. We will select a 13-card bridge hand with ten cards of the same suit in three steps. First, let us select the suit of the 10 cards; there are $\binom{4}{1}$ or 4 ways to do this. Next, let us select 10 of the 13 possible cards in the suit which will be in our bridge hand. There are $\binom{13}{10}$ ways to do this, with

$$\binom{13}{10} = \frac{13!}{10! \times 3!} = \frac{13 \times 2 \times 11}{3 \times 2 \times 1} = 286 \text{ ways to choose the 10 cards.}$$

Last, we must select the three remaining cards. These three cards must not be in the same suit as the 10 cards we have previously chosen. Instead they must be from the remaining three suits, or 39 cards. There are $\binom{39}{3}$ ways to select these cards and

$$\binom{39}{3} = \frac{39!}{3! \times 36!} = \frac{39 \times 38 \times 37}{3 \times 2 \times 1} = 9139.$$

By the Fundamental Principle of Counting, the number of different hands containing 10 cards in the same suit is the product of the number of ways in which each of these steps might be carried out. This product is

$$\binom{4}{1} \times \binom{13}{10} \times \binom{39}{3} = 4 \times 286 \times 9{,}139 = 10{,}455{,}016 \text{ .This is the}$$

number of all the possible bridge hands which have 10 cards all of the same suit.

We can now calculate the probability of being dealt a hand with 10 cards in the same suit. This probability is the

$$\frac{\text{number of hands with ten cards in the same suit}}{\text{total number of possible bridge hands}} \text{ .}$$

This equals

$$\frac{\binom{4}{1} \times \binom{13}{10} \times \binom{39}{3}}{\binom{52}{13}} = 0.000016 \text{ .}$$

SHORT ANSWER QUESTIONS FOR REVIEW

Choose the correct answer.

1. In order to work Venn diagrams, one must use (a) arithmetic only. (b) algebra only. (c) trigonometry only. (d) both arithmetic and algebra.

2. There are 37 men and 33 women. Nine women are non-smokers and 18 men smoke but don't drink. Thirteen men and 7 women drink but don't smoke. Which is the best example of a subset? (a) Women who smoke but don't drink (b) Set of smokers (c) Set of drinkers (d) Set of women

3. In Venn diagrams, a set is (a) a diagram. (b) cardinality. (c) a pictorial diagram. (d) a collection of objects.

4. A pictorial representation of the relationship between sets is known as (a) a Venn diagram. (b) a graph. (c) a correlation table. (d) a proof.

5. The probability of drawing a "4" from a well-shuffled deck of cards is (a) 33.51 percent. (b) zero. (c) 7.6923+ percent. (d) 50 percent.

Fill in the blanks.

6. The probability of drawing a diamond from a well-shuffled deck of cards is _____ percent.

7. Six chocolate bars, three peanut bars, and seven taffy bars are placed in a bag. If one bar is withdrawn from the bag, the probability of withdrawing either a peanut bar or a taffy bar is _____ percent.

8. When tossing two dice, the probability of getting an 11 or 12 is _____ percent.

9. In a single throw of a pair of dice, the probability that a total of two, three, or four will be thrown is _____ percent.

10. The probability of obtaining an 11 in one throw of a pair of dice is _____ percent.

Determine whether the following statements are true or false.

11. The probability of getting a 1, 2, or 3 in a single throw of a die is 40 percent.

12. If a card is drawn from a well-shuffled deck of playing cards, the probability that it will be a face card is 20 percent.

13. If a pair of dice is tossed three times, the probability of obtaining 7 on all three tosses is 0.463 percent.

14. If a dime is tossed three times, the probability of getting heads is 12.5 percent.

15. The number of objects in a particular set is the cardinality of a set.

ANSWER KEY

1. d   2. a   3. d

4. a   5. c   6. 25

7. $62\frac{1}{2}$ 8. $8\frac{1}{3}$ 9. $16\frac{2}{3}$

10. 5.555+   11. False   12. False

13. True   14. True   15. True

CHAPTER 2

COUNTING

FUNDAMENTAL PRINCIPLE OF COUNTING

● PROBLEM 2-1

How many ways can r different balls be placed in n different boxes? Consider the balls and boxes distinguishable.

SOLUTION:

If the balls are placed one at a time, then each ball may be placed in one of n boxes. That is, there are n boxes in which to place the first ball, n boxes for the second, n boxes for the third, and finally, n boxes for the rth.

By the Fundamental Principle of Counting there are $\underbrace{n \times n \times n \times \ldots \times n}_{r \text{ terms}}$ or

n^r ways to place r different balls in n boxes.

How many different three-digit numbers can be formed from the numbers 1, 2, 3, 4, 5 if (a) repetitions are allowed? (b) repetitions are not allowed? How many of these numbers are even in either case?

SOLUTION:

(a) If repetitions are allowed, there are five choices for the first digit, five choices for the second, and five choices for the third. By the Fundamental Principle of Counting, there are 5 × 5 × 5 = 125 possible three-digit numbers. If the number is even, the final digit must be either 2 or 4, giving two choices. So there will be five choices for the first digit, five choices for the second, and two for the third, or 5 × 5 × 2 = 50 such numbers.

(b) If repetitions are not allowed, there are five choices for the first digit. After this has been picked, there will be four choices left for the second digit, and three choices left for the third. Hence, 5 × 4 × 3 = 60 such numbers can be selected. If the number must be even, then there are two choices for the final digits, 2 or 4. This leaves four choices for the next digit and three choices for the first digit. Hence, there are 4 × 3 × 2 = 24 possible even numbers that can be selected in this way.

● PROBLEM 2-3

There are two roads between towns A and B. There are three roads between towns B and C. How many different routes may one travel between towns A and C?

SOLUTION:

If we take road 1 from town A to town B and then any road from B to C, there are three ways to travel from A to C. If we take road 2 from A to B and then any road from B to C, there are again three ways to travel from A to C. These two possibilities are the only ones available to us. Thus, there are 3 + 3 = 6 ways to travel from A to C.

This problem illustrates the Fundamental Principle of Counting. This principle states that if an event can be divided into k components, and there are n_1 ways to carry out the first component, n_2 ways to carry out the second, n_i ways to carry out the ith, and n_k ways to carry out the kth, then there are $n_1 \times n_2 \times n_3 \times \ldots \times n_k$ ways for the original event to take place.

PERMUTATIONS

● **PROBLEM 2-4**

Calculate the number of permutations of the letters a, b, c, and d taken two at a time.

SOLUTION:

The first of the two letters may be taken in four ways (a, b, c, d). The second letter may therefore be selected from the remaining three letters in three ways. By the Fundamental Principle, the total number of ways of selecting two letters is equal to the product of the number of ways of selecting each letter, or

$4 \times 3 = 12$

The list of these permutations is:

ab	ba	ca	da
ac	bc	cb	db
ad	bd	cd	dc

● **PROBLEM 2-5**

Calculate the number of permutations of the letters a, b, c, and d taken four at a time.

SOLUTION:

The number of permutations of the four letters taken four at a time equals the number of ways the four letters can be arranged or ordered. Consider four places to be filled by the four letters. The first place can be filled in four ways, choosing from the four letters. The second place may be filled in three ways, selecting one of the three remaining letters. The third place may be filled in two ways with one of the two still remaining.

The fourth place is filled one way with the last letter. By the Fundamental Principle, the total number of ways of ordering the letters equals the product of the number of ways of filling each ordered place, or $4 \times 3 \times 2 \times 1 = 24 = P(4, 4) = 4!$ (read "four factorial").

In general, for n objects taken r at a time,

$$P(n, r) = n (n - 1) (n - 2) \ldots (n - r + 1) = \frac{r!}{(n - r)!} \quad (r < n).$$

For the special case where $r = n$,
$$P(n, n) = n (n - 1) (n - 2) \ldots (3) (2) (1) = n!,$$
since $(n - r)! = 0!$ which equals one by definition.

● **PROBLEM 2-6**

In how many different ways may three books be placed next to each other on a shelf?

SOLUTION:

We construct a pattern of three boxes to represent the places where the three books are to be placed next to each other on the shelf:

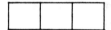

Since there are three books, the first place may be filled in three ways. There are then two books left, so that the second place may be filled in two ways. There is only one book left to fill the last place. Hence, our boxes take the following form:

3	2	1

The Fundamental Principle of Counting states that if one task can be performed in a different ways and, when it is performed in any one of these ways, a second task can be performed in b different ways, and a third task can be done in c ways, ... then all the tasks in succession can be performed in $a \times b \times c \ldots$ different ways. Thus, the books can be arranged in $3 \times 2 \times 1 = 6$ ways. This can also be seen as follows. Since the arrangement of books on the shelf is important, this is a permutations problem. Recalling the general formula for the number of permutations of n items taken r at a time,

$_nP_r = \dfrac{n!}{(n-r)!}$, we replace n by 3 and r by 3 to obtain

$$_3P_3 = \frac{3!}{(3-3)!} = \frac{3!}{0!} = \frac{3 \times 2 \times 1}{1} = 6 .$$

● PROBLEM 2-7

Determine the number of distinct permutations of the letters in the word "banana."

SOLUTION:

In solving this problem we use the fact that the number of permutations P of n objects taken all at a time [P (n, n)], of which n_1 are alike, n_2 others are alike, n_3 others are alike, etc. is

$$P = \frac{n!}{n_1! \; n_2! \; n_3!\dots}, \qquad \text{with } n_1 + n_2 + n_3 + \dots = n .$$

In the given problem there are six letters ($n = 6$), of which two are alike, (there are two N's so that $n_1 = 2$), three others are alike (there are three A's, so that $n_2 = 3$), and one is left (there is one B, so $n_3 = 1$). Notice that $n_1 + n_2 + n_3 = 2 + 3 + 1 = 6 = n$; thus,

$$P = \frac{6!}{2! \; 3! \; 1!} = \frac{6 \times 5 \times 4 \times 3!}{2 \times 1 \times 3! \times 1} = 60 .$$

Thus, there are 60 permutations of the letters in the word "banana."

● PROBLEM 2-8

Find the number of distinct permutations of the seven letters in the word "algebra."

SOLUTION:

A permutation is an ordered arrangement of a set of objects. For example, if you are given four letters a, b, c, and d and you choose two at a time, some permutations you can obtain are: ab, ac, ad, ba, bc, bd, ca, and cb.

For n items, we can arrange the first object in n different ways, the second in $n - 1$ different ways, the third in $n - 2$ different ways, etc. Thus, the n objects can be arranged in order in

$$n! = n \times (n - 1) \times (n - 2) \ldots 1 \text{ ways.}$$

Temporarily place subscripts, 1 and 2, on the a's to distinguish them, so that we now have $7! = 5{,}040$ possible permutations of the seven distinct objects. Of these 5,040 arrangements, half will contain the a's in the order a_1, a_2 and the other half will contain them in the order a_2, a_1. If we assume the two a's are indistinct, then we apply the following theorem. The number P of distinct permutations of n objects taken at a time, of which n_1 are alike, n_2 are alike of another kind, ... n_k are alike of still another kind, with

$n_1 + n_2 + \ldots + n_k = n$, is $P = \dfrac{n!}{n_1! \, n_2! \, \ldots \, n_k!}$. Then in this example, the two

a's are alike so $P = \dfrac{7!}{2!} = 2{,}520$ permutations of the letters in the word al-

gebra, when the a's are indistinguishable.

● PROBLEM 2-9

In how many ways may a party of four women and four men be seated at a round table if the women and men are to occupy alternate seats?

SOLUTION:

If we consider the seats indistinguishable, then this is a problem in circular permutations, as opposed to linear permutations. In the standard linear permutation approach, each chair is distinguishable from the others. Thus, if a woman is seated first, she may be chosen four ways, then a man seated next to her may be chosen four ways, the next woman can be chosen three ways and the man next to her can be chosen three ways... Our diagram to the linear approach shows the number of ways each seat can be occupied.

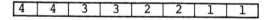

By the Fundamental Principle of Counting there are thus $4 \times 4 \times 3 \times 3 \times 2 \times 2 \times 1 \times 1 = 576$ ways to seat the people.

However, if the seats are indistinguishable, then so long as each person has the same two people on each side, the seating arrangement is considered the same. Thus, we may suppose one person, say a woman, is seated in a particular place, and then arrange the remaining three women and four men relative to her. Because of the alternate seating scheme, there are three possible places for the remaining three women and four possible places for the four men. Hence, the total number of arrangements is (3!) – (4!) = 6 × 24 = 144. In general, the formula for circular permutations of n items and n other items which are alternating is $(n - 1)! \, n!$. In our case, we have
$$(4 - 1)! \, 4! = 3! \, 4! = 3 \times 2 \times 4 \times 3 \times 2 = 144 \, .$$

COMBINATIONS

● **PROBLEM 2-10**

How many sums of money can be obtained by choosing two coins from a box containing a penny, a nickel, a dime, a quarter, and a half dollar?

SOLUTION:

The order makes no difference here, since a selection of a penny and a dime is the same as a selection of a dime and a penny insofar as the sum is concerned. This is a case of combinations, then, rather than permutations. The number of combinations of n different objects taken r at a time is equal to

$$\frac{n(n-1) \dots (n-r+1)}{1 \times 2 \dots r} \, .$$

In this example, $n = 5$, $r = 2$, therefore,

$$C\,(5,\,2) = \frac{5 \times 4}{1 \times 2} = 10 \, .$$

How many baseball teams of nine members can be chosen from among 12 boys, without regard to the position played by each member?

SOLUTION:

Since there is no regard to position, this is a combinations problem (if order or arrangement had been important, it would have been a permutations problem). The general formula for the number of combinations of n items taken r at a time is

$$C(n, r) = \frac{n!}{r! \, (n-r)!} \, .$$

We have to find the number of combinations of 12 items taken nine at a time. Hence, we have

$$C(12, 9) = \frac{12!}{9! \, (12-9)!} = \frac{12!}{9! \, 3!} = \frac{12 \times 11 \times 10 \times 9!}{3 \times 2 \times 1 \times 9!} = 220 \, .$$

Therefore, there are 220 possible teams.

How many words, each consisting of two vowels and three consonants, can be formed from the letters in the word "integral"?

SOLUTION:

To find the number of ways to choose vowels or consonants from letters, we use combinations. The number of combinations of n different objects taken r at a time is defined to be

$$C(n, r) = \frac{n!}{r! \, (n-r)!} \, .$$

We first select the two vowels to be used from among the three vowels in "integral"; this can be done in $C(3, 2) = 3$ ways. Next, we select the three consonants from the five in "integral"; this yields $C(5, 3) = 10$ possible choices. To find the number of ordered arrangements of five letters selected five at a time, we need to find the number of permutations of choosing r from n objects. Symbolically, it is $P\{n, r\}$, which is defined to be

$$P\{n, r\} = \frac{n!}{(n-r)!}.$$

We permute the five chosen letters in all possible ways, of which there are $P\{5, 5\} = 5! = 120$ arrangements since no two letters are the same. Finally, to find the total number of words which can be formed, we apply the Fundamental Principle of Counting, which states that if one event can be performed in m ways, another one in n ways, and another in k ways, then the total number of ways in which all events can occur is $m \times n \times k$. Hence, the total number of possible words is, by the Fundamental Principle,

$$C(3, 2) \ C(5, 3) \ P\{5, 5\} = 3 \times 10 \times 120 = 3,600.$$

● PROBLEM 2-13

How many different bridge hands are there?

SOLUTION:

A bridge hand contains 13 cards dealt from a 52-card deck. The order in which the cards are dealt is not important. The number of hands that might be dealt is the same as the number of hands it is possible to select, if one were allowed to select 13 cards at random from a standard deck. The question now becomes: how many ways may 52 objects be taken in combinations of 13 at a time? Let us denote this number by $_{52}C_{13}$.

The solution is $\begin{pmatrix} 52 \\ 13 \end{pmatrix} = \dfrac{52!}{13! \ 39!}.$

With the help of tables for $n!$, we find the number of possible bridge hands to be about 635,000,000,000.

SHORT ANSWER QUESTIONS FOR REVIEW

Choose the correct answer.

1. The act of changing the order of elements arranged in a particular order is called (a) deposition. (b) permutation. (c) juxtaposition. (d) disposition. (e) combination.

2. How does a combination differ from a permutation? (a) No difference. (b) A combination is changing the order of elements in a group while a permutation is the arrangement of elements into various groups without regard to their order in the group. (c) A permutation is changing the order of elements in a group while a combination is the arrangement of elements into various groups without regard to their order in the group. (d) None of the above.

3. If cards are selected from a deck at random, this means (a) without definite aim or pattern. (b) selecting with regard to suit but not with regard to the card's numerical value. (c) selecting with regard to the card's numerical value but not with regard to the card's suit. (d) selecting with regard to both numerical value and suit.

Fill in the blanks.

4. There are four roads from Harrisonville to Madisonville, and there are three other roads from Madisonville to Sioux Center. The number of different routes one may travel from Harrisonville to Sioux Center is _____ .

5. _____ two-digit numbers can be formed from the numbers 1, 2, and 3 if repetitions are allowed.

6. Four pamphlets can be placed next to each other on a shelf in _____ ways.

7. The number of permutations possible from the letters in the word "Chicago" is _____ .

Determine whether the following statements are true or false.

8. Six statues can be placed in line on a table in 720 different ways.

9. A party of three men, three women, and three children can be seated in 56 distinct ways if one man, one woman, and one child are to be seated in that order.

10. Using the letters in the word "Tampa," the number of permutations, using each of the five letters, that can be formed is 60.

ANSWER KEY

1. b	2. c	3. a
4. 12	5. 9	6. 24
7. 2,520	8. True	9. False
10. True		

CHAPTER 3

DISCRETE DISTRIBUTIONS

GENERAL CONCEPTS

● **PROBLEM 3-1**

Determine the probability distribution of the number of spades in a five-card poker hand from an ordinary deck of 52 cards.

SOLUTION:

Let X = number of spades in a five-card poker hand, which can take on the values 0, 1, 2, 3, 4, or 5.

To find the probability distribution of X, we calculate

$$P\{X = k\} = \frac{\text{number of poker hands with } k \text{ spades}}{\text{total number of poker hands}}.$$

The total number of poker hands is the number of ways five objects may

be selected from 52 objects. Thus, the total number of poker hands is $\binom{52}{5}$.

To count the number of poker hands with k spades, we first count the number of ways k spades may be chosen from the 13 spades available.

There are $\begin{pmatrix} 13 \\ k \end{pmatrix}$ ways to do this. If k of the cards in the hand are spades, $5 - k$ cards must be non-spades. The number of ways the remaining $5 - k$ cards may be selected from the available non-spades is

$$\begin{pmatrix} 52 - 13 \\ 5 - k \end{pmatrix} = \begin{pmatrix} 39 \\ 5 - k \end{pmatrix} .$$

Thus, the total number of poker hands with k spades is the product of these two expressions, or

$$\begin{pmatrix} 13 \\ k \end{pmatrix} \begin{pmatrix} 39 \\ 5 - k \end{pmatrix} .$$

Thus, $P (X = k) = \dfrac{\begin{pmatrix} 13 \\ k \end{pmatrix} \begin{pmatrix} 39 \\ 5 - k \end{pmatrix}}{\begin{pmatrix} 52 \\ 5 \end{pmatrix}}$ for $k = 0, 1, 2, 3, 4, 5$.

● PROBLEM 3–2

Let X be the random variable denoting the result of the single toss of a fair coin. If the toss is heads, $X = 1$. If the toss results in tails, $X = 0$. What is the probability distribution of X?

SOLUTION:

The probability distribution of X is a function which assigns probabilities to the values X may assume. A proper discrete probability distribution will satisfy $\sum P \{X = x\} = 1$ and $P \{X = x\} \geq 0$ for all x. The variable X in this problem is discrete as it only takes on the values 0 and 1. To find the probability distribution of X, we must find $P \{X = 0\}$ and $P \{X = 1\}$. Let $p_0 = P \{X = 0\}$ and $p_1 = P \{X = 1\}$. If the coin is fair, the events $X = 0$ and $X = 1$ are equally likely. Thus, $p_0 = p_1 = P$. We must have $p_0 > 0$ and $p_1 > 0$. In addition, $P \{X = 0\} + P \{X = 1\} = 1$, or $p_0 + p_1 = P + P = 1$, or $2 P = 1$, and

$p_0 = p_1 = P = \dfrac{1}{2}$, so the probability distribution of X is $f (x)$: where

$$f(0) = P\{X = 0\} = \frac{1}{2},$$

$$f(1) = P\{X = 1\} = \frac{1}{2}, \text{ and}$$

$f(k) = P\{X = k\} = 0$ for k other than 0 or 1. We see that this is a proper probability distribution for our variable X.

GEOMETRIC DISTRIBUTION

● **PROBLEM 3-3**

An absent-minded professor has five keys. One of the keys opens the door to his apartment. One night he arrives at his building, reaches into his pocket, and selects a key at random from those on his chain. He tries it in the lock. If it doesn't work, he replaces the key and again selects at random from the five keys. He continues this process until he finally finds his key, then stops. Let X be the number of attempts the professor makes. What is the probability distribution of X?

SOLUTION:

This is a special type of binomial random variable. Each time the professor reaches into his pocket can be considered a trial. The professor always replaces the key, so we assume that the trials are independent except if the correct key is chosen. There are five keys and he is selecting at random. The probability of "success" on a given trial is thus $\frac{1}{5}$ and the

probability that he selects the wrong key is $\frac{4}{5}$. We are not sure how many

attempts he will make, but we know that if he selects the correct key he will stop the process. We compute the probability distribution of X as

$P\{X = 1\}$ = probability that he picks the right key on the first draw

$$= \frac{1}{5}.$$

$P \{X = 2\}$ = probability that he picks a wrong key first and the right key second = $\left(\dfrac{4}{5}\right)\left(\dfrac{1}{5}\right)$.

$P \{X = 3\}$ = probability that he picks two wrong keys first and the right key third = $\left(\dfrac{4}{5}\right)\left(\dfrac{4}{5}\right)\left(\dfrac{1}{5}\right)$.

In general, $P (X = k)$ = probability that $k - 1$ wrong keys are tried and the kth key selected is the correct one.

$$P \{X = k\} = \left(\dfrac{4}{5}\right)^{k-1}\left(\dfrac{1}{5}\right).$$

This distribution is known as the geometric distribution.

● PROBLEM 3-4

Let X be the number of days between the time you purchase a stock and the stock price rises. X is a discrete variable with the probability distribution

$$f(x) = \left(\dfrac{1}{2}\right)^x, \qquad x = 1, 2, \ldots$$

$$= 0 \qquad \text{otherwise.}$$

Find the probability that the stock price decreases and then increases.

SOLUTION:

If the stock price decreases and then increases, then $x = 2$. Now

$$P \{x = 2\} = \left\{\dfrac{1}{2}\right\}^2 = \dfrac{1}{4}.$$

● PROBLEM 3-5

Find the probability that a person flipping a balanced coin requires four tosses to get a head.

SOLUTION:

Suppose one performs a series of repeated Bernoulli trials until a success is observed, and then stops. The total number of trials is random and equal to the number of failures plus one for the success. The probability that there will be k trials is equal to the probability that there are $k - 1$ failures followed by a success. If the probability of a success is p,

$$P\,(X = k) = \frac{\overbrace{(1-P)\,(1-P)\,\ldots\,(1-P)}^{k-1 \text{ times}}\,P}{}$$

In other words $f(x) = (1 - p)^{x-1}\,p; \quad x = 1, 2, 3, \ldots$

This is called the geometric distribution. Our problem is one of this type.

We have $p = 1 - p = \dfrac{1}{2}$. We want $f(4) = \left(\dfrac{1}{2}\right)^{4-1}\dfrac{1}{2} = \left(\dfrac{1}{2}\right)^{4} = \dfrac{1}{16}$.

● PROBLEM 3-6

In order to attract customers, a grocery store has started a SAVE game. Any person who collects all four letters of the word SAVE gets a prize. A diligent Mrs. Y, who has the letters S, A, and E, keeps going to the store until she gets the fourth letter, V. The probability that she gets the letter V on any visit is 0.002 and remains the same from visit to visit. Let X denote the number of times she visits the store (after her visits during which she obtained the other letters) until she gets the letter V for the first time. Find:

(a) the probability function of X;
(b) the probability that she gets the letter V for the first time on the twentieth visit; and
(c) the probability that she will not have to visit more than three times to obtain the V.

SOLUTION:

The process consists of a number of failures before a success, the obtaining of a V. The distribution is therefore geometric and

$$f(x) = (1 - p)^{x-1}\,p; \qquad \text{for } x = 1, 2, 3, \ldots.$$

In this case $p = 0.002$ and $f(x) = (1 - 0.002)^{x-1}(0.002) = (0.002)(0.998)^{x-1}$.

    (a) $f(x) = (0.002)(0.998)^{x-1}$.

    (b)   We want $f(20) = (0.002)(0.998)^{19} = (0.002)(0.963) = 0.0019$.

    (c) $P\{x \le 3\} = P\{x = 1\} + P\{x = 2\} + P\{x = 3\}$

$$= f(1) + f(2) + f(3)$$
$$= (0.002)(0.998)^{1-1} + (0.002)(0.998)^{2-1} + (0.002)(0.998)^{3-1}$$
$$= 0.002 + (0.002)(0.998) + (0.002)(0.998)^2$$
$$= 0.002 + 0.001996 + 0.001992$$
$$= 0.005988$$

● PROBLEM 3-7

A recent graduate is looking for a job. Let X be the number of jobs to which he applied before he gets an offer. Is the geometric distribution a reasonable model?

SOLUTION:

The assumptions required for the geometric distribution to apply are that the trials are independent and each has the same success probability. This may, in fact, be the case. More likely, however, the candidate would hone his interviewing skills during this process, thereby increasing his success probability, in violation of the geometric distribution.

POISSON DISTRIBUTION

● PROBLEM 3-8

Defects occur along the length of a cable at an average of six defects per 4,000 feet. Assume that the probability of k defects in t feet of cable is given by the Poisson probability mass function. Find the probability that a 3,000-foot cable will have at most two defects.

SOLUTION:

Since on average there are six defects per 4,000 feet, we would expect $\dfrac{(6) \times (3,000)}{(4,000)} = 4.5$ defects per 3,000 feet. Now we refer to the table of Poisson probabilities to find

$$P \text{ \{at most two defects\}} = P \text{ \{zero defects\}} + P \text{ \{one defect\}}$$
$$+ P \text{ \{two defects\}}$$

● **PROBLEM 3-9**

Suppose that flaws in plywood occur at random with an average of one flaw per 50 square feet. What is the probability that a four foot × eight foot sheet will have no flaws? At most one flaw? To get a solution, assume that the number of flaws per unit area is Poisson distributed.

SOLUTION:

Calculate the expected value and use that as λ. We expect one flaw per 50 square feet. Hence, we expect $\dfrac{1}{50}$ flaws per square foot. We have 4 × 8 = 32 sq. ft. We expect $\lambda = \dfrac{32}{50}$ flaws, so

$$P \text{ (no flaws)} = P \{X = 0\} = \frac{e^{-\frac{32}{50}} \left(\dfrac{32}{50}\right)^0}{0!} = e^{-\frac{32}{50}} = e^{-0.64},$$

$$P \text{ \{at most one flaw\}} = P \text{ \{no flaws\}} + P \text{ \{1 flaw\}}$$

$$= e^{-0.64} \left[\frac{e^{-\frac{32}{50}} \left(\dfrac{32}{50}\right)^1}{1!} + 1 \right]$$

$$= e^{-0.64} + 0.64 \, e^{-0.64}$$

Given that the random variable X has a Poisson distribution with mean $\mu = 2$, find the variance.

SOLUTION:

We are given that the mean $\mu = 2$, but we are not given the variance. Recall, however, that a Poisson random variable has the unique property that the expectation equals the variance. Hence

$$V(x)\ \lambda = 2.$$

Harvey the waiter drops, on the average, 2.5 dishes per hour. Determine, with the aid of a cumulative Poisson table, the probability that Harvey drops (a) at most four dishes, (b) exactly four dishes.

SOLUTION:

We are told that $E(x) = 2.5$. In a Poisson distribution, the parameter $\lambda = E(x)$. Hence, $\lambda = 2.5$.

Refer to a table of cumulative Poisson probabilities. Look at the table under expected value 2.5. There is no column for 2.5 so we will have to average the values for 2.4 and 2.6. In the row $c = 4$, we find $P_{2.4}\ \{X \le 4\} = 0.904$ and $P_{2.6}\ \{X \le 4\} = 0.877$. Therefore,

$$P_{2.5}\ \{X \le 4\} = \frac{0.904 + 0.877}{2} = 0.891 \text{ approximately.}$$

To find $P\ \{X = 4\}$, we will find $P\ \{X \le 3\}$. Now $P\ \{X = 4\} = P\ \{X \le 4\} - P\ \{X \le 3\}$. We will approximate $P_{2.5}\{X \le 3\}$ by taking the average of $P_{2.4}\{X \le 3\}$ and $P_{2.6}\{X \le 3\}$. From the table this is

$$\frac{0.779 + 0.736}{2} = 0.758 \ .$$

Therefore,
$$P\ \{X = 4\} = 0.891 - 0.758 = 0.133 \ .$$

● PROBLEM 3-12

The average number of traffic accidents that take place on the Hollywood freeway on a weekday between 7:00 A.M. and 8:00 A.M. is 0.7 per hour. Use tables to determine the probability that more than two accidents would occur on the Hollywood freeway on Tuesday morning between 7:00 A.M. and 8:00 A.M. Assume a Poisson distribution.

SOLUTION:

Note that $P\{X > 2\} = 1 - P\{X \le 2\}$. Using the cumulative Poisson tables we will find $P\{X \le 2\}$. We look under the column for expected value 0.70 and across the row $c = 2$ to find $P\{X \le 2\} = 0.966$. Hence $P\{X > 2\} = 1 - 0.966 = 0.034$.

● PROBLEM 3-13

A lot is accepted if and only if there is one or less defective items in a random sample of $n = 50$. Find the probability of accepting a lot which is two percent defective.

SOLUTION:

This is a binomial problem with parameters $n = 50$ and $p = 2\% = 0.02$.

$$P\{X \le 1\} = \sum_{k=0}^{1} \binom{50}{k} p^k (1-p)^{n-k} .$$

But this is a very hard computation. In the last problem we saw that a Poisson distribution can approximate a binomial.

We state this result formally: if the probability of success in a single trial p approaches 0 while the number of trials n becomes infinite in such a manner that the mean $\mu = np$ remains fixed, then the binomial distribution will approach the Poisson distribution with mean μ.

We apply this result to the present problem $\mu = np = 50\,(.02) = 1$. Hence,

$$P\{accepting\} = P\{x = 0\} + P\{x = 1\} = 0.736,$$

from the table of Poisson probabilities.

Given that four percent of the items in an incoming lot are defective, what is the probability that at most one defective item will be found in a random sample of size 30?

SOLUTION:

We use the binomial distribution for three reasons: (1) the selection of the 30 items can be considered a sequence of success–failure trials, because each item is either defective or nondefective; (2) the probability that an item is defective (or nondefective) does not change; (3) the outcome of each trial is independent of the results of the other trials.

Since the events (there are no defectives in the sample of 30 items) and (there is exactly one defective in the sample) are exclusive (they cannot both occur), we can add the probabilities of their occurrence to find
$$P \{d \leq 1\} = P \{d = 0\} + P \{d = 1\},$$
where d is the number of defective items. Now

$$P \{d \leq 1\} = \sum_{d=0}^{d=1} \binom{30}{d} (0.04)^d (0.96)^{30-d}$$

$$= \binom{30}{0} (0.04)^0 (0.96)^{30-0} + \binom{30}{1} (0.04)^1 (0.96)^{29}$$

$$= \frac{30!}{30! \; 0!} (1) (0.96)^{30} + 30 (0.04) (0.96)^{29}$$

$$= (0.96)^{30} + 30 (0.04) (0.96)^{29} = 0.661$$

Consider a production process of making ball bearings where the probability of a defective bearing is 0.01. In determining the probability of having 10 defective bearings out of 1,000, which distribution would you use?

41

SOLUTION:

Since this process involves repeated independent Bernoulli trials, each with the same success probability, the binomial distribution should be used. However, since n is very large and p is small, we can use the Poisson approximation to the binomial with $\lambda = E[x] = np = 1,000 \times 0.01 = 10$.

● PROBLEM 3-16

Let the probability of exactly one blemish in one foot of wire be $\dfrac{1}{1,000}$, and let the probability of two or more blemishes in that length be, for all practical purposes, zero. Let the random variable X be the number of blemishes in 3,000 feet of wire. Find $P\{X = 5\}$.

SOLUTION:

Let $n = 3,000$ feet of wire and $p = \dfrac{1}{1,000}$ be the probability of exactly one blemish in one foot. We are dealing with a binomial random variable with parameters $n = 3,000$ and $p = \dfrac{1}{1,000}$. The exact answer to this is therefore

$$P\{X = 5\} = \binom{3,000}{5}\left(\frac{1}{1,000}\right)^5\left(\frac{999}{1,000}\right)^{2,995}.$$

This is an incredibly tedious computation. Instead, since n is large and p is small, we will use a Poisson approximation. We know that $\lambda = \dfrac{3,000}{1,000} = 3$. Note that $P\{X = 5\} = P\{X \leq 5\} - P\{X \leq 4\}$. The last two values can be read off the cumulative tables under expectation 3. Hence, $P\{X = 5\} = 0.916 - 0.815 = 0.101$.

● PROBLEM 3-17

Suppose X has a Poisson distribution. Then $p(k + 1) = \dfrac{\lambda}{k+1} \, p(k)$, where $p(k) = P \{X = k\}$. If $\lambda = 2$, then use this recursive relation to compute $p(1)$, $p(2)$, $p(3)$, and $p(4)$. Note that $p(0) = 0.135$

SOLUTION:

Since $\lambda = 2$, $\dfrac{P(k+1)}{P(k)} = \dfrac{\lambda}{n+1} = \dfrac{2}{n+1}$. Thus,

$$p(1) = \frac{\lambda}{k+1} \, p(0) = \frac{2}{0+1} \, (0.135) = 0.271,$$

$$p(2) = \frac{\lambda}{1+1} \, p(1) = \frac{2}{2} \, (0.271) = 0.271,$$

$$p(3) = \frac{\lambda}{2+1} \, p(2) = \frac{2}{3} \, (0.271) = 0.180, \text{ and}$$

$$p(4) = \frac{\lambda}{3+1} \, p(3) = \frac{2}{4} \, (0.180) = 0.090.$$

● PROBLEM 3-18

A merchant knows that the number of a certain kind of item that he can sell in a given period of time is Poisson distributed. How many such items should the merchant stock so that the probability will be 0.95 that he will have enough items to meet the customer demand for a time period of length T?

SOLUTION:

Let v denote the mean rate of occurrence per unit time and let k be the unknown number of items the merchant should stock. The problem stipulates that there should be a 95 percent probability that enough is stocked.

This is an example of the Poisson process discussed in the previous problem. Hence by that discussion, the parameter for the Poisson distribution is vT. Assuming K items are stocked, P {having enough items} = P {having a demand for K items or less}. In general we have to find K such that this is ≥ 0.95.

In particular, if the merchant sells an average of two such items a day, how many should he stock so that he will have a probability of at least 0.95 of having enough items to meet demand for a 30-day month? Here $v = 2$ and $T = 30$.

From cumulative Poisson tables, for $K \geq 73$, $F(K) \geq 0.95$.

● **PROBLEM 3-19**

Customers enter Macy's "at random" at a rate of four per minute. Assume that the number entering Macy's in any given time interval has a Poisson distribution. Determine the probability that at least one customer enters the store in a given half-minute interval.

SOLUTION:

We again are discussing the specific occurrence of events in a length of time. The problem describes a Poisson process. The mean rate of occurrence is $\lambda = \dfrac{4}{2} = 2$ per half-minute interval. We want $P\{X \geq 1\}$. Note that

$$P\{X \geq 1\} = 1 - P\{X = 0\} = 0.865,$$

from the table of Poisson probabilities.

● **PROBLEM 3-20**

Suppose X_t, the number of phone calls that arrive at an exchange during a period of length t, has a Poisson distribution with parameter λt. The probability that an operator answers any given phone call is equal to p, $0 \leq p \leq 1$. If Y_t denotes the number of phone calls answered, find the distribution of Y_t.

SOLUTION:

We want to find $P(Y_t = k)$, $k = 0, 1, 2, \ldots$

This is an advanced exercise in conditional probability. If we are given $X_t = r$, we have r Bernoulli trials and a success constitutes the operator answering the call. Hence, given $X_t = r$, Y_t is binomially distributed, or

$$P\{Y_t = k \mid X_t = r\} = \binom{r}{k} p^k (1 - p)^{r-k}, \; k = 0, 1, 2, \dots r.$$

By the Law of Total Probability:

$$P\{Y_t = k\} = \sum_{r=k}^{\infty} P\{Y_t = k \cap X_t = r\}$$

$$= \sum_{r=k}^{\infty} \{P\{Y_t = k \mid X_t = r\}\}\{P\{X_t = r\}\}$$

from the definition of conditional probability

$$= \sum_{r=k}^{\infty} \binom{r}{k} p^k \{1 - p\}^{r-k} e^{-\lambda t} \frac{(\lambda t)^r}{r!}$$

$$= \frac{e^{-\lambda t}(\lambda t)^k p^k}{k!} \sum_{r=k}^{\infty} \frac{(1-p)^{r-k}(\lambda t)^{r-k}}{(r-k)!}.$$

Let $i = r - k$. We see that:

$$P\{Y_t = k\} = \frac{e^{-\lambda t}(\lambda t)^k p^k}{k!} \sum_{i=0}^{\infty} \frac{(1-p)^i(\lambda t)^i}{i!}$$

$$= \frac{e^{-\lambda t}(\lambda t)^k p^k}{k!} \sum_{i=0}^{\infty} \frac{\left[(1-p)\lambda t\right]^i}{i!}$$

$$= \frac{e^{-\lambda t}(\lambda t)^k p^k}{k!} e^{(1-p)\lambda t}$$

$$= \frac{e^{-\lambda t} e^{\lambda t} e^{-\lambda pt}(\lambda pt)^k}{k!}$$

$$= \frac{e^{-\lambda pt}(\lambda pt)^k}{k!}$$

In conclusion, we see that Y_t has a Poisson distribution with parameter $p\lambda t$. This is referred to as a thinned Poisson process.

SHORT ANSWER QUESTIONS FOR REVIEW

Choose the correct answer.

1. What is a "discrete distribution"? (a) Combined (b) Separate (c) Neither of these.

2. A quantity or function that may assume any given value or set of values is (a) an analysis. (b) an integer. (c) a variable. (d) a combination. (e) a permutation.

3. A whole number, whether zero, positive, or negative, is called (a) a fraction. (b) a section. (c) an integer. (d) a distribution.

4. A limiting form of a binomial probability distribution for small values of the probability of success and for large numbers of trial is known as (a) proper distribution. (b) limited distribution. (c) Harrison distribution. (d) Poisson distribution.

5. An expression that is a sum or difference of two terms, such as $2x + 3y$, is called (a) a binomial. (b) an ampersand. (c) a trinomial. (d) a mononomial. (e) None of these.

Fill in the blanks.

6. If a coin is tossed 1,000 times, the probability that it will come up tails is _____ percent.

7. The relative possibility that an event will occur, as expressed by the ratio of the number of actual occurrences to the total number of possible occurrences, is defined as _____ .

8. If a phone averages 20 calls per hour, the number of calls received per minute on average is _____ .

9. S. D. Poisson, discoverer of the Poisson distribution, was a mathematician from _____ .

10. Comparing the number of happenings or occurrences within a specific length of time is a classic example of a _____ process.

Determine whether the following statements are true or false.

11. Poisson distribution equations are particularly useful in work dealing with bacteria and industrial quality control.

12. Problems using Poisson distributions consist of tables only.

13. Limits, boundaries, or guidelines in mathematics are referred to as parameters.

14. In mathematics, using a rule or procedure that can be applied repeatedly is called recursive.

15. Repeated independent experiments having two possible outcomes for each experiment, with the probability for each outcome remaining constant throughout the experiment, as in tossing a coin several times, are called thinned processes.

ANSWER KEY

1. b	2. c	3. c
4. d	5. a	6. 50
7. probability	8. $\dfrac{1}{3}$	9. France
10. Poisson	11. True	12. False
13. True	14. True	15. False

CHAPTER 4

BINOMIAL AND MULTINOMIAL DISTRIBUTIONS

BINOMIAL PROBABILITIES

● **PROBLEM 4-1**

What is the probability of obtaining exactly three heads in five flips of a balanced coin?

SOLUTION:

We have here the situation often referred to as a Bernoulli trial. There are two possible outcomes, head or tail, each with a finite probability. Each flip is independent. This is the type of situation to which the binomial distribution,

$$P \{X = k\} = \binom{n}{k} p^k (1 - p)^{n-k} ,$$

applies. The a priori probability of tossing a head is $p = \dfrac{1}{2}$. The probability of a tail is $q = 1 - p = 1 - \dfrac{1}{2} = \dfrac{1}{2}$. Also $n = 5$ and $k = 3$ (number of heads required). We have

$$P\{X = 3\} = \binom{5}{3}\left(\frac{1}{2}\right)^3\left(1 - \frac{1}{2}\right)^2 = \frac{5!}{3!\,2!}\left(\frac{1}{2}\right)^3\left(\frac{1}{2}\right)^2$$

$$= \frac{5 \times 4 \times 3 \times 2 \times 1}{3 \times 2 \times 1 \times 2 \times 1}\left(\frac{1}{2}\right)^5 = \frac{10}{2^5} = \frac{10}{32} = \frac{5}{16}$$

● **PROBLEM 4-2**

A quarterback completed 60 percent of his passes one season. Assuming he is as good a quarterback the next fall, what is the probability that he will complete 80 of his first 100 passes?

SOLUTION:

Since we are working with sequences of independent successes and failures, the binomial distribution is the correct one to use. The probability of 80 percent success is given by substitution in the formula $\binom{n}{x} p^x (1 - p)^{n-x}$, where n is the number of trials. In this case, $n = 100$, x is the number of desired successes ($x = 80$ here), and p, the probability of success in any trial ($p = \dfrac{60}{100}$ here). We define $\binom{n}{x}$, the number of combinations of n trials taken x at a time, to be $\dfrac{n!}{x!\,(n-x)!}$. The distribution $p\,(x) = \binom{n}{x} p^x (1 - p)^{n-x}$ is called binomial since for each integer value of x, the probability of x corresponds to a term in the binomial expansion

$$(q + p)^n = q^n + \binom{n}{1} q^{n-1} p + \binom{n}{2} q^{n-2} p + \dots + p^n .$$

We interpret p to be the probability of success in any trial and $q = 1 - p$ the probability of failure because

$$p + q = p + (1 - p) = (p - p) + 1 = 1 .$$

We have, therefore,

$$p(x) = \binom{n}{x} p^x (1 - p)^{n-x} = \binom{100}{80}\left(\frac{60}{100}\right)^{80}\left(\frac{40}{100}\right)^{20}$$

$$= \frac{100!}{80!\ 20!}\left(\frac{6}{10}\right)^{80}\left(\frac{4}{10}\right)^{20} = 1.053\left(10^{-5}\right)$$

Thus, the probability that the quarterback completes exactly 80 of his first 100 passes in the upcoming football season is about 10^{-5} .

● PROBLEM 4-3

Expand $(x + 2y)^5$.

SOLUTION:

Apply the binomial theorem. If n is a positive integer, then

$$(a + b)^n = \binom{n}{0} a^n b^0 + \binom{n}{1} a^{n-1} b + \binom{n}{2} a^{n-2} b^2 + \dots + \binom{n}{r} a^{n-r} b^r +$$

$$\dots + \binom{n}{n} a^0 b^n.$$

Note that $\binom{n}{r} = \dfrac{n!}{r!\ (n-r)!}$ and that $0! = 1$. Then we obtain:

$$(x + 2y)^5 = \binom{5}{0} x^5 (2y)^0 + \binom{5}{1} x^4 (2y)^1 + \binom{5}{2} x^3 (2)^2 + \binom{5}{3} x^2 (2y)^3 +$$

$$\binom{5}{4} x^1 (2y)^4 + \binom{5}{5} x^0 (2y)^5$$

$$= \frac{5!}{0!\ 5!} x^5 + \frac{5!}{1!\ 4!} x^4 (2y) + \frac{5!}{2!\ 3!} x^3 (4y^2) + \frac{5!}{3!\ 2!} x^2 (8y^3) +$$

$$\frac{5!}{4!\ 1!} x (16y^4) + \frac{5!}{5!\ 0!} 1 (32y^5)$$

$$= x^5 + \frac{5! \cdot 4!}{4!} x^4 (2y) + \frac{5! \cdot 4! \cdot 3!}{2! \cdot 1! \cdot 3!} x^3 (4y^2) + \frac{5! \cdot 4! \cdot 3!}{3! \cdot 2! \cdot 1!} x^2 (8y^3) +$$

$$\overset{1}{} \qquad\qquad\qquad \overset{2}{} \qquad\qquad\qquad \overset{2}{}$$

$$\frac{5! \cdot 4!}{4! \cdot 1!} x (16y^4) + \frac{5!}{5! \cdot 0!} (32y^5)$$

$$= x^5 + 10x^4y + 40x^3y^2 + 80x^2y^3 + 80xy^4 + 32y^5$$

Find the expansion of $(x + y)^6$.

SOLUTION:

Use the binomial theorem, which states that

$$(a + b)^n = \frac{1}{0!} a^n b^0 + \frac{n}{1!} a^{n-1} b^1 + \frac{n(n-1)}{2!} a^{n-2} b^2 + \ldots + na^1 b^{n-1} + a^0 b^n .$$

Replacing a by x and b by y gives:

$$(x + y)^6 = \frac{1}{0!} x^6 y^0 + \frac{6}{1!} x^5 y + \frac{6 \cdot 5}{2!} x^4 y^2 + \frac{6 \cdot 5 \cdot 4}{3!} x^3 y^3 + \frac{6 \cdot 5 \cdot 4 \cdot 3}{4!} x^2 y^4$$

$$+ \frac{6 \cdot 5 \cdot 4 \cdot 3 \cdot 2}{5!} x^1 y^5 + \frac{6 \cdot 5 \cdot 4 \cdot 3 \cdot 2 \cdot 1}{6!} x^0 y^6$$

$$= \frac{1}{1} x^6 + \frac{6}{1} x^5 y + \frac{6 \cdot 5}{2 \cdot 1} x^4 y^2 + \frac{6 \cdot 5 \cdot 4}{3 \cdot 2 \cdot 1} x^3 y^3 + \frac{6 \cdot 5 \cdot 4 \cdot 3}{4 \cdot 3 \cdot 2 \cdot 1} x^2 y^4$$

$$+ \frac{6 \cdot 5 \cdot 4 \cdot 3 \cdot 2}{5 \cdot 4 \cdot 3 \cdot 2 \cdot 1} xy^5 + \frac{6 \cdot 5 \cdot 4 \cdot 3 \cdot 2 \cdot 1}{6 \cdot 5 \cdot 4 \cdot 3 \cdot 2 \cdot 1} y^6$$

$$(x + y)^6 = x^6 + 6x^5 y + 15x^4 y^2 + 20x^3 y^3 + 15x^2 y^4 + 6xy^5 + y^6 .$$

Give the expansion of $\left(r^2 - \dfrac{1}{s}\right)^5$.

SOLUTION:

Write the given expression as the sum of two terms raised to the 5th power:

$$\left(r^2 - \frac{1}{s}\right)^5 = \left[r^2 + \left(\frac{-1}{s}\right)\right]^5 . \tag{1}$$

The binomial theorem can be used to expand the expression on the right side of equation (1). The binomial theorem is stated as:

$$(a + b)^n = a^n b^0 + na^{n-1} b^1 + \frac{n(n-1)}{1 \cdot 2} a^{n-2} b^2 + \frac{n(n-1)(n-2)}{1 \cdot 2 \cdot 3} a^{n-3} b^3$$

$$+ \dots + na^1 b^{n-1} + a^0 b^n ,$$

where a and b are any two numbers.

Let $a = r^2$, $b = -\dfrac{1}{s}$, and $n = 5$. Then, using the binomial theorem:

$$\left(r^2 - \frac{1}{s}\right)^5 = \left[r^2 + \left(\frac{-1}{s}\right)\right]^5$$

$$= (r^2)^5 + 5(r^2)^{5-1}\left(-\frac{1}{s}\right) + \frac{5(5-1)}{1 \cdot 2}(r^2)^{5-2}\left(-\frac{1}{s}\right)^2$$

$$+ \frac{5(5-1)(5-2)}{1 \cdot 2 \cdot 3}(r^2)^{5-3}\left(-\frac{1}{s}\right)^3$$

$$+ \frac{5(5-1)(5-2)(5-3)}{1 \cdot 2 \cdot 3 \cdot 4}(r^2)^{5-4}\left(-\frac{1}{s}\right)^4$$

$$+ \frac{5(5-1)(5-2)(5-3)(5-4)}{1 \cdot 2 \cdot 3 \cdot 4 \cdot 5}(r^2)^{5-5}\left(-\frac{1}{s}\right)^5$$

$$= r^{10} - \frac{5(r^2)^4}{s} + \frac{5(4)}{1 \cdot 2}(r^2)^3 \left(\frac{1}{s^2}\right)^2 - \frac{5(4)(3)}{1 \cdot 2 \cdot 3}(r^2)^2 \left(\frac{1}{s^3}\right)^2$$

$$+ \frac{5(4)(3)(2)}{1 \cdot 2 \cdot 3 \cdot 4}(r^2)^1 \left(\frac{1}{s^4}\right) - \frac{5(4)(3)(2)(1)}{1 \cdot 2 \cdot 3 \cdot 4 \cdot 5}(r^2)^0 \left(\frac{1}{s^5}\right)(r^2)^0$$

$$= r^{10} - \frac{5r^8}{s} + \frac{10r^6}{s^2} - \frac{10r^4}{s^3} + \frac{5r^2}{s^4} - (1)\,(1)\,\left(\frac{1}{s^5}\right)$$

$$\left(r^2 - \frac{1}{s}\right)^5 = r^{10} - \frac{5r^8}{s} + \frac{10r^6}{s^2} - \frac{10r^4}{s^3} + \frac{5r^2}{s^4} - \left(\frac{1}{s^5}\right)$$

On three successive flips of a fair coin, what is the probability of observing three heads? Three tails?

SOLUTION:

The three successive flips of the coin are three independent events. Since the coin is fair, the probability of throwing a head on any particular toss is $p = \frac{1}{2}$. Let X equal the number of heads observed in three tosses of the coin. We wish to find $P\,(X = 3)$. By our assumptions, X is binomially distributed with parameters $n = 3$ and $p = \frac{1}{2}$. Thus,

$$P\,(X = 3) = \binom{3}{3}\left(\frac{1}{2}\right)^3 \left(\frac{1}{2}\right)^0 = \left(\frac{1}{2}\right)^3 \left(\frac{1}{2}\right)^0 = \frac{1}{8}\ .$$

Similarly, let T = the number of tails observed in three successive flips of a fair coin. T is distributed binomially, with parameters $n = 3$ and $p = \frac{1}{2}$ = the probability that a tail is observed on a particular toss of the coin. Thus,

$$P\{T = 3\} = \binom{3}{3}\left(\frac{1}{2}\right)^3\left(\frac{1}{2}\right)^0 = 1 \cdot \frac{1}{8} \cdot 1 = \frac{1}{8}.$$

● **PROBLEM 4-7**

Find the probability that in three rolls of a pair of dice, exactly one total of seven is rolled.

SOLUTION:

Consider each of the three rolls of the pair as a trial and of rolling a total of seven as a "success." Assume that each roll is independent of the others. If X is the number of successes, then we want to find

$$P\{X = 1\} = \binom{3}{1}p^1\,(1 - p)^2.$$

where p is the probability of rolling a total of seven on a single roll. The total number of combinations is 36 and six combinations have a total equal to seven. This probability is $\frac{6}{36} = \frac{1}{6}$, and hence the probability of rolling a total of seven exactly once in three rolls is

$$P\{X = 1\} = \binom{3}{1}\left(\frac{1}{6}\right)^1\left(\frac{5}{6}\right)^2 = 3 \cdot \frac{1}{6} \cdot \frac{25}{36} = \frac{25}{72}.$$

● **PROBLEM 4-8**

What is the probability of obtaining exactly four "sixes" when a die is rolled seven times?

SOLUTION:

Let X equal the number of "sixes" observed when a die is rolled seven times. If we assume that each roll is independent of each other roll and that the probability of rolling a six on one roll is $\frac{1}{6}$, then X is binomially distributed with parameters $n = 7$ and $p = \frac{1}{6}$.

Thus, $P\{X = 4\} = P$ {exactly four "sixes" on seven rolls}

$$= \binom{7}{4}\left(\frac{1}{6}\right)^4\left(\frac{5}{6}\right)^{7-4}$$

$$= \frac{7\cdot6\cdot5\cdot4\cdot3\cdot2\cdot1}{4\cdot3\cdot2\cdot1\cdot3\cdot2\cdot1}\left(\frac{1}{6}\right)^4\left(\frac{5}{6}\right)^3$$

$$= 35\left(\frac{1}{6}\right)^4\left(\frac{5}{6}\right)^3$$

$$P\{X = 4\} = 35\left(\frac{1}{1,296}\right)\left(\frac{125}{216}\right) = \frac{4,375}{279,936} = 0.0156$$

● **PROBLEM 4-9**

A deck of cards can be dichotomized into black cards and red cards. If p is the probability of drawing a black card on a single draw and q the probability of drawing a red card, then $p = \frac{1}{2}$ and $q = \frac{1}{2}$. Six cards are sampled with replacement. What is the probability on six draws of obtaining four black and two red cards? Of obtaining all black cards?

SOLUTION:

Let $X =$ the number of black cards observed in six draws from this deck. Then $P\{X = 4\}$ is the probability that four black cards and two red cards are in this sample of six. The probability of drawing a black card on a single draw is $p = \frac{1}{2}$ and since each draw is independent, X is distributed binomially with parameters of 6 and $\frac{1}{2}$. Thus,

$$P\{X=4\} = \binom{6}{4}\left(\frac{1}{2}\right)^4\left(\frac{1}{2}\right)^2 = 15\left(\frac{1}{2}\right)^6 = \frac{15}{64}$$

and $$P\{X=6\} = \binom{6}{6}\left(\frac{1}{2}\right)^6\left(\frac{1}{2}\right)^0 = \left(\frac{1}{2}\right)^6 = \frac{1}{64}.$$

In a family of four children, what is the probability that there will be exactly two boys?

SOLUTION:

The case of the sex of a born child is classically described by the binomial distribution. There are two possible outcomes, boy or girl. The probability of giving birth to a boy is $p = \frac{1}{2}$. The probability of having a girl is $q = 1 - p = 1 - \frac{1}{2} = \frac{1}{2}$. Also, $n = 4$ (number of children) and $k = 2$ (number of boys).

Furthermore, $P\{X=k\} = \binom{n}{k}p^k(1-p)^{n-k}$

$$P\{X=2\} = \binom{4}{2}\left(\frac{1}{2}\right)^2\left(\frac{1}{2}\right)^{4-2} = \frac{4!}{2!\,2!}\left(\frac{1}{2}\right)^2\left(\frac{1}{2}\right)^2$$

$$= \frac{4\cdot3\cdot2\cdot1}{2\cdot1\cdot2\cdot1}\left(\frac{1}{2}\right)^4 = \frac{6}{24}$$

$$= \frac{3\cdot2}{2^2\cdot2} = \frac{3}{2^3} = \frac{3}{8}$$

Suppose that the probability of parents to have a child with blond hair is $\frac{1}{4}$. If there are four children in the family, what is the probability that exactly half of them have blond hair?

SOLUTION:

We assume that the probability of parents having a blond child is $\frac{1}{4}$. In order to compute the probability that two of four children have blond hair, we must make another assumption. We must assume that the event consisting of a child being blond when it is born is independent of whether any of the other children are blond. The genetic determination of each child's hair color can be considered one of four independent trials with the probability of success, observing a blond child, equal to $\frac{1}{4}$.

If X is the number of children in the family with blond hair, we are interested in finding $P(X = 2)$. By our assumptions X is binomially distributed with $n = 4$ (total number of children) and $p = \frac{1}{4}$.

Thus, $P\{X = 2\} = P$ (exactly half the children are blond)

$$= \binom{4}{2}\left(\frac{1}{4}\right)^2\left(\frac{3}{4}\right)^2 = \frac{4!}{2!\,2!}\left(\frac{1}{4}\right)^2\left(\frac{3}{4}\right)^2$$

$$= \frac{4\cdot3}{2\cdot1}\left(\frac{1}{16}\right)\left(\frac{9}{16}\right) = \frac{27}{128} = 0.21$$

If a fair coin is tossed four times, what is the probability of obtaining at least two heads?

SOLUTION:

Let X = the number of heads observed in four tosses of a fair coin. Then

X is binomially distributed if we assume that each toss is independent. If the coin is fair, then $p = P$ (a head is observed on a single toss) $= \dfrac{1}{2}$.

Thus, P (at least two heads in four tosses) $= P \ (X \geq 2)$

$$= \sum_{x=2}^{4} \binom{4}{x} \left(\frac{1}{2}\right)^{x} \left(\frac{1}{2}\right)^{4-x}$$

$$= \binom{4}{2}\left(\frac{1}{2}\right)^{2}\left(\frac{1}{2}\right)^{2} = \binom{4}{3}\left(\frac{1}{2}\right)^{2}\left(\frac{1}{2}\right) + \binom{4}{4}\left(\frac{1}{2}\right)^{3}\left(\frac{1}{2}\right)$$

$$= \frac{6}{16} + \frac{4}{16} + \frac{1}{16} = \frac{11}{16}$$

● **PROBLEM 4–13**

A baseball player has a 0.250 batting average (one base hit every four times, on the average). Assuming that the binomial distribution is applicable, if he is at bat four times on a particular day, what is (a) the probability that he will get exactly one hit? (b) the probability that he will get at least one hit?

SOLUTION:

Considering a hit as a "success," we have P (success) $= \dfrac{1}{4}$,

(a) P (exactly one hit in four trials) $= \binom{4}{1}\left(\dfrac{1}{4}\right)^{1}\left(\dfrac{3}{4}\right)^{3}$

$$= 4\left(\frac{1}{4}\right)\left(\frac{27}{64}\right) = \frac{27}{64}$$

(b) P (one hit or two hits or three hits or four hits), since these are mutually exclusive events, equals

$$4\left(\frac{1}{4}\right)^{1}\left(\frac{3}{4}\right)^{3} + \binom{4}{2}\left(\frac{1}{4}\right)^{2}\left(\frac{3}{4}\right)^{2} + \binom{4}{3}\left(\frac{1}{4}\right)^{3}\left(\frac{3}{4}\right) + \binom{4}{4}\left(\frac{1}{4}\right)^{4}\left(\frac{3}{4}\right)^{0}$$

$$= \frac{27}{64} + 6 \cdot \frac{1}{16} \cdot \frac{9}{16} + 4 \cdot \left(\frac{1}{64}\right) \cdot \frac{3}{4} + 1 \cdot \frac{1}{256} \cdot 1$$

$$= \frac{27}{64} + \frac{27}{128} + \frac{3}{64} + \frac{1}{256} = \frac{30}{64} + \frac{27}{128} + \frac{1}{256} = \frac{175}{256}$$

There is a simpler way if we notice that the batter getting at least one hit and the batter going hitless are two mutually exclusive and exhaustive events. Because of this fact we know that

P {one hit} + P {two hits} + P {three hits} + P {four hits} +
$$P \text{ \{zero hits\} } = 1 \text{ , so}$$

P {at least one hit} + P {zero hits} = 1

or P {at least one hit} = 1 – P (zero hits) .

But $P \text{ \{zero hits\} } = \binom{4}{0}\left(\frac{1}{4}\right)^0 \left(\frac{3}{4}\right)^4 = 1 \cdot 1 \cdot \frac{81}{256}$

and $P \text{ \{at least one hit\} } = 1 - \frac{81}{256} = \frac{175}{256}$.

● PROBLEM 4–14

If a deck of cards is dichotomized into hearts and all other cards, what is the probability p of drawing a heart on a single draw? What is the probability q of drawing a spade, club, or diamond? When seven cards are sampled with replacement, what is the probability of drawing no hearts at all? What is the probability of drawing four hearts? What is the probability of drawing two hearts out of the first four draws and then two hearts out of the next three? Is this result more or less probable than "four hearts out of seven"? Why?

SOLUTION:

Using the classical model of probability, $P = \dfrac{\text{favorable outcomes}}{\text{total outcomes}}$. Of the 52 cards (total possible outcomes), 13 are hearts (favorable outcomes).

Therefore, P {heart} $= \dfrac{13}{52} = \dfrac{1}{4}$. The total probability of all events must equal one. Hence, P {spade, club, or diamond} $= 1 - P$ (heart) $= 1 - \dfrac{1}{4} = \dfrac{3}{4}$. Since

there is replacement, the probability of not drawing a heart remains $\dfrac{3}{4}$ on

each draw. Therefore, by the multiplication rule,

$$P \text{ (no hearts in seven)} = \frac{3}{4} \times \frac{3}{4} \times \frac{3}{4} \times \frac{3}{4} \times \frac{3}{4} \times \frac{3}{4} \times \frac{3}{4} = \left(\frac{3}{4}\right)^7 .$$ For the

probability of drawing four hearts, we use the binomial distribution. We do this since we have independent trials with two possible outcomes, success

or failure, each with constant probabilities, $\dfrac{1}{4}$ and $\dfrac{3}{4}$. According to the

binomial distribution, $P \{X = k\} = \dbinom{n}{k} p^k (1 - p)^{n-k}$. In our case

$$P \{X = 4\} = \binom{7}{4}\left(\frac{1}{4}\right)^4\left(\frac{3}{4}\right)^3 .$$

Again, we use the binomial distribution for the same reasons.

$$\text{When } n = k, P \{X = 2\} = \binom{4}{2}\left(\frac{1}{4}\right)^2\left(\frac{3}{4}\right)^2 ;$$

$$\text{when } n = 3, P \{X = 2\} = \binom{3}{2}\left(\frac{1}{4}\right)^2\left(\frac{3}{4}\right)^1 .$$

By the multiplication rule for independent events,
P {two of first four and two of last three}
$\quad\quad = P$ {two of first four} $\times P$ {two of last three}

$$= \binom{4}{2}\left(\frac{1}{4}\right)^2\left(\frac{3}{4}\right)^2 \cdot \binom{3}{2}\left(\frac{1}{4}\right)^2\left(\frac{3}{4}\right)^1 .$$

The second result is less because it restricts the number of ways the total of four hearts can be arranged. The first probability includes such arrangements as three in the first four, one in the second three, and so on.

If the probability of hitting a target on a single shot is 0.8, what is the probability that in four shots, the target will be hit at least twice?

SOLUTION:

Each shot at the target is an independent trial with constant probability, $p = 0.8$, of a success. The only other possibility is failure. This type of situation calls for the binomial distribution,

$$P \{X = k \text{ successes}\} = \binom{n}{k} p^k (1 - p)^{n - k} .$$

Since the events of two, three, or four successes are mutually disjoint, we use the addition rule for probabilities and

$$P \{\text{two or three or four}\} = P \{2\} + P \{3\} + P \{4\} ,$$

$$P \{X = 2\} = \frac{4!}{2! (4 - 2)!} (0.8)^2 (0.2)^{4 - 2} = \frac{4!}{2! \ 2!} (.8)^2 (.2)^2$$

$$= \frac{4 \cdot 3 \cdot \overset{2}{2} \cdot 1}{2 \cdot 1 \cdot 2 \cdot 1} (0.64) (0.04)$$

$$= 6 (0.0256) = 0.1536 ,$$

$$P \{X = 3\} = \frac{4!}{3! (4 - 3)!} (0.8)^3 (0.2)^{4 - 3} = \frac{4!}{3! \ 1!} (0.8)^3 (|0|)$$

$$= 4 (0.512) (0.2) = 0.4096 ,$$

$$P \{X = 4\} = \frac{4!}{4! (4 - 4)!} (0.8)^4 (0.2)^{4 - 4} = \frac{4!}{4! \ 0!} (0.8)^4 (0.2)^0$$

$$= (0.8)^4 = 0.4096 .$$

Now $\frac{4!}{4!} = 1$, $0! = 1$, and any number raised to the zero power ισ one. Thus,

$P \{\text{two or three or four}\} = 0.1536 + 0.4096 + 0.4096 = 0.9728 .$

Records of an insurance company show that $\frac{3}{1,000}$ of the accidents reported to the company involve a fatality. Determine:
  (a) the probability that no fatality is involved in 30 accidents reported.
  (b) the probability that four fatal accidents are included in 20 accidents reported.

SOLUTION:

Let X be the number of fatalities involved in n accidents. Then X may be assumed to be binomially distributed with parameters n and $\pi = \frac{3}{1,000}$.

This assumption will be a valid one if the number of fatalities observed can be considered the sum of the results of n independent trials. On each trial (or accident) a fatality will occur with the probability $\frac{3}{1,000}$.

(a) The probability that there are no fatalities in 30 accidents is $P(X = 0)$ with $n = 30$ accidents reported and $\pi = \frac{3}{1,000}$ involve a fatality. Now

$$P\{X = 0\} = \binom{30}{0}\left(\frac{3}{1,000}\right)^9\left(\frac{997}{1,000}\right)^9$$

$$= (1)(1)(0.997)^{30} = 0.9138$$

(b) The probability that there are four fatalities in 20 accidents is $P\{X = 4\}$ with $n = 20$.

$$P\{X = 4\} = \binom{20}{4}\left(\frac{3}{1,000}\right)^4\left(\frac{997}{1,000}\right)^{16}$$

$$= 0.374 \times 10^{-6}$$

● PROBLEM 4-17

Given that 40 percent of entering college students do not complete their degree programs, what is the probability that out of six randomly-selected students, more than half will get their degrees?

SOLUTION:

Since 40 percent of the entering students drop out, $100\% - 40\% = 60\%$ receive their degrees. We use the binomial probability function because (1) the selection of six students can be thought of as a sequence of success-failure trials, in which success indicates graduation from college; (2) each trial is independent of the result of the other five trials; (3) the probability of success is the same in every trial. The probability that four students out of six will graduate is

$$P\{4\} = \binom{6}{4}(0.6)^4 (0.4)^{6-4}$$

$$= \binom{6}{4}(0.6)^4 (0.4)^2 = \frac{6!}{4!\,(6-4)!}(0.6)^4 (0.4)^2$$

$$= (15)\,(0.1296)\,(0.16) = 0.311040 \,,$$

$$P\{5\} = \frac{6!}{5!\,(6-5)!}(0.6)^5 (0.4)^{6-5} = 6\,(0.7776)\,(0.4)$$

$$= 0.186624 \,,$$

$$P\{6\} = \frac{6!}{6!\,(6-6)!}(0.6)^6 (0.4)^0 = (0.6)^6 = 0.046656 \,.$$

No two of the events that four or five or six students out of the six selected graduate can occur together. We say they are mutually exclusive. Therefore, we can add their individual probabilities to find
$$P\{\text{four or five or six}\} = 0.311040 + 0.186624 + 0.046656 = 0.54432 \,.$$

● PROBLEM 4-18

The probability that a basketball player makes at least one of six free throws is equal to 0.999936. Find (a) the probability function of X, the number of times he scores; and (b) the probability that he makes at least three baskets.

SOLUTION:

This problem involves the binomial distribution for three reasons: (1) there are six independent trials (the outcome of each throw is independent of the others); (2) each throw has only two outcomes—score or no score;

63

(3) since the player is shooting "free throws" (from a standing position), we can assume that the probability of a score remains the same from throw to throw.

In order to determine the probability function of the number of scores, we need to know the probability that any free throw will score. The event that no free throw scores is the complement of the event that one or more throws score. By the binomial distribution,

$$P \{\text{no scores}\} = \binom{6}{0} p^0 (1 - p)^{6 - 0} = 1 \cdot 1 \cdot (1 - p)^6$$

$$= (1 - p)^6 ,$$

since $\binom{6}{0} = \dfrac{6!}{0! \, (6-0)!} = \dfrac{6!}{1 \cdot 6!} = 1$ and $p^0 = 1$.

Now $P \{\text{at least one score}\} + P \{\text{no scores}\} = 1$, since the events are complementary. Substituting $(1 - p)^6$ for $P \{\text{no scores}\}$, the equation becomes $P \{\text{at least one score}\} + (1 - p)^6 = 1$. Using the given information, this becomes

$$P \{\text{at least one score}\} = 0.999936 = 1 - (1 - p)^6$$
$$= (1 - p)^6 = 0.000064,$$

so $1 - p = \sqrt[6]{0.000064} = 0.2$ and so $p = 0.8$. Again, using the binomial distribution, where r is the number of scores in six throws,

$$P \{r\} = \binom{6}{r} (0.8)^r (0.2)^{6-r} .$$

Substitution of any integer from one to six inclusive for r will yield the probability of that number of scores in six free throws.

For example, the probability of four scores ($r = 4$) is

$$P \{4\} = \binom{6}{4} (0.8)^4 (0.2)^2 .$$

$$= 15 \, (0.4096) \, (0.04)$$
$$= 0.24576$$

Part (b) asks for the probability of at least three scores. This includes four possibilities: exactly three scores; exactly four scores; exactly five score; or exactly six scores in six throws. Since only one of these events can occur, these events are mutually exclusive. It follows that their probabilities can be added to give the probability that any one event will occur. Using summation notation, P {three or more scores in six throws}

$$= \sum_{r=3}^{6} \binom{6}{r} (0.8)^r (0.2)^{6-r}.$$

By the table, P {three scores} = 0.082, P {4} = 0.246, P {5} = 0.393, and P {6} = 0.262. Then, P (three or more) = 0.082 + 0.246 + 0.393 + 0.262 = 0.983.

Many binomial tables give values for $p \leq 0.5$. Since in our example $p = 0.8$, we would have to convert the binomial distribution to an equivalent form in the following way:

Let $P \{X = k\} = \binom{n}{k} p^k (1 - p)^{n-k}$ with $p \geq 0.5$. If $p \geq 0.5$, then $1 - p \leq 0.5$.

We will find a probability for a new random variable Y with probability of success $1 - p \leq 0.5$. Now

$$P \{X = k\} = \binom{n}{k} p^k (1 - p)^{n-k}$$

$$= \binom{n}{n-k} p^k (1 - p)^{n-k} = P(Y = n - k)$$

Remember that $\binom{n}{k} = \dfrac{n!}{(n-k)! \, k!} = \binom{n}{n-k}.$

We can thus use the table to find $P \{Y = n - k\}$ where the probability of success is $1 - p$ and we can thus find $P \{X = k\}$ when the probability of success is p.

● PROBLEM 4-19

Forty percent of a company's employees are in favor of a proposed new incentive-pay system. Develop the probability distribution for the number of employees out of a sample of two who would be in favor of the incentive system by the use of a tree diagram. Use F for a favorable reaction and F' for an unfavorable reaction.

SOLUTION:

Imagine that the two employees are sampled in succession. The tree diagram describing the possible outcomes is

Because 40 percent of the employees favor the new incentive-pay system, the probability of selecting a single employee who favors the new plan is 0.4, $P\{F\} = 0.4$ and $P\{F'\} = 1 - P\{F\} = 1 - 0.4 = 0.6$.

The tree diagram for a single employee with the probabilities labeled is

After one employee is picked and his opinion is recorded, the second employee will be picked. The probabilities for the second employee will be the same. Using the multiplication rule, the extended tree diagram is

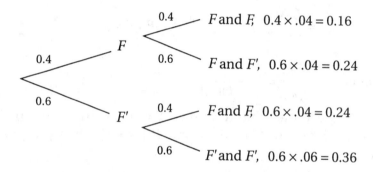

This diagram lists all the possible outcomes and probabilities associated with this sampling procedure. Let X be the number of people in the sample who favor the new plan. Then X can take on the values 0, 1, or 2. We will compute the probability distribution of X from the tree diagram.

$P\{X = 0\}$ = P {both sampled do not favor the new plan}
$= P\{F' \text{ and } F'\} = 0.6 \times 0.6 = 0.36$

$P\{X = 1\}$ = P {one favors and one does not}
$= P\{F \text{ and } F' \text{ or } F' \text{ and } F\} = (0.4) \times (0.6) + (0.6)(0.4)$
$= 0.24 + 0.24 = 0.48$

$P\{X = 2\}$ = P {both favor the new plan}
$= P\{F \text{ and } F\} = 0.16$

An alternative method is to notice that X is binomially distributed with parameters $n = 2$ and $\pi = 0.4$.

Thus, $P\{X = 0\} = \binom{2}{0}(0.4)^0 (0.6)^2 = (1)\ (1)\ (0.36) = 0.36$

$P\{X = 1\} = \binom{2}{1}(0.4)^1 (0.6)^1 = (2)\ (0.4)\ (0.6) = 0.48$

$P\{X = 2\} = \binom{2}{2}(0.4)^2 (0.6)^0 = (1)\ (0.4)^2\ (1) = 0.16$

● **PROBLEM 4-20**

Over a long period of time a certain drug has been effective in 30 percent of the cases in which it has been prescribed. If a doctor is now administering this drug to four patients, what is the probability that it will be effective for at least three of the patients?

SOLUTION:

Let X be the number of patients on which the drug is effective. Then X is binomially distributed. There are assumed to be four independent trials, the administration of the drug to the four patients. The probability of "success" in a particular trial is the probability that the drug is effective on a patient and P (drug is effective on a patient) $= p = 0.30$. The probability that the drug is effective on at least three patients is the probability that X is equal to three or four. Since these two events are mutually exclusive, P $(X = 3 \text{ or } X = 4) = P\ (X = 3) + P\ (X = 4)$ by the addition rule. Now X is distributed binomially with parameters 4 and 0.3. Thus,

$$P\{X = 3\} = \binom{4}{3}(0.3)^3 (0.7)^1 = 4\ (0.027)\ (0.7) = 0.0756$$

$$P\{X = 4\} = \binom{4}{4}(0.3)^4 (0.7)^0 = 1 \cdot (0.0081) \cdot 1 = 0.0081$$

and $P\{X = 3 \text{ or } X = 4\} = 0.0756 + 0.0081 = 0.0837$. This means that 8.37% of the time this drug will be effective on at least three patients.

You are told that nine out of ten doctors recommend Potter's Pills. Assuming this is true, suppose you plan to choose four doctors at random. What is the probability that no more than two of these four doctors will recommend Potter's Pills?

SOLUTION:

Let X be the number of doctors among the four chosen that will recommend Potter's Pills. If each doctor is selected at random and the probability of selecting a doctor that recommends Potter's Pills is 0.9, then X is a binomially distributed random variable with parameters $n = 4$ and $p = 0.9$.

In order to make this assumption we needed to know that each trial on which a doctor was selected was independent of any other trial. This is guaranteed by our selection of doctors at random and the fact that we may treat the population as infinite for all practical purposes.

We wish to find P {no more than two of these four doctors will recommend Potter's Pills}. This equals P {$X = 0$, 1, or 2}. Each of these outcomes is mutually exclusive, so

$$P\{X = 0, 1, \text{ or } 2\} = P\{X = 0\} + P\{X = 1\} + P\{X = 2\}$$

$$= \binom{4}{0}(0.9)^0 (0.1)^4 + \binom{4}{1}(0.9)^1 (0.1)^3 + \binom{4}{2}(0.9)^2 (0.1)^3$$

$$= (0.1)^4 + 4 (0.9) (0.1)^3 + \frac{4 \cdot 3 \cdot 2 \cdot 1}{2 \cdot 1 \cdot 2 \cdot 1}(0.9)^2 (0.1)^2$$

$$= (0.1)^4 + (3.6) (0.1)^3 + 6 (0.9)^2 (0.1)^2$$

$$= (1 \times 10^{-1})^4 + (3.6) (1 \times 10^{-1})^3 + 6 (0.81) (1 \times 10^{-1})^2$$

$$= 1 \times 10^{-4} + 36 \times 10^{-4} + 486 \times 10^{-4}$$

$$= 523 \times 10^{-4} = 0.0523$$

● **PROBLEM 4-22**

The most common application of the binomial theorem in industrial work is in lot-by-lot acceptance inspection. If there are a certain number of defectives in the lot, the lot will be rejected as unsatisfactory.

It is natural to wish to find the probability that the lot is acceptable even though a certain number of defectives are observed. Let p be the fraction of defectives in the lot. Assume that the size of the sample is small compared to the lot size. This will insure that the probability of selecting a defective item remains relatively constant from trial to trial. Now choose a sample of size 18 from a lot in which 10 percent of the items are defective. What is the probability of observing zero, one, or two defectives in the sample?

SOLUTION:

Imagine that the items are drawn successively from the lot until 18 have been chosen. The probability of selecting a defective item is $p = 0.10$, the fraction of defectives in the lot. Hence, the probability of selecting a non-defective item is $1 - 0.10 = 0.90$. If X is the number of defective items observed, X is the sum of the number of defective items observed on 18 independent trials and is hence binomially distributed with parameters $n = 18$ and $p = 0.10$.

We wish to determine $P \{X = 0, 1, \text{ or } 2\}$. This probability is the sum of the probabilities of three mutually exclusive events. Hence, $P \{X = 0, 1, \text{ or } 2\} = P \{X = 0\} + P \{X = 1\} + P \{X = 2\}$.

Now X is binomially distributed so

$$P \{X = 0\} = \binom{18}{0}(0.10)^0 + (0.90)^{18} = 0.150$$

$$P \{X = 1\} = \binom{18}{1}(0.10)^1 + (0.90)^{17} = 0.300$$

$$P \{X = 2\} = \binom{18}{2}(0.10)^2 + (0.90)^{16} = 0.284$$

and $P \{X = 0, 1, \text{ or } 2\} = 0.150 + 0.300 + 0.284 = 0.734$.

● PROBLEM 4–23

Over a period of some years, a car manufacturing firm finds that 18 percent of their cars develop body squeaks within the guarantee period. In a randomly selected shipment, 20 cars reach the end of the guarantee period and none develop squeaks. What is the probability of this?

SOLUTION:

The car can either squeak or not squeak. The probability of a car squeaking is 18 percent or 0.18. The probability of it not squeaking is $q = 1 - p = 1 - 0.18 = 0.82$. The situation we have here is a dichotomy of the type that fits the binomial distribution. There are independent trials with two possible outcomes each with a constant probability.

According to the binomial distribution,

$$P\{X = k\} = \binom{n}{k} p^k (1 - p)^{n-k}.$$

Here, $p = 0.18$, $1 - p = 0.82$, $n = 20$, and $k = 0$. Hence,

$$P\{X = 0\} = \binom{20}{0} (0.18)^0 (0.82)^{20} = \frac{20!}{20! \cdot 0!} (0.18)^0 (0.82)^{20}$$

$$= (0.82)^{20} = 0.019$$

● PROBLEM 4–24

A sample of four fuses is selected without replacement from a lot consisting of 5,000 fuses. Assuming that 20 percent of the fuses in the lot are known to be defective, what is the probability that the sample would contain exactly two defective items?

SOLUTION:

Since the sample constitutes a very small fraction of the population, the probability of getting a defective fuse, π, is approximately the same on each selection. The probability of selecting a defective fuse is 0.20, since 20 percent of the fuses are known to be defective. If the probability of getting a defective fuse is the same on each draw, it follows that the outcome of each selection is independent from the outcome of any other selection.

Let X be the number of defective fuses observed in a sample of four fuses. By our assumptions, X is binomially distributed with parameters $n = 4$ and $p = 0.2$. Now P {sample contains exactly two defective fuses}

$$= P\{X = 2\} = \binom{4}{2} (0.2)^2 (0.8)^2 = \frac{4!}{2! \cdot 2!} (0.2)^2 (0.8)^2$$

$$= 6 (0.4) (0.64) = 0.1536$$

An industrial process produces items of which one percent are defective. If a random sample of 100 of these are drawn from a large consignment, calculate the probability that the sample contains no defectives.

SOLUTION:

If X is the number of defectives in a sample of 100, then X is distributed binomially with parameters $n = 100$ and $p = 1\%$ or 0.01. Thus,

$$P\{X = 0\} = P\{\text{no defective in sample}\}$$

$$= \binom{100}{0}(0.1)^0 (1 - 0.01)^{100}$$

$$= (0.99)^{100} = 0.366$$

A proportion p of a large number of items in a batch is defective. A sample of n items is drawn and if it contains no defective items, the batch is accepted, while if it contains more than two defective items the batch is rejected. If, on the other hand, it contains one or two defectives, an independent sample of m is drawn, and if the combined number of defectives in the samples does not exceed two, the batch is accepted. Calculate the probability of accepting this batch.

SOLUTION:

The batch will be accepted only if:
  (1) the first sample contains no defectives, or
  (2) the first sample contains one defective and the second sample contains zero or one defective, or
  (3) the first sample contains two defectives and the second sample contains zero defectives.

These three probabilities are mutually exclusive. If one occurs then none of the others can occur. Thus, if we compute the probability of each of these events, the sum of the three will be the probability of acceptance.

Let: X = the number of defectives in the first sample.
       Y = the number of defectives in the second sample.

If the sampling is done with replacement, then X will be binomially distributed with the parameter n equal to the number of trials (or size of sample) and p equal to the probability of selecting a defective on one trial. Similarly, Y is binomially distributed with parameters m and p.

Again by the addition law, P {acceptance} $= P$ {0 defectives in first batch} $+ P$ {one in first and zero or one in second} $+ P$ {two in first and zero in second} $= P\{X = 0\} + P\{X = 1, Y = 0 \text{ or } 1\} + P\{X = 2, Y = 0\}$.

Now $P\{X = 0\} = \binom{n}{0} p^0 (1 - p)^{n-0}$, and

$$P\{X = 1, Y = 0 \text{ or } 1\} = P\{X = 1, Y = 0\} + P\{X = 1, Y = 1\}$$

by the addition rule, since we are dealing with mutually exclusive events. Thus, $P\{X = 1, Y = 0\} = P\{X = 1\} \cdot P\{Y = 0\}$ by the multiplication law. Hence,

$$P\{X = 1, Y = 0\} = \binom{n}{1} p^1 (1 - p)^{n-1} \cdot \binom{m}{0} p^0 (1 - p)^m .$$

Similarly, $P\{X = 1, Y = 1\} = P(X = 1) \cdot P(Y = 1)$

$$= \binom{n}{1} p^1 (1 - p)^{n-1} \cdot \binom{m}{1} p^1 (1 - p)^{m-1}$$

For similar reasons, $P(X = 2, Y = 0) = P(X = 2) \cdot P(Y = 0)$.

$$P\{Y = 0\} = \binom{n}{2} p^2 (1 - p)^{n-2} \cdot \binom{m}{0} p^0 (1 - p)^m .$$

Hence, P (acceptance)

$$= \binom{n}{0} p^0 (1 - p)^{n-0} + \binom{n}{1} p^1 (1 - p)^{n-1} \binom{m}{0} p^0 (1 - p)^m +$$

$$\binom{n}{1} p^1 (1 - p)^{n-1} \binom{m}{1} p^1 (1 - p)^{m-1} +$$

$$\binom{n}{2} p^2 (1 - p)^{n-2} \binom{m}{0} p^0 (1 - p)^m$$

$$= (1 - p)^n + np (1 - p)^{m+n-1} + nmp^2 (1 - p)^{m+n-2}$$

$$+ \frac{1}{2} n (n - 1) p^2 (1 - p)^{m-n-2}$$

Letting $1 - p = q$, we can write this more concisely as

$$P \text{ (acceptance)} = q^n + npq^{m-1} + mnp^2 q^{m-2} + \frac{1}{2} n (n - 1) p^2 q^{m-2} .$$

CUMULATIVE BINOMIAL PROBABILITIES
n=4

x	π=	01	02	03	04	05	06	07	08	09	10	
1		0394	0776	1147	1507	1855	2193	2519	2836	3143	3439	3
2		0006	0023	0052	0091	0140	0199	0267	0344	0430	0523	2
3				0001	0002	0005	0008	0013	0019	0027	0037	1
4										0001	0001	0

| x | | 99 | 98 | 97 | 96 | 95 | 94 | 93 | 92 | 91 | 90 =π | x |

n = 4

x	π=	11	12	13	14	15	16	17	18	19	20	
1		3726	4003	4271	4530	4780	5021	5254	5479	5695	5904	3
2		0624	0732	0847	0968	1095	1228	1366	1509	1656	1808	2
3		0049	0063	0079	0098	0120	0144	0171	0202	0235	0272	1
4		0001	0002	0003	0004	0005	0007	0008	0010	0013	0016	0

| x | | 89 | 88 | 87 | 86 | 85 | 84 | 83 | 82 | 81 | 80 =π | x |

n = 4

x	π=	21	22	23	24	25	26	27	28	29	30	
1		6105	6298	6485	6664	6836	7001	7160	7313	7459	7599	3
2		1963	2122	2285	2450	2617	2787	2959	3132	3307	3483	2
3		0312	0356	0403	0453	0508	0566	0628	0694	0763	0837	1
4		0019	0023	0028	0033	0039	0046	0053	0061	0071	0081	0

| x | | 79 | 78 | 77 | 76 | 75 | 74 | 73 | 72 | 71 | 70 = | x |

n = 4

x	π=	31	32	33	34	35	36	37	38	39	40	
1		7733	7862	7985	8103	8215	8322	8425	8522	8615	8704	3
2		3660	3837	4015	4193	4370	4547	4724	4900	5075	5248	2
3		0915	0996	1082	1171	1265	1362	1464	1596	1679	1792	1
4		0092	0105	0119	0134	0150	0168	0187	0209	0231	0256	0

| x | | 69 | 68 | 67 | 66 | 65 | 64 | 63 | 62 | 61 | 60 =π | x |

n = 4

x	π=	41	42	43	44	45	46	47	48	49	50	
1		8788	8868	8944	9017	9085	9150	9211	9269	9323	9375	3
2		5420	5590	5759	5926	6090	6252	6412	6569	6724	6875	2
3		1909	2030	2155	2283	2415	2550	2689	2831	2977	3125	1
4		0283	0311	0342	0375	0410	0448	0488	0531	0576	0625	0

| x | | 59 | 58 | 57 | 56 | 55 | 54 | 53 | 52 | 51 | 50 =π | x |

CUMULATIVE BINOMIAL PROBABILITIES

● **PROBLEM 4–27**

Let X be a binomially distributed random variable with parameters n and π, where n is the number of independent trials and π is the probability of success on a particular trial. Use the table above to find $P\{X \geq 2\}$ and $P\{X = 2\}$ if $n = 4$ and $\pi = 0.23$.

SOLUTION:

To find $P\{X \geq 2\} = P\{X = 2 \text{ or } 3 \text{ or } 4\}$, we resort to the table of cumulative binomial probabilities. First find $\pi = 0.023$ in the body of this table. Then read down the left side of the table until $X = 2$. The number in the row of $X = 2$ and $\pi = 0.023$ is $P\{X \geq 2\}$. We see that $P\{X \geq 2\} = 0.2285$.

To find $P\{X = 2\}$ from the cumulative binomial table, we must first express an exact probability in terms of a cumulative probability. Thus,

$$P\{X = 2\} = P\{X = 2\} + P\{X = 3\} + P\{X = 4\} - \{P(X = 3) + P(X = 4)\}$$
$$= P\{X \geq 2\} - P\{X \geq 3\}$$

We now find the two cumulative probabilities, $P\{X \geq 2\}$ and $P\{X \geq 3\}$, from the table. Reading down the column headed by $\pi = .023$ and from the left across the row labeled $x = 3$, we find $P\{X \geq 3\} = 0.0403$.

Thus, $P\{X = 2\} = P\{X \geq 2\} - P\{X \geq 3\}$
$$= 0.2285 - 0.0403 = 0.1882.$$

● **PROBLEM 4–28**

For $n = 4$ and $\pi = 0.73$, find (a) $P\{X \leq 2\}$ and $P\{X = 2\}$.

SOLUTION:

The table used in the previous problem can be used again here. First read through the body of the table until $\pi = 0.73$ is found. This is in the third section from the top. We wish to find $P\{X \leq 2\}$, where X is binomially distributed with parameters $n = 4$ independent trials and $\pi = 0.73$, the probability of success on any particular trial.

Now $P\{X \le 2\} = P\{X = 0\} + P\{X = 1\} + P\{X = 2\}$. We can find this probability in two ways.

(1) In the section where $\pi = 0.73$, read up the column on the right until $X = 2$ is reached. Then read across from right to left until the column labeled $\pi = 0.73$ is found. This gives $P\{X \le 2\} = 0.2959$.

(2) The second method is as follows. Notice that a binomial probability is really two probabilities. To illustrate this, let X be a binomially distributed random variable with $n = 4$ and $\pi = 0.73$. Let Y be a binomially distributed random variable with $n = 4$ and $\pi = 0.27$.

A probability about X is also a probability about Y.

$$P\{X = 1\} = \binom{4}{1}(0.73)^1 (0.27)^3 = \binom{4}{3}(0.27)^3 (0.73)^1$$

$$= P\{Y = 3\}, \text{ since}$$

$$\binom{4}{1} = \frac{4!}{1! \cdot 3!} = \binom{4}{3}$$

A cumulative probability for X is also a cumulative probability for Y. Namely,

$$P\{X = 0, 1, \text{ or } 2\} = P\{X \le 2\} = \sum_{x=0}^{2} (0.73)^x (0.27)^{4-x} .$$

Let $Y = 4 - X$, then $X = 4 - Y$ and

$$P\{X \le 2\} = \binom{4}{0}(0.73)^0 (0.27)^4 + \binom{4}{1}(0.73)^1 (0.27)^3 + \binom{4}{2}(0.73)^2 (0.27)^2$$

$$= \binom{4}{0}(0.27)^4 (0.73)^0 + \binom{4}{3}(0.27)^3 (0.73)^1 + \binom{4}{2}(0.27)^2 (0.73)^2$$

$$= P\{Y = 4\} + P\{Y = 3\} + P\{Y = 2\}.$$

We have shown that
$$P\{X \le 2\} = P\{Y \ge 2\}.$$

The second method of using a table of cumulative binomial probabilities uses this fact. We wish to find $P\{X \le 2\}$ where X is distributed with parameters $n = 4$ and $\pi = 0.73$. This is equal to $P\{Y \ge 2\}$ where Y is distributed with parameters $n = 4$ and $\pi = 0.27$. We find $P\{Y \ge 2\}$. To do this we read through the table until we find $\pi = 0.27$ and then read down the column on the right until we reach the row headed by 2. Reading from left to right across this row and down the column headed by $\pi = 0.27$, our answer is found to be the intersection of this row and column or $P\{X \le 2\} = P\{Y \ge 2\} = 0.2959$.

To find $P\{X = 2\}$ from this table, we convert from cumulative probabilities to single probabilities.

$$P\{X = 2\} = [P\{X = 0\} + P\{X = 1\} + P\{X = 2\}] - [P\{X = 0\} + P\{X = 1\}].$$

Thus, $P\{X = 2\} = P\{X \leq 2\} - P\{X \leq 1\}$.

To find the $P\{X \leq 1\}$, we read up the column in which $\pi = 0.73$ and across the row from right to left labeled 1. We see that $P\{X \leq 1\} = 0.0628$. Hence,

$$P\{X = 2\} = 0.2959 - 0.0628 = 0.2331.$$

● PROBLEM 4-29

Given the following cumulative binomial distribution, find (a) $P(X = 1)$; (b) $P\{X = 4\}$; and (c) $P\{X = 5\}$.

$$(n = 5,\ p = 0.31)$$

x	$P(X > x)$
0	1.0000
1	0.8436
2	0.4923
3	0.1766
4	0.0347
5	0.0029

SOLUTION:

(a) The probabilities in the table, $P(X \geq x)$, give the values of the probabilities that a specific occurrence of a random variable will be at least as great as the given x. For example, 1 is the only value at least as great as 1, but not at least as great as 2. Therefore, the probability that $X = 1$ is the probability that X is at least 1 but NOT at least 2.

The addition rule for mutually exclusive probabilities therefore says $P\{X \geq 1\} = P\{X = 1\} + P\{X \geq 2\}$.

Equivalently, $P\{X = 1\} = P\{X \geq 1\} - P\{X \geq 2\}$

$$= 0.8436 - 0.4923 = 0.3513.$$

(b) $P\{X = 4\} = P\{X \geq 4\} - P\{X \geq 5\} = 0.0347 - 0.0029 = 0.0318$.

(c) Since 5 is the only possible value at least as large as 5, $P\{X = 5\} = P\{X \geq 5\} = 0.0029$.

Given the following binomial distribution, find (a) $P\{X = 4\}$; (b) $P\{X = 1\}$; and (c) $P\{X = 0\}$.

$$(n = 5, \; p = 0.69)$$

x	$P(X \leq x)$
0	0.0029
1	0.0347
2	0.1766
3	0.4923
4	0.8436
5	1.0000

SOLUTION:

(a) The events $\{X \leq 3\}$ and $\{X = 4\}$ are disjoint and therefore $P\{X = 4\} \cup P\{X \leq 3\} = P\,(X \leq 3) + P\{X = 4\}$ by the addition rule, or

$P\{X \leq 4\} = P\{X \leq 3\} + P\{X = 4\}$.

Equivalently, $P\{X = 4\} = P\{X \leq 4\} - P\{X \leq 3\}$

$$= 0.8436 - 0.4923 = 0.3513.$$

(b) Similarly, $P\{X = 1\} = P\{X \leq 1\} - P\{X \leq 0\}$

$$= 0.0347 - 0.0029 = 0.0318.$$

(c) $P\{X = 0\} = P\{X \leq 0\} = 0.0029$.

You might notice that the previous problem had the same solution. The similarity can be explained if the binomial formula,

$$P\{X = k\} = \binom{n}{k} p^k \, (1 - p)^{n-k} \,,$$

is used to solve both examples. In the first one, $n = 5$, $p = 0.31$, $1 - p = 0.69$, and

$$P\{X = 1\} = \binom{5}{1}(0.31)^1 \, (0.69)^4 = \frac{5!}{1! \cdot 4!}(0.31)^1 \, (0.69)^4 = 0.3513.$$

In this example $n = 5$, $p = 0.69$, $1 - p = 0.31$, and

$$P\{X = 4\} = \binom{5}{4}(0.69)^4 \, (0.31)^1 = 0.3513.$$

Similar operations can be performed on (b) and (c).

The probability of hitting a target on a shot is $\frac{2}{3}$. Let X denote the number of times a person hits the target in eight shots. Find:

(a) $P\{X = 3\}$
(b) $P\{1 < X \le 6\}$
(c) $P\{X > 3\}$

SOLUTION:

If we assume that each shot is independent of any other shot, then X is a binomially distributed random variable with parameters $n = 8$ and $\pi = \frac{2}{3}$.

Thus, $P\{X = 3\} = \binom{8}{3}\left(\frac{2}{3}\right)^3\left(\frac{1}{3}\right)^{8-3} = \frac{8!}{3!\cdot 5!}\left(\frac{2}{3}\right)^3\left(\frac{1}{3}\right)^5$

$= \frac{8\cdot 7\cdot 6}{3\cdot 2\cdot 1}\left(\frac{8}{27}\right)\left(\frac{1}{243}\right) = \frac{448}{6,561} = 0.06828$, and

$P\{1 < X \le 6\} = P(X = 2, 3, 4, 5, \text{ or } 6)$.

These events are mutually exclusive and thus

$P\{X = 2, 3, 4, 5, \text{ or } 6\} = P\{X = 2\} + P\{X = 3\} + P\{X = 4\} + P\{X = 5\} + P\{X = 6\}$

$= \sum_{n=2}^{6} P\{X = n\}$

$= \sum_{n=2}^{6} \binom{8}{n}\left(\frac{2}{3}\right)^n\left(\frac{1}{3}\right)^{8-n}$

Using tables of cumulative probabilities and the fact that $P\{1 < X \le 6\} = P\{X \le 6\} - P\{X \le 1\}$, or calculating single probabilities and adding, we see that $P\{1 < X \le 6\} = 0.8023$.

Finally, $P\{X > 3\} = P\{X = 4, 5, 6, 7, \text{ or } 8\}$

$= P\{X = 4\} + P\{X = 5\} + P\{X = 6\} + P\{X = 7\} + P\{X = 8\}$

$= \sum_{n=4}^{8} P\{X = n\}$

$$= \sum_{n=4}^{8} \binom{8}{n} \left(\frac{2}{3}\right)^{n} \left(\frac{1}{3}\right)^{8-n}$$

Again, using a table of cumulative probabilities or calculating each single probability, we see that $P(X > 3) = 0.912$.

MULTINOMIAL DISTRIBUTION

● PROBLEM 4-32

A bag contains three white, two black, and four red balls. Four balls are drawn at random with replacement. Calculate the probabilities that

(a) the sample contains just one white ball, and
(b) the sample contains just one white ball given that it contains just one red ball.

SOLUTION:

Since there are nine balls and we are sampling with replacement and choosing the balls at random on each draw.

$$P \text{ \{white ball\}} = \frac{3}{9} = \frac{1}{3} \ ,$$

$$P \text{ \{black ball\}} = \frac{2}{9} \ ,$$

$$P \text{ \{red ball\}} = \frac{4}{9} \ .$$

(a) On each draw, P {white} + P {black or red} = 1. Let X be the number of white balls. Then X is distributed binomially with $n = 4$ trials and

P {white ball} = $\frac{1}{3}$. Thus,

$$P \text{ \{just one white\}} = P(X = 1)$$

$$= \binom{4}{1}\left(\frac{1}{3}\right)^1 \left(1 - \frac{1}{3}\right)^{4-1}$$

$$= 4\left(\frac{1}{3}\right)\left(\frac{2}{3}\right)^3 = \frac{32}{81}.$$

(b) P {just one white | just one red}

$$= \frac{P\{\text{just one white and just one red}\}}{P\,(\text{just one red})}$$

If Y is the number of red balls, then Y is distributed binomially with parameters $n = 4$ and $p = \frac{4}{9}$.

Thus, P {just one red} $= P\,(Y = 1)$

$$= \binom{4}{1}\left(\frac{4}{9}\right)^1 \left(1 - \frac{4}{9}\right)^{4-1}$$

$$= 4\,\left(\frac{4}{9}\right)\left(\frac{5}{9}\right)^3 \text{, and}$$

P {just one white and just one red}
$= P$ {one white, one red, and two blacks} .

Any particular sequence of outcomes in which one white ball is chosen, one red ball is chosen, and two black balls are chosen has probability $\left(\frac{3}{9}\right)^1 \left(\frac{2}{9}\right)^2 \left(\frac{4}{9}\right)^1$. We now must find the number of such distinguishable arrangements. There are $\binom{4}{1}$ ways to select the position of the white ball. There are now three positions available to select the position of the red ball and $\binom{3}{1}$ ways to do this. The position of the black balls are now fixed. There are thus

$$\binom{4}{1}\binom{3}{1} = \frac{4!}{1! \cdot 3!}\frac{3!}{1! \cdot 2!} = \frac{4!}{1! \cdot 2! \cdot 1!}$$

distinguishable arrangements.

Thus, P {one red ball, one white ball, and two black balls}

$$= \frac{4!}{1! \cdot 2! \cdot 1!} \cdot \left(\frac{3}{9}\right)\left(\frac{2}{9}\right)^2\left(\frac{4}{9}\right)^1 = \frac{4 \cdot 3 \cdot 3 \cdot 4 \cdot 4}{9^4} \text{, so}$$

$$P \text{ \{just one white I just one red\}} = \frac{\dfrac{4 \cdot 3 \cdot 3 \cdot 4 \cdot 4}{9^4}}{4\left(\dfrac{4}{9}\right)\left(\dfrac{5}{9}\right)^3}$$

$$= \frac{4 \cdot 3 \cdot 3 \cdot 4 \cdot 4}{4 \cdot 4 \cdot 5 \cdot 5 \cdot 5} = \frac{36}{125}$$

● PROBLEM 4-33

Three electric motors from a factory are tested. A motor is either discarded, returned to the factory, or accepted. If the probability of acceptance is 0.7, the probability of return is 0.2, and the probability of discard is 0.1, what is the probability that of three randomly selected motors one will be returned, one will be accepted, and one will be discarded? What is the probability that two motors will be accepted, one returned, and zero discarded?

SOLUTION:

Let the probability that one is returned, one accepted, and one discarded be denoted by $P \{1, 1, 1\}$. Since the motors are selected at random, each selection is independent and the probability that an arrangement consisting of one returned, one accepted, and one discarded is observed is $(0.7)(0.2)(0.1) = 0.14$. We now count the number of possible arrangements in which one engine is discarded, one returned, and one accepted.

Let us count the number of arrangements in the following way. First choose the one motor from three that will be returned. There are $\binom{3}{1}$ ways to do this. Now choose one motor from the remaining two which will be accepted. There are $\binom{2}{1}$ ways to do this. Once the one motor that will be accepted is chosen from the remaining two, the motor that will be discarded is left over and hence selected automatically. Altogether there are $\binom{3}{1}$ arrangements of motors that will consist of one accepted, one returned, and one discarded.

Hence, $P\{1, 1, 1\} = \binom{3}{1}\binom{2}{1}(0.7)\,(0.2)\,(0.1) = \dfrac{3!}{1!\cdot2!}\dfrac{2!}{1!\cdot1!}(0.014)$

$$= 6 \times (0.014) = 0.084$$

Similarly, the probability of selecting two motors that will be accepted, one returned, and one discarded is computed in two steps. The probability of observing one particular arrangement of this form is $(0.7)^2\,(0.2)^1\,(0.1)^0$. We now count the number of arrangements which lead to this observation.

There are $\binom{3}{2}$ ways to choose the two motors that will be accepted. There are $\binom{1}{1}$ ways to choose the one motor that will be returned. Multiplying from the remaining one, we see that there are $\binom{3}{2}\binom{1}{1} = \dfrac{3!}{2!\cdot1!\cdot0!}$ possible arrangements. The probability of observing a sample in which two motors are accepted is thus

$$\dfrac{3!}{2!\cdot1!\cdot0!}(0.7)^2\,(0.2)^1\,(0.1)^0 = 3\,(0.7)^2\,(0.2)^1\,(0.1)^0 = 0.294.$$

The coefficient $\binom{n}{k_1, k_2, \ldots k_r}$ is called the multinomial coefficient and counts the number of ways n objects can be labeled in r ways; k_1 in the first category, k_2 in the second, up to k_r in the rth, with $k_1 + k_2 + \ldots + k_r = n$, and

$$\binom{n}{k_1, k_2, \ldots k_r} = \dfrac{n!}{k_1!\ k_2!\ \ldots k_r!}.$$

A survey was made of the number of people who read classified ads in a newspaper. Thirty people were asked to indicate which one of the following best applies to them: (1) read no ads (N); (2) read "articles for sale" ads (S); (3) read "help wanted" ads (H); and (4) read all ads (A).

(a) Use the multinomial theorem for the expansion of
$$(N + S + H + A)^{30}$$
to find the coefficients of the terms involving
(1) _____ $N^{10} A^{10} H^{10}$
(2) _____ $N^5 S^{10} H^{10} A^5$

(b) Assuming the following probabilities, what is the probability that 10 read no ads, 10 read "help wanted" ads, and 10 read all ads?

$$P\{N\} = \frac{30}{100}$$

$$P\{S\} = \frac{40}{100}$$

$$P\{H\} = \frac{20}{100}$$

$$P\{A\} = \frac{10}{100}$$

SOLUTION:

(a) We can generalize the binomial distribution to instances in which the independent, identical "trials" have more than just two possible outcomes. Recall that the binomial distribution had its origins in connection with a sequence of Bernoulli trials, each of which had only two possibilities for an outcome. Now consider a sequence of independent trials, each trial having k possible outcomes, $O_1, O_2, O_3, \ldots, O_k$ with respective probabilities $p_1, p_2, p_3, \ldots, p_k$. There is the relation $p_1 + p_2 + p_3 + \ldots + p_k = 1$, so that any one probability can be obtained from the remaining $k - 1$. Consider the random variables $X_1, \ldots, X_k$, where X_i is the frequency of O_i among n trials. Note that $X_1 + X_2 + \ldots + X_k = n$ since all trials must have some outcome. The joint distribution of $(X_1, \ldots, X_k)$ is called multinomial. We can derive the probability function of the k-nomial distribution by a method similar to the binomial. For a particular sequence of results, $f_1 A_1$'s, $f_2 A_2$'s, etc., the probability, according to the multplication rule, is simply the product of the corresponding probabilities:

$$p_1^{f_1} p_2^{f_2} \cdots p_k^{f_k} \, .$$

Such a sequence can come in many orders—the number of which is the number of ways of arranging n objects, f_1 of one kind, ..., and f_k of the kth kind. This is $n!$ divided by a factorial for each group of like objects. Hence, the total probability for all sequences with given frequencies is

$$P\{X = f_1, \ \ldots \ \text{and} \ X_k = f_k\} = \frac{n!}{r_1! \ r_k!} p_1^{f_1} p_2^{f_2} \cdots p_k^{f_k} \, ,$$

provided $\sum_i f_i = n$. We use the term "multinomial" since (as in the particular case $k = 2$) the probabilities we have are the terms in a multinomial expansion:

$$(p_1 + \ldots + p_k)^n = \sum \frac{n!}{f_1! \cdots f_k!} p_1^{f_1} p_2^{f_2} \cdots p_k^{f_k} = 1.$$

The sum extends to all sets of nonnegative integers that sum to n.

In our problem, we have four possible outcomes N, A, S, and H.

(1) We are looking for the coefficient of p_1^{10}, p_2^{10}, p_3^{10}, p_4^{10}. It is

$$\frac{30!}{10! \cdot 10! \cdot 10! \cdot 0!} \ \text{but since 0! is 1, we have} \ \frac{30!}{10! \cdot 10! \cdot 10!} \, .$$

(2) We are looking for the coefficient of p_1^5, p_2^5, p_3^{10}, p_4^{10}. By our

multinomial derivation it is $\dfrac{30!}{5! \cdot 5! \cdot 10! \cdot 10!}$.

(b) In part (a–1) we substitute

$$p_1 = \frac{30}{100} = 0.3, \ p_2 = \frac{10}{100} = 0.1, \ p_3 = \frac{40}{100} = 0.4, \ \text{and} \ p_4 = \frac{20}{100} = 0.2 \, .$$

$$\frac{30!}{10! \cdot 10! \cdot 10!} P(N)^{10} \, P(A)^{10} \, P(H)^{10} = \frac{30!}{10! \cdot 10! \cdot 10!} (0.3)^{10} (0.2)^{10} (0.1)^{10} \, .$$

● PROBLEM 4–35

Find the coefficient of $a_1^2 a_2 a_3$ in the expansion of $(a_1 + a_2 + a_3)^4$.

SOLUTION:

The binomial theorem states that if n is a positive integer, then

$$(a + b)^n = a^n b^0 + na^{n-1} b^1 + \frac{n(n-1)}{1 \cdot 2} a^{n-2} b^2 + \frac{n(n-1)(n-2)}{1 \cdot 2 \cdot 3} a^{n-3} b^3$$
$$+ \ldots + na^1 b^{n-1} + a^0 b^n .$$

Use the binomial theorem, but for convenience, associate the terms $(a_2 + a_3)$, then expand the expression.

$$[a_1 + (a_2 + a_3)]^4 = a_1^4 + 4a_1^3 (a_2 + a_3) + \frac{4 \cdot 3}{1 \cdot 2} a_1^2 + (a_2 + a_3)^2$$

$$+ \frac{4 \times 3 \times 2}{1 \times 2 \times 3} a_1 + (a_2 + a_3)^3 + (a_2 + a_3)^4 .$$

Notice that the only term involving $a_1^2 a_2 a_3$ is the third term with

coefficient $\frac{4 \cdot 3}{2}$ and, further, that $(a_2 + a_3)^2$ must be expanded also. This

expansion is

$$(a_2 + a_3)^2 = a_2^2 + 2a_2 a_3 + a_3^2 .$$

Therefore, the third term becomes

$$\frac{4 \times 3}{1 \times 2} a_1^2 (a_2 + a_3)^2 = \frac{4 \cdot 3}{1 \cdot 2} a_1^2 (a_2^2 + 2a_2 a_3 + a_3^2)$$
$$= 6a_1^2 a_2^2 + 12 a_1^2 a_2 a_3 + 6a_1^2 a_3^2$$

Hence, the coefficient of $a_1^2 a_2 a_3$ is 12.

● PROBLEM 4-36

A package in the mail can be lost, delivered, or damaged while being delivered. The probability of loss is 0.2, the probability of damage is 0.1, and the probability of delivery without damage is 0.7. If 10 packages are sent, then what is the probability that six arrive safely, two are lost, and two are damaged?

SOLUTION:

If each package being sent can be considered an independent trial with three outcomes, the event of six safe arrivals, two losses, and two smashed packages can be assumed to have a multinomial distribution. Thus,

$$P \{\text{six, two, and two}\} = \binom{10}{6, 2, 2}(0.7)^6 (0.2)^2 (0.1)^2$$

$$= \frac{10!}{6! \cdot 2! \cdot 2!}(0.7)^6 (0.2)^2 (0.1)^2 = 0.059$$

A die is tossed 12 times. Let X_i denote the number of tosses in which i dots come up for $i = 1, 2, 3, 4, 5,$ and 6. What is the probability that we obtain two of each value?

SOLUTION:

We have a series of independent successive trials with six possible outcomes each with constant probability $\frac{1}{6}$. The multinomial distribution,

$$P \{X_1 = f_1, X_2 = f_2, \ldots, X_k = f_k\}$$

$$= \frac{n!}{f_1! \; f_2! \; \cdots f_k!} p_1^{f_1} p_2^{f_2} \cdots p_k^{f_k},$$

is called for. Hence,

$$P \{X_1 = 2, X_2 = 2, X_3 = 2, X_4 = 2, X_5 = 2, X_6 = 2\}$$

$$= \frac{12!}{2! \cdot 2! \cdot 2! \cdot 2! \cdot 2! \cdot 2!}\left(\frac{1}{6}\right)^2 \left(\frac{1}{6}\right)^2 \cdots \left(\frac{1}{6}\right)^2$$

$$= \frac{12!}{2^6}\left[\left(\frac{1}{6}\right)^2\right]^6 = \frac{1,925}{559,872} = 0.0034.$$

SHORT ANSWER QUESTIONS FOR REVIEW

Choose the correct answer.

1. A listing of all outcomes of an experiment and their corresponding probabilities is called a (a) probability distribution. (b) frequency distribution. (c) random variable. (d) subjective probability.

2. A fire chief estimates that the probability that an arsonist will be arrested for deliberately setting a fire is 0.30. The probability that exactly three arsonists will be arrested in the next five deliberately set fires is (a) 0.312. (b) 0.213. (c) 0.132. (d) 0.231.

3. The probability that two of five students randomly selected to participate in a psychological experiment are altruistic, if the class of ten students contains three altruistic students is (a) 0.40. (b) 0.30. (c) 0.2592. (d) 0.417.

4. A firm has a four percent defective rate. If 100 items are randomly selected, the probability that at least one out of the 100 items is defective is (a) 0.98. (b) 0.09. (c) 0.91. (d) 0.02.

5. Assume that the probability of a boy being born is 0.50. If a couple plan on having six children, the probability that all are boys or all are girls is (a) 0.312. (b) 0.032. (c) 0.016. (d) 0.984.

6. A company that manufactures color television sets claims that only five percent of its sets will need to be adjusted by a technician before being sold. If an appliance dealer sells 20 of these sets, the likelihood that more than three of them need to be adjusted is (a) 0.510. (b) 0.150. (c) 0.501. (d) 0.015.

7. Among a department store's 16 delivery trucks, five emit excessive amounts of pollutants. If eight of the trucks are randomly selected for inspection, the probability that this sample will include at least three of the trucks which emit excessive pollutants is (a) 0.005. (b) 0.050. (c) 0.500. (d) 0.555.

8. In a very large city, network TV has 40 percent of the viewing audience on Friday nights, a local channel has 20 percent, cable TV has 30 percent, and 10 percent are viewing video cassettes. The probability

that among seven television viewers randomly selected in that city on Friday night, two will be viewing network TV, one will be watching the local channel, three will be watching cable TV, and one will be watching a video cassette is (a) 0.306. (b) 0.036. (c) 0.630. (d) 0.063.

Fill in the blanks.

9. A probability is a number that expresses the likelihood that an _____ occurs.

10. The sum of all probabilities in any probability distribution is always _____ .

11. The various values of a random variable form a list of _____ _____ events.

12. The binomial distribution is symmetric when π (the probability of success in a single trial) is equal to _____ .

13. A binomial experiment is one that meets all the following requirements:

(a) The experiment must have a _____ number of trials.

(b) There are only _____ possible outcomes of each trial, _____ or _____ .

(c) The trials must be _____ of each other.

(d) The probability of a success, π, is always a _____ from trial to trial.

14. According to one study conducted at the University of Texas at Austin, 2/3 of all Americans can do routine computations. If an employer were to hire eight randomly selected Americans, the probability that exactly five of them can do routine computations is equal to _____ .

Determine whether the following statements are true or false.

15. Each of the following formulas can serve as the probability distribution of some random variable, x:

(a) $f(x) = \dfrac{x-2}{5}$ for $x = 1, 2, 3, 4, 5$.

(b) $f(x) = \dfrac{x^2}{30}$ for $x = 0, 1, 2, 3, 4$.

(c) $f(x) = \dfrac{x+3}{15}$ for $x = 1, 2, 3$.

16. Given that the probability of x, $P\{x\}$ ιο $\dfrac{cx}{6}$ for $x = 1, 2$, the value of c so that a probability distribution is determined is equal to 3.

17. A binomial probability distribution requires at least 50 observations.

18. (a) 6! (six factorial) means $6 \times 5 \times 4 \times 3 \times 2 \times 1$.

(b) $\dbinom{5}{2} = \dfrac{5!}{3!}$.

19. A student is given a five-question multiple-choice quiz. He has not studied the material to be quizzed, and therefore decides to answer the five questions by randomly guessing the answers without reading the questions or the answers. If there are three answers to each question of which only one is correct, then the probability that

(a) all questions are answered incorrectly is $P\{5\} = \left[\dfrac{1}{3}\right]^5$.

(b) all questions are answered correctly is $P\{5\} \approx 0.004$.

20. A local elementary school holds four open houses annually. Records show that the probability that a child's parents (one or both) attend from 0 to 4 of the open houses is as shown in the following table:

Number of Open Houses (x)	0	1	2	3	4
P $\{x\}$	0.12	0.38	0.30	0.12	0.08

The probability that an individual child's parents attend at least one of the open houses is given by $P\{\text{at least one}\} = 0.88$.

ANSWER KEY

1. a   2. c   3. d

4. a   5. b   6. d

7. c   8. b   9. event

10. one   11. mutually exclusive 12. 0.50

13. (a) fixed (b) two, success, failure (c) independent (d) constant

14. 0.273   15. (a) False (b) True (c) True

16. False   17. False   18. (a) True (b) False

19. (a) False (b) True 20. True

CHAPTER 5

CONTINUOUS DISTRIBUTIONS

GENERAL CONCEPTS

● PROBLEM 5-1

Let X be a continuous random variable. Find a density function such that the probability that X falls in an interval (a, b) $(0 < a < b < 1)$ is proportional to the length of the interval (a, b). Check that this is a proper probability density function.

SOLUTION:

The probabilities of a continuous random variable are computed from a continuous function called a density function in the following way. If $f(x)$ is graphed,

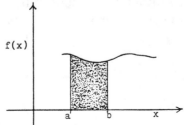

the $P\{a \le X \le b\}$ = the area under the curve $f(x)$ from a to b.

With this definition some conditions on $f(x)$ must be imposed. Namely, $f(x)$ must be nonnegative and the total area between $f(x)$ and the x-axis must be equal to 1.

We also see that if probability is defined in terms of area under a curve, the probability that a continuous random variable is equal to a particular value, $P\{X = a\}$, is the area under $f(x)$ at the point a. The area of a line is zero, thus $P\{X = a\} = 0$. Therefore,

$$P\{a < X < b\} = P\{a \le X \le b\}.$$

To find a density function for $0 < X < 1$, such that $P\{a < X < b\}$ is proportional to the length of (a, b), we look for a function $f(x)$ that is positive and the area under $f(x)$ between zero and one is equal to one. It is reasonable to expect that the larger the interval the larger the probability that X is in the interval.

A Density function that satisfies these criteria is

$$f(x) = \begin{cases} 1 & 0 < x < 1 \\ \\ 0 & \text{otherwise} \end{cases}$$

A graph of this density function is

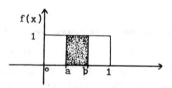

The probability that X is between a and b is the area of the shaded region. This is the area of a rectangle. The area of a rectangle is base × height. Thus,

$$P\{a \le X \le b\} = (b - a) \times 1 = b - a.$$

Similarly, $P\{X \le k\} = (k - 0) \times 1 = k$ for $0 < k < 1$.

Often the density function is more complicated and integration must be used to calculate the area under the density function.

To check that this is a proper probability density function, we must check that the total area under $f(x)$ is one. The total area under this density function is $(1 - 0) \times 1 = 1$.

Given that the random variable X has density function

$$f(x) = \begin{cases} 2x & 0 < x < 1 \\ \\ 0 & \text{otherwise} \end{cases}$$

Find $P\left\{\dfrac{1}{2} < x < \dfrac{3}{4}\right\}$ and $P\left\{-\dfrac{1}{2} < x < \dfrac{1}{2}\right\}$.

SOLUTION:

Since $f(x) = 2x$ is the density function of a continuous random variable,

$P\left\{\dfrac{1}{2} < x < \dfrac{3}{4}\right\}$ = area under $f(x)$ from $\dfrac{1}{2}$ to $\dfrac{3}{4}$.

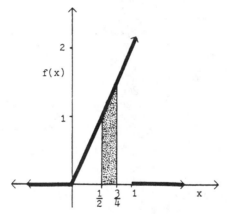

$f(x)$ is indicated by the heavy line.

The area under $f(x)$ is the area of the triangle with vertices at $(0, 0)$, $(1, 0)$ and $(1, 2)$.

The area of this triangle is $A = \dfrac{1}{2}bh$, where b equals the base of the triangle and h is the altitude.

Thus, $A = \dfrac{1}{2}(1) \times 2 = \dfrac{2}{2} = 1$,

proving that $f(x)$ is a proper probability density function.

To find the probability that $\frac{1}{2} < x < \frac{3}{4}$, we find the area of the shaded region in the diagram. This shaded region is the difference between the area of the right triangle with vertices $(0, 0)$, $\left(\frac{1}{2}, 0\right)$, and $\left(\frac{1}{2}, f\left(\frac{1}{2}\right)\right)$ and the area

of the triangle with vertices $(0, 0)$, $\left(\frac{3}{4}, 0\right)$, and $\left(\frac{3}{4}, f\left(\frac{3}{4}\right)\right)$.

This difference is $P\left\{\frac{1}{2} < x < \frac{3}{4}\right\} = \frac{1}{2}\left(\frac{3}{4}\right)f\left(\frac{3}{4}\right) - \frac{1}{2}\left(\frac{1}{2}\right)f\left(\frac{1}{2}\right)$

$$= \frac{1}{2}\left[\frac{3}{4} \cdot \frac{6}{4} - \frac{1}{2} \cdot 1\right]$$

$$= \frac{1}{2}\left[\frac{9}{8} - \frac{1}{2}\right] = \frac{1}{2} \cdot \frac{5}{8} = \frac{5}{16}$$

The probability that $-\frac{1}{2} < x < \frac{1}{2}$ is $P\left\{-\frac{1}{2} < x < \frac{1}{2}\right\} =$ Area under $f(x)$ from

$-\frac{1}{2}$ to $\frac{1}{2}$. Because $f(x) = 0$ from $-\frac{1}{2}$ to 0, the area under $f(x)$ from $-\frac{1}{2}$ to 0 is 0. Thus,

$$P\left\{-\frac{1}{2} < x < \frac{1}{2}\right\} = P\left\{0 < x < \frac{1}{2}\right\} = \text{area under } f(x) \text{ from 0 to } \frac{1}{2}$$

$$= \frac{1}{2}\left(\frac{1}{2}\right)f\left(\frac{1}{2}\right)$$

$$= \frac{1}{2}\left(\frac{1}{2}\right) \times 1 = \frac{1}{4}.$$

Let X be the lifetime of a certain species, in years. Given that the continuous random variable X has distribution function $F(x) = 0$ when $x < 1$ and $F(x) = 1 - \dfrac{1}{x^2}$ when $x \geq 1$, graph $F(x)$. What do you find peculiar?

SOLUTION:

Plotting several values of $\left(x, 1 - \dfrac{1}{x^2}\right)$ and joining these points smoothly results in the following plot.

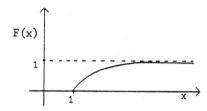

It is peculiar that each member of this population must live at least one year.

Let a distribution function, F, be given by
$$F(x) = 0 ; \qquad x < 0$$
$$= \frac{x+1}{2} ; \qquad 0 \leq x < 1$$
$$= 1 ; \qquad 1 \leq x .$$

Find $P\left\{-3 < x \leq \dfrac{1}{2}\right\}$ and sketch F.

SOLUTION:

First note that

$$P\left\{-3 < x \le \frac{1}{2}\right\} = P\left\{x \le \frac{1}{2}\right\} - P\ (x \le -3)\ .$$

By definition, this is

$$F\left(\frac{1}{2}\right) - F(-3) = \frac{\frac{1}{2}+1}{2} - 0 = \frac{\frac{1}{2}+1}{2}$$

$$= \frac{\frac{3}{2}}{2} = \frac{3}{4}\ .$$

The graph of F follows:

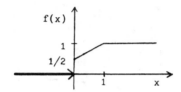

● **PROBLEM 5-5**

Let X be a continuous random variable representing the proportion of voters who are in favor of a certain bill. If $f(x) = 3x^2$; $0 < x < 1$, then determine whether, in a randomly selected county, it is likely or unlikely that this bill will pass.

SOLUTION:

We plot this density below:

insert artwork

Since the area between $\frac{1}{2}$ and 1 is obviously larger than the area between 0 and $\frac{1}{2}$, it is likely that the bill will pass.

96

The cumulative distribution function (CDF) of the longitude angle $\phi(w)$ of the random orientation on the earth's surface is

$$F_\phi(\lambda) = \begin{cases} 0 & ; & \lambda < 0 \\ \dfrac{\lambda}{2\pi} & ; & 0 \le \lambda \le 2\pi \\ 1 & ; & \lambda > 2\pi \end{cases}$$

Find the probability that this angle is no greater than π.

SOLUTION:

Using the CDF given, we compute

$$P\{\phi \le \pi\} = F_\phi(\pi)$$
$$= \frac{\pi}{2\pi}$$
$$= \frac{1}{2}$$

UNIFORM DISTRIBUTION

Let X be the distance (in miles) that wind blows some pollen. Let the probability density function for X be given as $f(x) = \dfrac{1}{3}$ for $0 < x < 3$ and 0 otherwise. Find $P\{X \le 2\}$.

SOLUTION:

We can easily plot this density function as

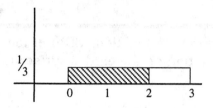

Notice that the entire area is $\left(\dfrac{1}{3}\right)(3)=1$. Now $P\{x \le 2\}$ = the area of the

shaded region $= \dfrac{2}{3}$.

Let X be as in the last problem. Find $P\{x \le 1\}$.

SOLUTION:

Here we need to find the area between 0 and 1. This is half the shaded

region. But the area of the shaded region was $\dfrac{2}{3}$. Thus,

$$P\{x \le 1\} = \frac{1}{2} P\{x \le 2\}$$

$$= \left(\frac{1}{2}\right)\left(\frac{2}{3}\right)$$

$$= \frac{1}{3}$$

Consider the hardness of steel as a random variable, X, with values between 50 and 70 on the Rockwell B scale. We can assume that the hardness has density function

$f(x) = 0$ when $x < 50$,

$f(x) = \dfrac{1}{20}$ when $50 \le x \le 70$,

$f(x) = 0$ when $x > 70$.

Graph this density function. Compute the probability that the hardness of a randomly selected steel specimen is less than 65.

SOLUTION:

Graph of $f(x)$.

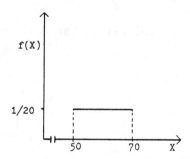

To compute $P\{X < 65\}$, we find the area between 50 and 65. This is

$$P\{x < 65\} = \frac{65 - 50}{70 - 50}$$

$$= \frac{15}{20}$$

$$= \frac{3}{4}$$

The simplest continuous random variable is the one whose distribution is constant over some interval (a, b) and zero elsewhere. This is the uniform distribution.

$$f(x) = \begin{cases} \dfrac{1}{b-a}, & a \le X \le b \\ 0, & \text{elsewhere} \end{cases}$$

Find the mean of this distribution.

SOLUTION:

By definition, the mean is the center of the distribution if the distribution is symmetric. Since this uniform distribution is symmetric about $\dfrac{a+b}{2}$, its mean must be $\dfrac{a+b}{2}$.

The length of hair of postal employees is uniformly distributed between 4 and 24 inches. Find the probability that Chris, a randomly chosen employee, has hair that is 19 inches long to the nearest inch.

SOLUTION:

To have hair that is 19 inches to the nearest inch, the length must fall in the interval $18.5 \le L \le 19.5$.

We have a uniform distribution.

$$f(L) = \begin{cases} \dfrac{1}{b-a}, & a \le L \le b \\ 0, & \text{otherwise} . \end{cases}$$

In this problem, $a = 4$ and $b = 24$.

$$f(L) = \begin{cases} \dfrac{1}{20}, & 4 \le L \le 24 \\ 0, & \text{otherwise}. \end{cases}$$

The probability now becomes

$$P\{18.5 \le L \le 19.5\} = \frac{19.5 - 18.5}{24 - 4} = \frac{1}{20}.$$

This problem will show an analogy between the geometric and exponential distributions. Show that the result of the last problem also holds if X is distributed geometrically.

SOLUTION:

We want to show that if X has the distribution $P\{X > x\} = (1 - p)^{x-1} \, p$, $x = 1, 2, 3, \dots$, then for nonnegative a and b

$$P\{X > a + b \mid X > a\} = P\{X > b\}.$$

First note that $P\{X > k\}$

$$= \sum_{x=k+1}^{\infty} P\{X > x\} = \sum_{x=k+1}^{\infty} (1 - p)^{x-1} \, p,$$

$$= p \sum_{x=k+1}^{\infty} (1 - p)^{x-1} = p \sum_{x=k+1}^{\infty} (1 - p)^{x}$$

$$= p \cdot \frac{(1 - p)^k}{1 - (1 - p)}$$

$$= p \, \frac{(1 - p)^k}{p} = (1 - p)^k$$

$$P \quad X \quad a \quad b \quad X \quad a$$

$$= \frac{P\{X > a + b \text{ and } X > a\}}{P\{X > a\}}$$

$$b \ge \qquad X \quad a \quad b, \qquad X \quad a$$

101

$$\frac{P\{X > a+b\}}{P\{X > a\}} = \frac{(1-p)a+b}{(1-p)}$$

$$= \frac{(1-p)^a (1-p)^b}{(1-p)^a}(1-p)^b$$

$$= P\{X > b\}$$

The last two problems may be interpreted as follows: if we have already spent some time in waiting, the distribution of further waiting time is the same as that of the initial waiting time. It is as if we waited in vain! A suggestive way of saying this is that the random variable X has no memory. This turns out to be a fundamental property of these two distributions and is basic for the theory of Markov processes. Distributions with this property are said to have the Markov property.

NORMAL DISTRIBUTION

● **PROBLEM 5–13**

If Z is a standard normal variable, use the table of standard normal probabilities to find:
(a) $P\{Z < 0\}$
(b) $P\{-1 < Z < 1\}$
(c) $P\{Z > 2.54\}$.

SOLUTION:

The normal distribution is the familiar "bell-shaped" curve. It is a continuous probability distribution that is widely used to describe the distribution of heights, weights, and other characteristics.

The density function of the standard normal distribution is

$$f(x) = \frac{1}{\sqrt{2\pi}}\exp\left(\frac{-x^2}{2}\right) \qquad -\infty < x < \infty .$$

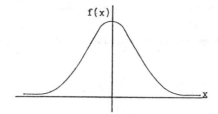

The probability of a standard normal variable being found in a particular interval can be found with the help of tables located in the backs of most statistics textbooks.

(a) To find the probability $P\{Z < 0\}$, we can take advantage of the fact that the normal distribution is symmetric about its mean of zero. Thus, $P\{Z > 0\} = P\{Z < 0\}$. We know that

$$P\{Z > 0\} + P\{Z < 0\} = 1$$

because $Z > 0$ and $Z < 0$ are essentially exhaustive events since $P\{Z = 0\} = 0$. Thus,

$$2P\{Z < 0\} = 1 \text{ or } P\{Z < 0\} = \frac{1}{2}.$$

(b) To find $P\{-1 < Z < 1\}$, we use the tables of the standard normal distribution. We obtain

$$P\{-1 < Z < 1\} = P\{Z < 1\} - P\{Z < -1\}.$$

Reading across the row headed by 1 and down the column labeled 0.00, we see that $P(Z < 1.0) = 0.8413$.

$P\{Z < -1\} = P\{Z > 1\}$ by the symmetry of the normal distribution. We also know that

$$P\{Z > 1\} = 1 - P\{Z < 1\}.$$

Substituting, we see that

$$P\{-1 < Z < 1\} = P\{Z < 1\} - [1 - P\{Z < 1\}]$$
$$= 2P\{Z < 1\} - 1 = 2\,(0.8413) - 1 = 0.6826.$$

(c) $P\{Z > 2.54\} = 1 - P\{Z < 2.54\}$ and reading across the row labeled 2.5 and down the column labeled 0.04, we see that $P\{Z < 2.54\} = 0.9945$. Substituting,

$$P\{Z > 2.54\} = 1 - 0.9945 = 0.0055.$$

Find $P\{-0.47 < Z < 0.94\}$.

SOLUTION:

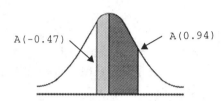

The probability $P\{-0.47 \leq Z \leq 0.94\}$ is equal to the shaded area above. To find the value of the shaded area, we add the areas labeled $A(-0.47)$ and $A(0.94)$. That is,

$P\{-0.47 \leq Z \leq 0.94\} = A(-0.47) + A(0.94)$.

By the symmetry of the normal distribution, $A(-0.47) = A(0.47) = 0.18082$ from the table. Also $A(0.94) = 0.32639$, so

$P\{-0.47 < Z < 0.94\} = 0.18082 + 0.32639 = 0.50721$.

Find $\Phi(-0.45)$.

SOLUTION:

Note that $\Phi(-0.45) = P\{Z \leq -0.45\}$, where Z is distributed normally with mean 0 and variance 1.

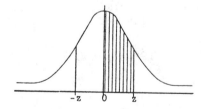

Let $A(Z)$ be the area under the curve from 0 to Z. From our table we find $A(0.45) = 0.17364$ and by the symmetry of the normal distribution,

A (−0.45) = A (0.45) = 0.17364.

We wish to find $\Phi(-0.45)$, the shaded area below.

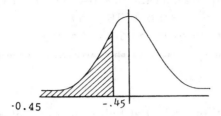

-0.45   -.45

We know that $\Phi(0) = 0.5000$ and from the diagram below we know that $\Phi(0) - A (-0.45) = \Phi(-0.45)$.

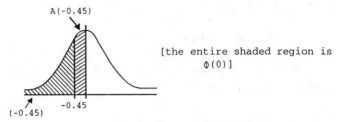

A(-0.45)

[the entire shaded region is $\Phi(0)$]

(-0.45)   -0.45

Substituting, we see that $\Phi(0) - A (-0.45) = 0.5000 - 0.17364 = \Phi(-0.45)$ and $\Phi(0.45) = 0.32636$.

● PROBLEM 5−16

Find P {− 0.47 < Z < 0.94} using $\Phi(-0.47)$ and $\Phi(0.94)$.

SOLUTION:

By definition
$$\Phi(-0.47) = 0.5000 - A (-0.47)$$
$$= 0.5000 - A (0.47)$$
and $\Phi(0.94) = 0.5000 + A (0.94)$. Hence,
$$P \{-0.47 < Z < 0.94\} = \Phi(0.94) - F(-0.47)$$
$$= [0.5000 + A (0.94)] - [0.5000 - A (0.47)]$$
$$= 0.82539 - 0.31918 = 0.50721$$

In a normal distribution, what is the Z-score equivalent of the median? What is the Z-score above which only 16 percent of the distribution lies? What percentage of the scores lie below a Z-score of +2.0?

SOLUTION:

The median is the number such that half of a probability distribution lies above or below it. Equivalently, the median is a number $\tilde{m}$ such that a random observation X from a distribution is equally likely to be above or below it. Thus,

$$P\{X \geq \tilde{m}\} = P\{X \leq \tilde{m}\} = \frac{1}{2}.$$

To find the Z-score equivalent of the median, we wish to find some number m such that

$$P\{Z \geq \tilde{m}\} = P\{Z \leq \tilde{m}\} = \frac{1}{2},$$

where Z is a normally distributed random variable with mean 0 and variance 1.

From the tables or from the fact that the normal distribution is symmetric about its mean we have

$$P\{Z \geq 0\} = P\{Z \leq 0\} = \frac{1}{2}.$$

Thus, the median is $\tilde{m} = 0$.

To find the Z-score above which 16 percent of the distribution lies, we find a constant C such that

$P\{Z \geq C\} = 16\% = 0.160$ or equivalently
$P\{Z \leq C\} = 1 - 0.160 = 0.840$

Searching for 0.8400 in the body of the table and then reading up the appropriate row and column, we find that
$P\{Z < 1\} = 0.84$, and thus $C = 1$.

To find the proportion of scores that lie below a Z-score of 2, we wish to find $P\{Z < 2.00\}$. Reading across the column labeled 2.0 and then down the row headed by 0.00, we find

$P\{Z < 2.00\} = 0.9772$,

but 0.9772 is 97.72% of 1; thus, 97.72% of the Z-scores lie below 2.00.

Given a random variable x with density

$$f(x) = \frac{1}{\sqrt{18\pi}}e^{-\left(\frac{x^2-10x+25}{18}\right)}, \quad -\infty < x < \infty .$$

Is this distribution normal? What is the maximum value of the density?

SOLUTION:

A normal distribution can be written in the form

$$f(x) = \frac{1}{\sigma\sqrt{2\pi}}\exp\left(-\frac{(x-\mu)^2}{2\sigma^2}\right), \quad \text{when} \quad -\infty < x < \infty .$$

Rewrite $(x^2 - 10x + 25)$ as $(x - 5)^2$ and 18 as $2 \times 9 = 2 \times 3^2$. Also, $\sqrt{18\pi} = \sqrt{9 \times 2\pi} = 3\sqrt{2\pi}$. Thus, $\mu = 5$ and $\sigma = 3$. Substitution gives

$$f(x) = \frac{1}{3\sqrt{2\pi}}e^{-\left(\frac{(x-5)^2}{2\times3^2}\right)} .$$

The density of a normal distribution reaches its maximum at $x = \mu$, so we substitute $x = 5$:

$$f(x) = \frac{1}{3\sqrt{2\pi}}e^{-\left(\frac{(5-5)^2}{2\times3^2}\right)} = \frac{1}{3\sqrt{2\pi}}e^0$$

$$= \frac{1}{3\sqrt{2\pi}}$$

Thus, the maximum value of $f(x)$ is $\dfrac{1}{3\sqrt{2\pi}}$.

● **PROBLEM 5-19**

Given that x has a normal distribution with mean 10 and standard deviation 4, find $P\{x < 15\}$.

SOLUTION:

A graph of this density function will look like this:

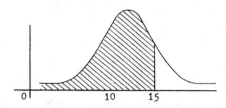

We wish to find $P\{x < 15\}$ or the area of the shaded region. It would be possible to construct tables which would supply such probabilities for many different values of the mean and standard deviation. Luckily this is not necessary. We may shift and scale our density function in such a way so that only one table is needed.

First, the mean is subtracted from x, giving a new random variable, $x - 10$. This new random variable is still normally distributed, but $E(x - 10)$, the mean of $x - 10$, is $E(x) - 10 = 0$. We have shifted our distribution so that it is centered at 0.

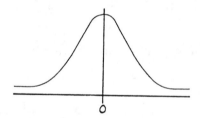

We can scale our new random variable by dividing by the standard deviation, thus creating a new random variable $z = \left(\dfrac{x-10}{4}\right)$; the variance of Z is

$$V(z) = \left(\frac{x-10}{4}\right) = \frac{V(x)}{4^2} = \frac{(\text{standard deviation of } x)^2}{16} = 1.$$

Fortunately, our new random variable Z is still normally distributed and has mean 0 and variance 1. This new random variable is referred to as a Z-score or standard normal random variable and tables for its probabilities are widespread.

To solve our problem we first convert an x-score to a Z-score and then consult the appropriate table. We find that

$$P\{x < 15\} = P\left\{\frac{x-10}{4} < \frac{15-10}{4}\right\}$$

$$= P\left\{Z < \frac{5}{4}\right\} = F\{1.25\} = 0.5000 + A(1.25)$$

$$= 0.5000 + 0.39439 = 0.89439$$

● **PROBLEM 5-20**

If a random variable X is normally distributed with a mean of 118 and a standard deviation of 11, what Z-scores correspond to raw scores of 115, 134, and 99?

SOLUTION:

To convert a raw score to a Z-score, we subtract the mean and divide by the standard deviation, or

$$Z\text{-score} = \frac{\text{raw score} - \text{mean}}{\text{standard deviation}}.$$

Thus, $\dfrac{115-118}{11} = \dfrac{-3}{11} = -0.27$ or

a Z-score of –0.27 corresponds to a raw score of 115. Also,

$$Z = \frac{134-118}{11} = \frac{16}{11} = -1.45 \text{ or}$$

a Z-score of 1.45 corresponds to a raw score of 134. And

$$Z = \frac{99-118}{11} = -1.73,$$

or a Z-score of –1.73 corresponds to a raw score of 99.

● **PROBLEM 5-21**

If X has a normal distribution with mean 9 and standard deviation 3, find $P\{5 < X < 11\}$.

SOLUTION:

First we convert our X-scores to Z-scores by subtracting the mean and dividing by the standard deviation. Next we consult tables for the standard normal distribution.

Thus, $P\{5 < X < 11\} = P\left\{\dfrac{5-9}{3} < \dfrac{X-9}{3} < \dfrac{11-9}{3}\right\}$

$$= P\left\{\dfrac{-4}{3} < Z < \dfrac{2}{3}\right\} = \Phi(0.66) - \Phi(-1.33)$$

$$= 0.74537 - 0.09176 = 0.65361$$

● PROBLEM 5-22

Given a mean of 50 and a standard deviation of 10 for a set of measurements that is normally distributed, find the probability that a randomly selected observation is between 50 and 55.

SOLUTION:

We wish to find $P\{50 \leq X \leq 55\}$ where X is normally distributed with mean 50 and standard deviation 10. We standardize X to convert our distribution of X-scores to a distribution of Z-scores. Let $Z = \dfrac{X-\mu}{\sigma}$, where μ is the mean of X-scores and σ is the standard deviation of the X-scores. Then

$$P\{50 \leq X \leq 55\} = P\left\{\dfrac{50-\mu}{\sigma} \leq \dfrac{X-\mu}{\sigma} \leq \dfrac{55-\mu}{\sigma}\right\}$$

$$= P\left\{\dfrac{50-50}{10} \leq Z \leq \dfrac{55-50}{10}\right\} = P\{0 \leq Z \leq 0.5\}$$

$$= P\{Z \leq 0.5\} - P\{Z \leq 0\}$$

From the table of standard normal,

$P\{Z \leq 0\} = 0.5$ P and $\{Z \leq 0.5\} = 0.691$

Substituting we see that

$P\{50 \leq X \leq 55\} = P\{0 \leq Z \leq 0.5\}$

$$= P\{Z \leq 0.5\} - P\{Z \leq 0\} = 0.691 - 0.500$$

$$= 0.191$$

An electrical firm manufactures light bulbs that have a lifetime that is normally distributed with a mean of 800 hours and a standard deviation of 40 hours. Of 100 bulbs, about how many will have lifetimes between 778 and 834 hours?

SOLUTION:

The probability that X, the lifetime of a randomly selected bulb, is between 778 and 834 hours is $P \{778 < X < 834\}$. Standardizing, we see that $P \{778 < X < 834\}$

$$= P \left\{ \frac{778-\mu}{\sigma} \le \frac{X-\mu}{\sigma} \le \frac{834-\mu}{\sigma} \right\}$$

$$= P \left\{ \frac{778-800}{40} \le Z \le \frac{834-800}{40} \right\}$$

$$= P \left\{ \frac{-22}{40} < Z < \frac{34}{40} \right\} = P \{-0.55 < Z < 0.85\}$$

$$= P \{Z < 0.85\} - P \{Z < -0.55\} = 0.802 - \{1 - 0.709\}$$

$$= 0.511$$

Thus, 51.1% of the bulbs manufactured will have lifetimes between 778 and 834 hours. On the average, 51 of 100 light bulbs will have lifetimes between 778 and 834 hours.

Given a normal population with $\mu = 25$ and $\sigma = 5$, find the probability that an assumed value of the variable will fall in the interval 20 to 30.

SOLUTION:

We wish to find the probability that a normally distributed random variable, X, with mean $\mu = 25$ and standard deviation $\sigma = 5$, will lie in the interval (20, 30), $P \{20 < X < 30\}$. We convert X from a normally distributed variable with mean 25 and standard deviation 5 to Z, a normally distributed random variable with mean 0 and standard deviation 1. The formula for conversion is $Z = \dfrac{X - \mu}{\sigma}$. Thus,

$$P\,(20 < X < 30) = P\left\{\frac{20 - \mu}{\sigma} < \frac{X - \mu}{\sigma} < \frac{30 - \mu}{\sigma}\right\}$$

$$= P\left\{\frac{20 - 25}{5} < Z < \frac{30 - 25}{5}\right\}$$

$$= P\,\{-1 < Z < 1\}$$

To find this probability involving the random variable Z, we resort to prepared tables which are usually found in statistics texts. There are a variety of such tables and we find $P\,\{-1 < Z < 1\}$ three different ways to illustrate the various types of tables.

(1)   This type of table gives $P\,\{0 < Z < a\}$. To find the $P\,\{-1 < Z < 1\}$, we first find $P\,\{0 < Z < 1\}$. This is $P\,(0 < Z < 1) = 0.341$. Next use the fact that the standard normal distribution is symmetric about 0, hence $P\,\{0 < Z < a\} = P\,\{-a < Z < 0\}$.

From this fact,

$$P\,\{-1 < Z < 0\} = P\,\{0 < Z < 1\} = 0.341$$
$$P\,\{-1 < Z < 1\} = P\,\{-1 < Z < 0\} + P\,\{0 < Z < 1\}$$
$$= 2\,(0.341) = 0.682.$$

(2)   Another type of table gives $P\,\{Z \le a\}$ for various values of a. To use this table we note that

$$P\,\{-1 \le Z \le 1\} = P\,\{Z \le 1\} - P\,\{Z \le -1\};$$

from the table we see that

$$P\,\{Z \le 1\} = 0.841 \quad \text{and} \quad P\,\{Z \le -1\} = 0.159\;.$$

Thus, $P\,\{-1 \le Z \le 1\} = 0.841 - 0.159 = 0.682.$

(3)   This type of table gives $P\,(Z \ge a)$ for certain values of a.

$$P\,\{-1 \le Z \le 1\} = P\,\{-1 \le Z\} - P\,\{1 \le Z\}$$

But $P\,\{-1 \le Z\} = P\,\{1 \ge Z\}$ by symmetry

$$= 1 - P\,\{1 \le Z\}$$

Thus, $P\,\{-1 \le Z \le 1\} = [1 - P\,\{1 \le Z\}] - P\,\{1 \le Z\}$

$$= 1 - 2\,P\,\{1 \le Z\} = 1 - 2\,(0.1587) = 0.682\;.$$

A television company manufactures transistors that have an average life span of 1,000 hours and a standard deviation of 100 hours. Find the probability that a transistor selected at random will have a life-span between 875 hours and 1,075 hours. Assume the distribution is normal.

SOLUTION:

The probability that a transistor selected at random will have a life span between 875 hours and 1,075 hours can be expressed symbolically as $P\{875 < X < 1,075\}$. Life spans of transistors are normally distributed, but we must standardize X (the random variable which represents life span) in order to use the standard normal table. We do this by subtracting its mean and dividing the resulting difference by its standard deviation. We are given that the mean (average life span) is 1,000 hours, and that the standard deviation is 100 hours.

Letting Z denote our standard normal random variable, $Z = \dfrac{X-\mu}{\sigma} =$

$\dfrac{X-1,000}{100}$. We want to find the area under the standard normal curve between the Z values for $X = 875$ and $X = 1,075$, so we compute

$$Z\,(875) = \frac{875-1,000}{100} = \frac{-125}{100} = -1.25, \text{ and}$$

$$Z\,(1075) = \frac{1,075-1,000}{100} = \frac{75}{100} = 0.75.$$

In terms of Z,
$$P\{875 < X < 1075\} = P\{-1.25 < Z < 0.75\}\,.$$

Since some tables give areas under the standard normal curve only for positive Z values, we put $P\{-1.25 < Z < 0.75\}$ in its equivalent form: $P\{0 < Z < 0.75\} + P\{0 < Z < 1.25\}$. The symmetry of the standard normal curve allows us to do this.

Reading the table we find $P\{0 < Z < 0.75\} = 0.2734$ and $P\{0 < Z < 1.25\} = 0.3944$. The total area between $Z = -1.25$ and $Z = 0.75$ is $0.2734 + 0.3944 = 0.6678$, and this is the probability that a randomly selected transistor will function between 875 and 1,075 hours.

The true weights of ten-pound sacks of potatoes processed at a certain packaging house have a normal distribution with mean 10 (pounds) and variance 0.01 (square pounds). What is the probability that a sack purchased at the grocery store will weigh at least 9 lbs. 14 oz.?

SOLUTION:

Let X be the true weight of a ten-pound sack of potatoes. Our question asks what is the $P \{9 \text{ lbs. } 14 \text{ oz. } \leq X\}$?

Now 9 lbs. 14 oz. $= 9\frac{14}{16}$ lbs. $= 9.875$ lbs.

We will subtract the mean, 10, and divide by the standard deviation, $\sqrt{0.01} = 0.1$, to standardize and convert the X-score to a Z-score. This results in

$$P \{9.875 \text{ lbs. } < X\} = P\left\{\frac{9.875-10}{0.1} < \frac{X-10}{0.1}\right\}$$

$$= P \{-1.25 < Z\} = 1 - P \{Z < -1.25\}$$
$$= 1 - \Phi (-1.25) = 1 - 0.10565 = 0.89435$$

If a distribution has a mean of 15 and a standard deviation of 2, what Z-score corresponds to a raw score of 19? What Z-score corresponds to a raw score of 14?

SOLUTION:

One interpretation of the conversion from X-scores to Z-scores is taken from the meaning of the standard deviation. If a distribution of X-scores has a certain known mean and standard deviation, the Z-score can be thought of as the number of standard deviations from the mean.

For example, in the current problem the distribution has a mean of 15 and a standard deviation of 2. To find the Z-score equivalent of 19, we can either standardize score 19 by subtracting the mean and dividing by the standard deviation or equivalently we can find how many standard deviations 19 is from 15.

The standard deviation is 2, and so 19 is a distance of 2 standard deviations from the mean, since 15 + 2 (2) = 19. The Z-score corresponding to 19 is two standard deviations from 15; thus, $Z = 2$ corresponds to 19 (that

is, $P\{X = 19\} = P\left\{\dfrac{19-15}{12}\right\} = P\{Z = 2\}$).

The Z-score that corresponds to an X-score of 14 is the number of standard deviations 14 is from 15. Since 14 is one unit below 15 and one

unit is $\dfrac{1}{2}$ the standard deviation, the Z-score corresponding to 14 is –0.5.

● PROBLEM 5–28

For a normal distribution of measurements whose mean is 50 and whose standard deviation is 10, what is the probability that a measurement chosen at random will be between the values of 35 and 45?

SOLUTION:

We wish to find $P\{35 < X < 45\}$, where X is normally distributed with mean 50 and standard deviation 10. To find the Z-scores, we ask how many standard deviations away is 35 from 50, and 45 from 50.

One standard deviation is a distance of 10, and half a standard deviation is a distance of 5. Thus, 35 is 15 units or 1.5 standard deviations below 50, and 45 is 5 units or 0.5 standard deviations below 50. Thus, the Z-score corresponding to 35 is –1.5 and the Z-score corresponding to 45 is –0.5. Hence,

$$P\{35 < X < 45\} = P\{-1.5 < Z < -0.5\}.$$
$$\text{But } P\{-1.5 < Z < -0.5\} = P\{Z < -0.5\} - P\{Z < -1.5\}$$
$$= 0.3085 - 0.0668 = 0.2417.$$

Given a population of values for which $\mu = 100$ and $\sigma = 15$, find the percentage of values that lie within one standard deviation of the mean. Assume a normal distribution.

SOLUTION:

The observations that will lie within one standard deviation of the mean are those values greater than $100 - 15 = 85$ and less than $100 + 15 = 115$.

$$P\{85 < X < 115\} = P\{-1 < Z < 1\}$$

because 85 is one standard deviation below the mean and 115 is one standard deviation above the mean. Now

$$P\{-1 < Z < 1\} = P\{Z < 1\} - P\{Z < -1\}$$
$$= 0.841 - 0.159 = 0.682$$

Thus, 68.2% of the values lie within one standard deviation of the mean.

Let X be a normally distributed random variable with mean $\mu = 2$ and $\sigma^2 = 9$. Find the probability that X is less than 8 and greater than 5.

SOLUTION:

Let $Z = \dfrac{X-\mu}{\sigma}$.

Then $P\{a < X \le b\} = P\left\{\dfrac{a-\mu}{\sigma} < \dfrac{x-\mu}{\sigma} \le \dfrac{b-\mu}{\sigma}\right\}$

$$= P\left\{Z > \dfrac{a-\mu}{\sigma}\right\} - P\left\{Z > \dfrac{b-\mu}{\sigma}\right\}$$

$$= P\left\{Z > \dfrac{5-2}{\sqrt{9}}\right\} - P\left\{Z > \dfrac{8-2}{\sqrt{9}}\right\}$$

$$= P\left\{Z > \dfrac{3}{3}\right\} - P\left\{Z > \dfrac{6}{3}\right\}$$

$$= P\{Z > 1\} - P\{Z > 2\}$$
$$= 0.1587 - 0.0228 = 0.1359,$$

making use of the normal table.

Suppose that a random variable X has the following probability density function:

$$f(x) = \frac{1}{2\sqrt{2\pi}} e^{-\frac{(x+4)^2}{8}}, \quad -\infty < x < \infty.$$

Compute:
(a) $P\{X \leq -2\}$ (b) $P\{-5 < X \leq -2\}$
(c) $P\{|X + 3| \leq 1\}$ (d) $P\{X \geq -6\}$

SOLUTION:

A random variable with this density function is normally distributed. The general density function of a normally distributed random variable with mean μ and variance σ^2 is:

$$f(x) = \frac{1}{\sigma\sqrt{2\pi}} e^{-\frac{(x-\mu)^2}{2\sigma^2}}, \quad -\infty < x < \infty.$$

The p.d.f., or probability density function, that has been given is identical to this with $\mu = -4$ and $\sigma = 2$. To find the probabilities asked for, we standardize the distribution and calculate the probabilities from the table of the standard normal distribution.

(a) $P\{X \leq -2\} = P\left\{\frac{x-\mu}{\sigma} \leq \frac{-2-\mu}{\sigma}\right\}$

$$= P\left\{Z \leq \frac{-2-(-4)}{2}\right\} = P\{Z \leq 1\} = 0.8413$$

(b) $P\{-5 < X \leq -2\} = P\{X \leq -2\} - P\{X \leq -5\}$

$$= P\left(\frac{x-\mu}{\sigma} \leq \frac{-2-\mu}{\sigma}\right) - P\left\{\frac{x-\mu}{\sigma} \leq \frac{-5-\mu}{\sigma}\right\}$$

$$= P\left\{Z \le \frac{-2-(-4)}{2}\right\} - P\left\{Z \le \frac{-5-(-4)}{2}\right\}$$

$$= P\{Z \le 1\} - P\{Z \le -0.5\}$$

$$= 0.8413 - 0.3085 = 0.5328$$

(c) $|X + 3| \le 1$ is the set of all $X =$ values such that

$X + 3 \le 1$ and $-(X + 3) \le 1$

or $X \le 1 - 3$ and $(X + 3) \ge -1$,

$X \le -2$ and $X \ge -4$.

Thus,

$$P\{|X + 3| \le 1\} = P\{X \le -2 \text{ and } X \ge -4\}$$
$$= P\{-4 \le X \le -2\}$$

Converting to Z-scores by subtracting the mean and dividing by the standard deviation, we see that

$$P\{|X + 3| \le 1\} = P\left\{\frac{-4-\mu}{\sigma} \le \frac{X-\mu}{\sigma} \le \frac{-2-\mu}{\sigma}\right\}$$

$$= P\left\{\frac{-4-(-4)}{2} \le Z \le \frac{-2-(-4)}{2}\right\}$$

$$= P\{0 \le Z \le 1\} = P\{Z \le 1\} - P\{Z \le 0\}$$

$$= 0.8413 - 0.5000 = 0.3413$$

(d) $P\{X \ge -6\} = P\left\{\frac{X-\mu}{\sigma} \ge \frac{-6-\mu}{\sigma}\right\}$

$$= P\left\{Z \ge \frac{-6-(-4)}{2}\right\} = P(Z \ge -1)$$

By the symmetry of the normal distribution,

$P\{Z \ge -1\} = P\{Z \le 1\} = 0.8413.$

Notice that the answer to parts (a) and (d) are the same. This is not surprising because the normal distribution is symmetric about its mean, $\mu = -4$.

The melting point of gold is known to be 1,060°C. This is an average figure, for unavoidable "experimental error" causes more or less variation from this figure whenever the test is actually performed. The best measure of these variations is the standard deviation (S). Suppose this has been calculated from a large series of tests and found to be 3°C. Now imagine that you are analyzing an unknown metal, and a test shows its melting point to be 1,072°C. Is it likely that this unknown metal is gold? In other words, what is the probability that a sample of gold would show a melting point as different from its average of 1,072°C?

SOLUTION:

Let X be the random variable denoting the observed melting point of gold. Now X is assumed to be normally distributed with mean 1,060°C and standard deviation 3°C. We wish to determine if an unknown sample, having an observed melting point of 1,072°C, is gold. We compute the probability that gold would have an observed melting point of 1,072°C. First, we convert the X observation 1,072 into a Z-score.

$$Z = \frac{X - \text{mean}}{\text{standard deviation}} = \frac{1,072 - 1,060}{3}$$

$$= \frac{12}{3} = 4$$

That is, this observation of 1,072 is four standard deviations from the mean. The probability of an observation lying four standard deviations from its mean is very small, virtually zero; 99.8% of the distribution lies within three standard deviations of the mean of a normal distribution. It is very unlikely that the unknown sample is, in fact, gold.

A food processor packages instant coffee in small jars. The weights of the jars are normally distributed with a standard deviation of 0.3 ounces. If five percent of the jars weigh more than 12.492 ounces, what is the mean weight of the jars?

SOLUTION:

Let X be the weight of a randomly selected jar. Five percent of the jars weigh more than 12.492 ounces. Thus, $P\{X > 12.492\} = 0.05$.

To find the mean of X given a standard deviation of $\sigma = 0.3$, we convert X-scores to Z-scores.

We know that

$$P\{X > 12.492\} = P\left\{\frac{X-\mu}{\sigma} > \frac{12.492-\mu}{\sigma}\right\}$$

$$= P\left\{Z > \frac{12.492-\mu}{\sigma}\right\}$$

$$= 0.05$$

From the table of the normal distribution,
$$P\{Z > 1.64\} = 0.05 .$$

Thus, $\dfrac{12.492-\mu}{\sigma} = 1.64$. Now

$\sigma = 0.3$, so $\mu = 12.492 - 1.64\ \sigma$
$= 12.492 - (1.64)\ (0.3) = 12.492 - 0.492$
$= 12$ ounces

● PROBLEM 5-34

The demand for meat at a grocery store during any week is approximately normally distributed with a mean demand of 5,000 lbs and a standard deviation of 300 lbs.
  (a) If the store has 5,300 lbs of meat in stock, what is the probability that it is overstocked?
  (b) How much meat should the store have in stock per week so as to not run short more than 10 percent of the time?

SOLUTION:

(a) Let the random variable X denote the demand for meat. If the demand is less than the quantity of meat the store has in stock, the store will be overstocked. Thus, if $X < 5,300$, the store will be overstocked. Then $P\{X < 5,300\}$ can be found by converting the X-score to a Z-score. That is,

$$P\{X < 5,300\} = P\left\{\frac{X-\mu}{\sigma} > \frac{5,300-\mu}{\sigma}\right\}$$

$$= P\left\{Z < \frac{5,300-5,000}{300}\right\} = P\{Z < 1\}$$

$$= 0.8413$$

Thus if the store keeps 5,300 lbs of meat in stock, demand will be less than supply 84.13% of the time.

(b) The store will not run short if $X > q$. We wish to find the number q such that $X < q$ 90% of the time. Equivalently, we wish to find q such that

$$P\{X < q\} = 0.90$$

$$P\{X < q\} = P\left\{\frac{X-\mu}{\sigma} > \frac{q-\mu}{\sigma}\right\} = 0.90$$

$$= P\left\{Z < \frac{q-5,000}{300}\right\} = 0.90$$

From the table of the standard normal distribution,

$$P\{Z < 1.282\} = 0.90. \text{ Thus, } \frac{q-5,000}{300} = 1.282$$

or $q = 5,000 + (1.282)\ 300 = 5,384.6$.

If the store orders 5,384.6 pounds of meat a week, they will run short only ten percent of the time.

● PROBLEM 5–35

A lathe produces washers whose internal diameters are normally distributed with mean equal to 0.373 inches and standard deviation of 0.002 inches. If specifications require that the internal diameters be 0.375 inches plus or minus 0.004 inches, what percentage of production will be unacceptable?

SOLUTION:

Let X be a random variable representing the internal diameter of a randomly selected washer. Now X is normally distributed with mean 0.373 inches and a standard deviation of 0.002 inches.

If X is greater than $0.375 + 0.004 = 0.379$ inches or less than $0.375 - 0.004 = 0.371$ inches, the washer will be unacceptable. Now

$P\{X > 0.379\} + P\{X < 0.371\}$

$$= P\left\{\frac{X-\mu}{\sigma} > \frac{0.379-\mu}{\sigma}\right\} + P\left\{\frac{X-\mu}{\sigma} < \frac{0.371-\mu}{\sigma}\right\}$$

$$= P\left\{Z > \frac{0.379-0.373}{0.002}\right\} + P\left\{Z < \frac{0.371-0.373}{0.002}\right\}$$

$$= P\left\{Z < \frac{0.006}{0.002}\right\} + P\left\{Z < \frac{-0.002}{0.002}\right\}$$

$$= P\{Z > 3\} + P\{Z < -1\}$$

$$= 0.001 + (1 - 0.841) = 0.001 + 0.159$$

$$= 0.160$$

Thus, P {washer is unacceptable' $= 0.160$ or 16% of the washers produced will be unacceptable.

● PROBLEM 5-36

The life of a machine is normally distributed with a mean of 3,000 hours. From past experience, 50% of these machines last less than 2,632 or more than 3,368 hours. What is the standard deviation of the lifetime of a machine?

SOLUTION:

Let X be the random variable denoting the life of this machine. We know that X is normally distributed with mean 3,000 and the probability that X is greater than 3,368 or less than 2,632 is

$P\{X < 2,632\} + P\{X > 3,368\} = 0.5$.

Converting X to a standard normal variable with mean 0 and standard deviation 1, we see that

$$P\{X < 2,632\} = P\left\{\frac{X-\mu}{\sigma} < \frac{2,632-\mu}{\sigma}\right\}$$

$$= P\left\{Z < \frac{2,632-\mu}{\sigma}\right\}$$

and

$$P \{X > 3{,}368\} = P \left\{ \frac{X - \mu}{\sigma} > \frac{3{,}368 - \mu}{\sigma} \right\}$$

$$= P \left\{ Z > \frac{3{,}368 - \mu}{\sigma} \right\}$$

Substituting $\mu = 3{,}000$ into these equations, we see that

$$P \{X < 2{,}632\} = P \left\{ Z < \frac{-368}{\sigma} \right\}$$

and

$$P \{X > 3{,}368\} = P \left\{ Z > \frac{368}{\sigma} \right\} .$$

By the symmetry of the normal distribution, we know that:
$$P \{Z < - C\} = P \{Z > C\} .$$

Thus, $P \{X < 2{,}632\} = P \left\{ Z < \frac{-368}{\sigma} \right\}$

$$= P \left\{ Z > \frac{368}{\sigma} \right\} = P \{X > 3{,}368\} .$$

Taking advantage of this fact, we let

$$P \{X < 2{,}632\} = P \{X > 3{,}368\} = P \left\{ Z > \frac{368}{\sigma} \right\} .$$

Thus,

$$P \left\{ Z > \frac{368}{\sigma} \right\} + P \left\{ Z > \frac{368}{\sigma} \right\} = 0.5$$

or $\quad P \left\{ Z > \frac{368}{\sigma} \right\} = \frac{0.5}{2} = 0.25 .$

Searching through the table of standardized Z-scores, we see that
$P \{Z > 0.67\} = 0.25$, very nearly.

Thus, $\dfrac{368}{\sigma} = 0.67$ or $s = \dfrac{368}{0.67} =$

The mean height of a soldier in an army regiment is 70 inches. Ten percent of the soldiers in the regiment are taller than 72 inches. Assuming that the heights of the soldiers in this regiment are normally distributed, what is the standard deviation?

SOLUTION:

Let X be the height of a randomly selected soldier. We are given that X is normally distributed with mean $\mu = E(X) = 70$ inches and $P\{X > 72\} = 0.10$.

To find the standard deviation of X, we convert X from an X-score to a Z-score by subtracting the mean and dividing by the unknown standard deviation. Thus,

$$P\{X > 72\} = P\left\{\frac{X-\mu}{\sigma} > \frac{72-\mu}{\sigma}\right\} = 0.10$$

$$= P\left\{Z > \frac{72-\mu}{\sigma}\right\} = 0.10$$

Checking the table of the standard normal distribution, we wish to find the value C such that $P\{Z > C\} = 0.10$. To do this we inspect the body of the table until the four-digit number closest to 0.10 is located. This is 0.1003. Reading across the row to the left and up the column, we see that $C = 1.28$. Thus,

$$P\{X > 1.28) = 0.10$$

We know that

$$P\left\{Z > \frac{72-\mu}{\sigma}\right\} = P(X > 1.28) = 0.10 \ .$$

Thus, $\dfrac{72-\mu}{\sigma} = 1.28$.

We have been given that $\mu = 70$; thus, substituting for μ and solving yields

$$\frac{72-70}{\sigma} = 1.28 \ , \qquad \sigma = \frac{72-70}{1.28} = \frac{2}{1.28} = 1.56 \text{ inches.}$$

The heights of soldiers are normally distributed. If 13.57% of the soldiers are taller than 72.2 inches and 8.08% are shorter than 67.2 inches, what are the mean and the standard deviation of the heights of the soldiers?

SOLUTION:

Let X be the random variable denoting the heights of the soldiers. If 13.57% of the soldiers are taller than 72.2 inches, the probability that a randomly selected soldier's height is greater than 72.2 is:

$P \{X > 72.2\} = 0.1357$.

Similarly, the probability that a randomly selected soldier's height is less than 67.2 inches is:

$P \{X < 67.2\} = 0.0808$.

To find the mean and variance of X from this information, we convert the X-scores to Z-scores by subtracting the mean and dividing by the standard deviation.

Thus, $P (X > 72.2) = 0.1357$

$$P \left\{ \frac{X - \mu}{\sigma} > \frac{72.2 - \mu}{\sigma} \right\} = 0.1357 \quad P \left\{ Z > \frac{72.2 - \mu}{\sigma} \right\} = 0.1357$$

From the table of Z-scores, we know that

$$P \{Z > 1.1\} = 0.1357. \text{ Thus, } \frac{72.2 - \mu}{\sigma} = 1.1.$$

Similarly, $P (X < 67.2) = 0.0808$ implies

$$P \left\{ \frac{X - \mu}{\sigma} < \frac{67.2 - \mu}{\sigma} \right\} = 0.0808 \text{ or}$$

$$P \left\{ Z < \frac{67.2 - \mu}{\sigma} \right\} = 0.0808$$

By the symmetry of the normal distribution,

$$P \{Z < -C\} = P \{Z > C\} ;$$

thus $\quad P \left\{ Z < \frac{67.2 - \mu}{\sigma} \right\} = P \left\{ Z > \frac{-67.2 + \mu}{\sigma} \right\}.$

From the table we see that $P (Z > 1.4) = 0.0808$

thus $\quad \dfrac{-67.2 + \mu}{\sigma} = 1.4$.

We now have two equations involving μ and σ. These are

$$\frac{72.2 - \mu}{\sigma} = 1.1 \text{ and } \frac{-67.2 + \mu}{\sigma} = 1.4 .$$

Multiplying both equations by σ and adding them together gives

$$72.2 - \mu = (1.1) \sigma$$

and

$$- 67.2 + \mu = (1.4) \sigma$$

$$\overline{ 5 = (2.5) \sigma}$$

Thus, $\sigma = \dfrac{5}{2.5} = 2$.

Substituting 2 into either of our original equations gives

$$\mu = 72.2 - (1.1) \, 2 = 70 .$$

Thus, the mean of the distribution of heights is $\mu = 70$ and the standard deviation is $\sigma = 2$.

● PROBLEM 5–39

Suppose the weights of adult males are normally distributed and that 6.68 percent are under 130 lbs in weight, and 77.45 percent are between 130 and 180 lbs. Find the parameters of the distribution.

SOLUTION:

Let the random variable X denote the weight of adult males. We are given that X is normally distributed and that $P \{X \le 130\} = 6.68\%$ and $P \{130 \le X \le 180\} = 77.45\%$. Equivalently, $P \{X \le 130\} = 0.0668$ and $P \{130 \le X \le 180\} = 0.7745$. We are asked to find the parameters of this distribution, μ and σ^2, the mean and variance. Now

$$P \{X \le 130\} + P \{130 \le X \le 180\}$$
$$= P \{X \le 130\} + [P \{X \le 180\} - P \{X \le 130\}]$$
$$= P (X \le 180)$$

Thus,

$$P \{X \le 180\} = 0.0668 + 0.7745 = 0.8413.$$

Converting from X-scores to Z-scores, we see that

$$P \left\{ \frac{X-\mu}{\sigma} \le \frac{130-\mu}{\sigma} \right\} = 0.0668$$

and $\quad P\left\{\dfrac{X-\mu}{\sigma} \le \dfrac{180-\mu}{\sigma}\right\} = 0.8413$

or $\quad P\left\{Z \le \dfrac{130-\mu}{\sigma}\right\} = 0.0668$

and $\quad P\left\{Z \le \dfrac{180-\mu}{\sigma}\right\} = 0.8413$

From the table of the standard normal distributions, we know that
$P\{Z < -1.5\} = 0.0668$ and $P\{Z \le 1\} = 0.8413$.

Thus, $\quad \dfrac{130-\mu}{\sigma} = -1.5$

and $\quad \dfrac{180-\mu}{\sigma} = 1$

or $\quad 130 = \mu - (1.5)\,\sigma$
and $\quad 180 = \mu + (1)\,\sigma$.

Subtracting these two equations, we see that
$\quad -50 = (-2.5)\,\sigma \quad$ or $\quad \sigma = 20 \quad$ and
$\quad 180 = \mu + 20 \quad$ or $\quad \mu = 180 - 20 = 160$.

● PROBLEM 5-40

The average grade on a mathematics test is 82, with a standard deviation of 5. If the instructor assigns A's to the highest 12 percent and the grades follow a normal distribution, what is the lowest grade that will be assigned A?

SOLUTION:

We relate the given information to the normal curve by thinking of the highest 12 percent of the grades as 12 percent of the area under the right side of the curve. Then the lowest grade assigned A is that point on the X-axis for which the area under the curve to its right is 12 percent of the total area.

12%

Lowest grade
assigned A

127

The standard normal curve is symmetric about the Y-axis; this means that if we take the additive inverse of any Z-score, its Y value will be unchanged. For example, the area to the right of $Z = 2$ is equal to the area to the left of $Z = -2$; $P\{Z \geq 2\} = P\{Z \leq -2\}$. It follows that the area under the curve to the right of $Z = 0$ is exactly half the total area under the curve. Therefore, the area between the Y-axis and the desired X-score is 50% − 12% = 38% of the total area, which is 1.

If we can find a K for which $P\{0 < Z < K\} = 0.38$, K can be converted to an X-score which is the lowest grade assigned A.

Using the table of areas under the standard normal curve, we locate 0.380 and see that its Z-score is 1.175. This means that $P\{0 < Z < 1.175\} = 0.380$. This is equivalent to $P\{Z > 1.175\} = 0.500 - 0.380 = 0.120$.

Now we can convert $Z = 1.175$ to an X-score by solving the equation $1.175 = \dfrac{X - \mu}{\sigma}$ for X. We are told that the average grade on the test is $82 = \mu$ (the mean) and the standard deviation is 5. Substituting we have $1.175 = \dfrac{X - 82}{5}$ and $5\,(1.175) = X - 82$, so that $X = 5\,(1.175) + 82 = 87.875$. This means that

$$P\{Z > 1.175\} = P\{X > 87.875\} = 0.120.$$

Since all grades are integers, the integer just above 87.875 is 88, which is the lowest grade assigned an A.

● **PROBLEM 5–41**

A teacher decides that the top 10 percent of students should receive A's and the next 25 percent B's. If the test scores are normally distributed with the mean 70 and the standard deviation 10, find the scores that should be assigned A's and B's.

SOLUTION:

We wish to find two numbers, a and b. If X is the random variable denoting a student's test score and X is assumed to be approximately normal, then any score such that $X > a$ will get an A. Any score such that $b < X < a$ will get a B. In addition, only 10 percent of the students should receive A's. We should choose a to reflect this fact. Thus, we wish to find a such that $P\{X > a\} = 0.10$. Similarly, if 25 percent of the students are to receive B's, b must be chosen so that $P\{b < X < a\} = 0.250$.

But,
$$P\{b < X < a\} + P\{x > a\} = P\{X > b\}$$
$$= 0.250 + 0.10 = 0.350$$

Thus, our conditions on a and b become
$$P\{X > b\} = 0.350$$
and $P\{X > a\} = 0.10$.

Since we know the mean and standard deviation of X to be 70 and 10, we can convert X-scores to Z-scores.

$$P\{X > b\} = P\left\{\frac{X-\mu}{\sigma} > \frac{b-\mu}{\sigma}\right\} = 0.350$$

$$= P\left\{Z > \frac{b-70}{10}\right\} = 0.350$$

and $P\{X > a\} = P\left\{\dfrac{X-\mu}{\sigma} > \dfrac{a-\mu}{\sigma}\right\} = 0.10$

$$= P\left\{Z > \frac{a-70}{10}\right\} = 0.10$$

From the table of the standard normal distribution,
$$P\{Z > 0.385\} = 0.35$$
and $P\{Z > 1.282\} = 0.10$.

Thus, $\dfrac{b-70}{10} = 0.385$ and $\dfrac{a-70}{10} = 1.282$

and $a = 70 + (1.282)\ 10$
$b = 70 + (0.385)\ 10$
or $a = 82.82$ and $b = 73.85$.

Thus, if a student scores over 83, he receives an A, while a student who scores between 74 and 83 receives a B.

● PROBLEM 5-42

The IQs of the army recruits in a given year are normally distributed with $\mu = 110$ and $\sigma = 8$. The army wants to give special training to the 10% of those recruits with the highest IQ scores. What is the lowest IQ score acceptable for this special training?

SOLUTION:

Let X denote the IQ score of a randomly selected recruit. We wish to find the number such that 10% of the distribution of IQ scores is above this number. Thus, this number K will be specified by

$P\{X \geq K\} = 0.10.$

Standardizing X by subtracting the mean of X, 110, and dividing by the standard deviation, 8, we obtain

$$P\{X \geq K\} = P\left\{\frac{X-110}{8} \geq \frac{K-110}{8}\right\} = 0.10.$$

But $\dfrac{X-110}{8} = Z$ is normally distributed with mean 0 and standard deviation 1. Thus, from the table of the standard normal,

$P\{Z > 1.282\} = 0.10.$ Hence, $\dfrac{K-110}{8} = 1.282,$

or $\quad K = 110 + 8\,(1.282) = 120.256.$

Thus, the lowest IQ score for this special training is 121. All recruits with IQ scores of 121 or above will receive this training.

● PROBLEM 5-43

Let X be a normally distributed random variable representing the hourly wage in a certain craft. The mean of the hourly wage is \$4.25 and the standard deviation is \$.75.
   (a) What proportion of workers receives an hourly wage between \$3.50 and \$4.90?
   (b) What hourly wage represents the 95th percentile?

SOLUTION:

(a) We seek
    $P\{3.50 \leq X \leq 4.90\}.$
    Converting to Z-scores, we see that

$$P\{3.50 \leq X \leq 4.90\} = P\left\{\frac{3.50-\mu}{\sigma} \leq Z \leq \frac{4.90-\mu}{\sigma}\right\}$$

130

$$= P\left\{\frac{3.50-4.25}{0.75} \le Z \le \frac{4.90-4.25}{0.75}\right\}$$

$$= P\left\{\frac{-0.75}{0.75} \le Z \le \frac{0.65}{0.75}\right\}$$

$$= P\{-1 \le Z \le 0.87\}$$
$$= P\{Z \le 0.87\} - P\{Z \le -1\}$$
$$= P\{Z \le 0.87\} - \{1 - P\{Z \ge -1\}$$
$$= P\{Z \le 0.87\} - [1 - P\{Z \le -1\}]$$
$$= 0.809 - [1 - 0.841] = 0.650$$

Thus, 65% of the hourly wages are between \$3.50 and \$4.90.

(b) The 95th percentile is that number Z_α such that
$$P\{X \le K\} = 0.95.$$

To find Z_α, we first convert to Z-scores. Thus,

$$P\{X \le Z_\alpha\} = P\left\{\frac{X-4.25}{0.75} \le \frac{K-4.25}{0.75}\right\} = 0.95$$

$$= P\left\{Z \le \frac{K-4.25}{0.75}\right\} = 0.95$$

But $P\{Z \le 1.645\} = 0.95$; thus $\dfrac{K-4.25}{0.75} = 1.645$,

$$K = 4.25 + (0.75)(1.645) = 5.48.$$

Thus, 95% of the craftsmen have hourly wages less than \$5.48.

● PROBLEM 5–44

A soft-drink machine can be regulated to discharge an average of seven ounces per cup. If the amount of drink dispensed per cup is normally distributed with a standard deviation of 0.3 ounces,
  (a) what fraction of the cups will contain more than 7.1 ounces?
  (b) if the cups hold exactly eight ounces, what is the probability that a cup will overflow?
  (c) what should be the cup size so that the cups will overflow only one percent of the time?

SOLUTION:

Let Y be the amount of drink discharged into a cup. Then Y is assumed to be a normally distributed random variable with a mean of 7 ounces and a standard deviation of 0.3 ounces.

(a) The fraction of cups which will contain more than 7.1 ounces is found from $P\{Y > 7.1\}$. Standardizing or converting the Y-score to a Z-score, we see that

$$P\{Y > 7.1\} = P\left\{\frac{Y-\mu}{\sigma} > \frac{7.1-\mu}{\sigma}\right\}$$

$$= P\left\{Z > \frac{7.1-7}{0.3}\right\} = P\left\{Z > \frac{0.1}{0.3}\right\}$$

$$= P\{Z > 0.33\} = 0.37$$

Thus, about 37% of the cups will contain more than 7.1 ounces.

(b) A cup will overflow if $Y > 8$. The probability of an overflow is

$$P\{Y > 8\} = P\left\{\frac{Y-\mu}{\sigma} > \frac{8-\mu}{\sigma}\right\} = P\left\{Z > \frac{8-7}{0.3}\right\}$$

$$= P\{Z > 3.33\}$$
$$= 0.0004$$

(c) The problem is to find a cup size such that the cups will overflow only one percent of the time. We wish to find some number, C, such that

$P\{Y > C\} = 0.01$.
$P\{Z > 2.33\} = 0.01$ and

$$\left\{\frac{Y-\mu}{\sigma} > \frac{C-\mu}{\sigma}\right\} = P\left\{Z < \frac{C-7}{0.3}\right\} = 0.01 .$$

The proper cup size, C, is thus determined by

$$\frac{C-7}{0.3} = 2.33 ;$$

$C = (0.3)(2.33) + 7 = 7.699.$

Thus, if the cups hold 7.7 ounces, they will overflow one percent of the time.

Three hundred college freshmen are observed to have grade point averages that are approximately normally distributed with the mean 2.1 and a standard deviation of 1.2. How many of these freshmen would you expect to have grade point averages between 2.5 and 3.5 if the averages are recorded to the nearest tenth?

SOLUTION:

To find the number of students with averages between 2.5 and 3.5, we first find the percentage of students with averages between 2.5 and 3.5. The averages are continuous random variables that are rounded to become discrete random variables. For example, any average from 2.45 to 2.55 would be recorded as 2.5. An average of 3.45 to 3.55 would be recorded as 3.5. Thus, in computing the probability of an average lying between 2.5 and 3.5, we must account for this rounding procedure. Hence,

$P \{2.5 < X^* < 3.5\} = P \{2.45 < X < 3.55\}$, where X is the GPA and X^* is the rounded GPA. We now find this probability by standardizing the X-scores and converting them to Z-scores. Thus,

$$P \{2.45 < X < 3.55\} = P \left\{ \frac{2.45-\mu}{\sigma} < \frac{X-\mu}{\sigma} < \frac{C-\mu}{\sigma} \right\}$$

$$= P \left\{ \frac{2.45-2.1}{1.2} < Z < \frac{3.55-2.1}{1.2} \right\}$$

$$= P \{0.292 < Z < 1.21\}$$

$$= P \{Z < 1.21\} - P \{Z < 0.292\}$$

$$= 0.8869 - 0.6141 = 0.2728$$

or 27.28 percent of the freshmen have grades between 2.5 and 3.5. So, 27.28 percent of 300 is 81.84, or approximately 82 students have grade point averages between 2.5 and 3.5.

Miniature poodles have a mean height of 12 inches and a standard deviation of 1.8 inches. If height is measured to the nearest inch, find the percentage of poodles having a height of at least 14 inches.

SOLUTION:

Let X be the height of a randomly selected poodle. Then X has mean 12 and standard deviation 1.8. Because the heights are measured to the nearest inch, any height that is greater than 13.5 and less than 14.5 is recorded as 14 inches.

To find the percentage of poodles such that height, X, is recorded as at least 14 inches, we must find the percentage of poodles whose true heights are greater than 13.5 inches.

Now $P\{X > 13.5\}$ can be found by converting X to a random variable Z that is normally distributed with mean 0 and variance 1.

$$P\{X > 13.5\} = P\left\{\frac{X-\mu}{\sigma} > \frac{13.5-\mu}{\sigma}\right\}$$

$$= P\left\{Z > \frac{13.5-12}{1.8}\right\} = P\{Z \geq 0.83\}$$

From the table this is found to be 0.2033.

Thus, about 20% of these miniature poodles have heights that are at least 14 inches.

● PROBLEM 5-47

A pair of dice is thrown 120 times. What is the approximate probability of throwing at least 15 sevens? Assume the rolls are independent.

SOLUTION:

The answer to this problem is a binomial probability. If X is the number of sevens rolled, then

$$P\{X \geq 15\} = \sum_{j=15}^{120}\binom{120}{j}\left(\frac{1}{6}\right)^j\left(\frac{5}{6}\right)^{120-j}.$$

This sum is quite difficult to calculate. There is an easier way. If n is large, $Pr_B(X \geq 15)$ can be approximated by $Pr_N(X \geq 14.5)$ where X is normally distributed with the same mean and variance as the binomial random variable. Remember that the mean of a binomially distributed random variable is np; n is the number of trials and p is the probability of "success" in a single trial. The variance of a binomially distributed random

134

variable is $np(1-p)$ and the standard deviation is $\sqrt{np(1-p)}$.

Because of this fact, $\dfrac{X-np}{\sqrt{np(1-p)}}$ is normally distributed with mean 0 and variance 1.

$$np = (120)\left(\frac{1}{6}\right) = 20$$

and $\sqrt{np(1-p)} = \sqrt{120\left(\frac{1}{6}\right)\left(\frac{5}{6}\right)} = \sqrt{\dfrac{50}{3}} = 4.08248.$

Thus $P\{X \geq 15\} = P\left\{\dfrac{X-20}{4.08248} > \dfrac{14.5-20}{4.08248}\right\}$

$$= P\{Z > -1.35\} = 1 - P\{Z < -1.35\}$$
$$= 1 - \Phi(-1.35) = 1 - 0.0885$$
$$= 0.9115$$

$$Pr_B\,(X \geq 15) \approx Pr_N\,(X \geq 14.5)\,.$$

The reason 15 has become 14.5 is that a discrete random variable is being approximated by a continuous random variable.

Consider the following example:

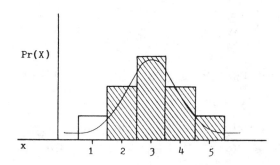

$Pr_B\,(2 \leq X \leq 5)$ = sum of the areas of the shaded rectangles. In approximating this area with a curve, we must start at the edge of the first shaded rectangle and move to the edge of the last shaded rectangle. This implies $Pr_B\,(2 \leq X \leq 5) \approx Pr_N\,(1.5 \leq X \leq 5.5)$.

Suppose that it is desired to estimate the proportion of voters in favor of a certain proposal by taking a sample of 200. What is the probability that a majority of the persons in the sample are against the proposal if, in reality, only 45 percent of the electorate is against the proposal? Assume that the population is sufficiently large so that the probability of "success" on each trial is constant, and that the trials are independent.

SOLUTION:

The desired probability is associated with a binomial experiment. In this problem each independent trial consists of selecting a voter from the electorate and checking to see if this voter favors the proposal or not. This procedure is carried out 200 times. Since 45% of the voters favor the proposal, the probability of selecting a voter from the electorate that favors the proposal is 0.45.

Let X be the number of voters sampled who favor the proposal. As we have seen, X is distributed binomially with parameters $n = 200$ and $p = 0.45$. We wish to find the probability that a majority of the sample favors the proposal, or $P\{X \geq 101\}$. Because n is large we may use the normal approximation to the binomial distribution

$$Pr_B(X \geq 101) \approx Pr_N \left(\frac{X - E(X)}{\sqrt{\mathrm{Var}\,X}} > \frac{100.5 - E(X)}{\sqrt{\mathrm{Var}\,X}} \right)$$

where $\dfrac{X - E(X)}{\sqrt{\mathrm{Var}\,X}}$ is normally distributed with mean 0 and variance 1. That is,

$$E(X) = \text{expected value of } X = np = (200)(0.45) = 90$$
$$\mathrm{Var}\,X = \text{variance of } X = np(1-p) = (200)(0.45)(0.55) = 49.5$$

and $\quad Z = \dfrac{X - E(X)}{\sqrt{\mathrm{Var}\,X}} = \dfrac{X - 90}{\sqrt{49.5}}$.

Thus, $P\{X \geq 101\} \approx P \dfrac{100.5 - 90}{\sqrt{49.5}}$

$$= P\{Z \geq 1.49\} = 1 - P\{Z < 1.49\}$$
$$= 1 - 0.9319 = 0.068$$

A binomial random variable has a mean of 6 and a standard deviation of 1.5. What percent of the area under the probability histogram is to the left of 5; to the right of 7.0?

SOLUTION:

Let X be the binomial random variable with a mean of 6 and a standard deviation of 1.5. The percent of area under the probability histogram to the left of 5 is $Pr_B (X \leq 5)$, a binomial probability. This probability can be approximated by a normal probability, so
$$Pr_B (X \leq 5) \cong Pr_N (Y \leq 5.5) \text{ where } Pr_N (Y \leq 5.5)$$
is the probability that a normally distributed variable Y is less than 5.5. The addition of 0.5 is necessary because a discrete distribution is being approximated by a continuous distribution.

The new normally distributed random variable Y has the same mean and standard deviation as X. Thus, the mean of Y is 6 and the standard deviation of Y is 1.5. To find
$$P \{X \leq 5\} \approx P \{Y \leq 5.5\}$$
we standardize the variable Y by subtracting the mean and dividing by the standard deviation. Thus,

$$P \{Y \leq 5.5\} = P \left\{ \frac{Y - \mu}{\sigma} \leq \frac{5.5 - \mu}{\sigma} \right\}$$

$$= P \left\{ Z \leq \frac{5.5 - 6}{1.5} \right\}$$

where Z is distributed normally with mean zero and variance 1.

Thus, $P \left\{ Z \leq \frac{5.5 - 6}{1.5} \right\} = P \{Z \leq -0.33\}$

and from the table of the standard normal distributions,
$$P \{Z \leq -0.33\} = 0.37.$$

Thus, the probability that X is less than 5 is approximately $P \{X \leq 5\} = 0.37$. The percentage to the right of 7.0 is the $P \{X \geq 7.0\}$, where X is binomially distributed with mean 6 and standard deviation 1.5. To correct for the approximation of a discrete random variable by a continuous random variable, subtract $\frac{1}{2}$ from 7.

Thus, $P\{X \geq 7\} \cong P\left\{Y \geq 7 - \dfrac{1}{2}\right\}$

$\cong P\{Y \geq 6.5\}$

where Y is normally distributed with mean 6 and standard deviation 1.5.

Standardizing Y by subtracting the mean and dividing by the standard deviation yields

$$P\{Y \geq 6.5\} = P\left\{\dfrac{Y-6}{1.5} \geq \dfrac{6.5-6}{1.5}\right\}$$

$$= P\left\{Z \geq \dfrac{0.5}{1.5}\right\},$$

where Z is normally distributed with mean 0 and standard deviation 1. From the table of the normal distributions

$$P\left\{Z \geq \dfrac{0.5}{1.5}\right\} = P\{Z \geq 0.33\} = 0.37$$

$$P\{X \geq 7\} \cong P\{Y \geq 6.5\} = P\{Z \geq 0.33\} = 0.37$$

● **PROBLEM 5-50**

A multiple-choice test has 200 questions, each with four possible answers, of which only one is correct. What is the probability that sheer guesswork yields from 25 to 30 correct answers from 80 of the 200 problems about which the student has no knowledge?

SOLUTION:

Let X be the number of correct answers in the 80 questions about which the student has no knowledge. If the student is guessing, the probability

of selecting the correct answer is $\dfrac{1}{4}$. It may also be assumed that random

guesswork will imply that each question is answered independently of any other question. With these assumptions, X is binomially distributed with

parameters $n = 80$ and $p = \dfrac{1}{4}$. Hence, $E(X) = np = 80 \times \dfrac{1}{4} = 20$ and

$$\sqrt{\text{Var } X} = \sqrt{np(1-p)} = \sqrt{80 \times \frac{1}{4} \times \frac{3}{4}} = \sqrt{15} = 3.87.$$

We wish to find $P(25 \le X \le 30)$. This probability is found exactly to be

$$P\{25 \le X \le 30\} = \sum_{j=25}^{30} \binom{80}{j} \left(\frac{1}{4}\right)^j \left(\frac{3}{4}\right)^{80-j}.$$

This expression is quite tedious to calculate and we thus use the normal approximation to the binomial. Let Y be normally distributed with mean np = 20 and standard deviation $\sqrt{np(1-p)}$ = 3.87. Then

$$P\{25 \le X \le 30\} \cong \left(25 - \frac{1}{2} \le Y \le 30 + \frac{1}{2}\right).$$

We add and subtract $\dfrac{1}{2}$ to improve the approximation of a discrete random variable by a continuous random variable. To calculate, P (24.5 $\le$ $Y \le$ 30.5), we standardize Y by subtracting the mean and then dividing by the standard deviation. Thus,

$$P\{24.5 \le Y \le 30.5\}$$

$$= P\left\{\frac{24.5-20}{3.87} \le \frac{Y-20}{3.87} \le \frac{30.5-20}{3.87}\right\}$$

$$= P\left\{\frac{4.5}{3.87} \le Z \le \frac{10.5}{3.87}\right\}$$

where Z is normally distributed with mean 0 and standard deviation 1. From the table of the standard normal distributions,

$$P\left\{\frac{4.5}{3.87} \le Z \le \frac{10.5}{3.87}\right\} = P\{1.163 \le Z \le 2.713\}$$

$$= P\{Z \le 2.713\} - P\{Z \le 1.163\}$$
$$= 0.9966 - 0.8776 = 0.1190$$

Thus, the approximate probability that the student correctly answers between 25 and 30 questions by sheer guesswork is 0.1190.

The records of a large university show that 40 percent of the student body are classified as freshmen. A random sample of 50 students is selected. Find
  (a) the expected number of freshmen in the sample,
  (b) the standard error of the number of freshmen in the sample, and
  (c) the probability that at least 45 percent of the students in this sample are freshmen.

SOLUTION:

Let the random variable X denote the number of freshmen in the random sample. Because 40 percent of the student body are freshmen, and because the university is large, the random variable X is approximately binomially distributed with parameters $n = 50$ and $p = 0.40$.

(a) To find the expected number of freshmen in the sample, we find the $E(X)$. The expected value of a binomially distributed random variable is

$$E(X) = np = 50\ (0.4) = 20.$$

(b) The standard error of X is the standard deviation of X.

$$\sqrt{\text{Var } X} = \sqrt{np(1-p)} = \sqrt{50\ (0.4)\ (0.6)} = 3.46$$

(c) Using the normal approximation to the binomial, the probability that $X \geq 45\%$ of 50, or $X \geq 22.5$, is

$$P\{X \geq 22.5\} \cong P\{Y > 22.5 - 0.5\}$$
$$\cong P\{Y > 22\},$$

where Y is normally distributed with mean $np = 20$ and standard deviation $\sqrt{np(1-p)} = 3.46$. Standardizing Y by subtracting the mean and dividing by the standard deviation, we see that

$$P\{Y > 22\} = P\left\{\frac{Y-20}{3.46} > \frac{22-20}{3.46}\right\}$$
$$= P\{Z > 0.578\}$$

where Z is normally distributed with mean 0 and standard deviation 1.

From the table of the standard normal distribution
$$P\{Z > 0.578\} = 1 - P\{Z \leq 0.578\}$$
$$= 1 - 0.7190$$
$$= 0.281$$

Thus, the probability of observing more than 45 percent of freshmen in the sample of 50 is approximately 0.281.

The student body of a large school has approximately an equal number of boys and girls. If a committee of eight is selected at random, what is the probability that it will contain exactly five girls?

SOLUTION:

Since the probability that a student picked at random is a boy (or girl) is $\frac{1}{2} = 0.5$, the binomial distribution with $n = 8$ (the number of committee members selected at random) and $p = 0.5$ is the approximate distribution of the number of girls. The probability of exactly five girls on the committee is

$$P\{X = 5\} = \binom{8}{5}(0.5)^5 (1 - 0.5)^{(8-5)}$$

$$= 56\,(0.5)^5\,(0.5)^3 = 0.2188$$

We can also find an approximate value of the probability by using the normal curve. Computing the standard deviation

$$\sigma = \sqrt{np(1-p)} = \sqrt{8\,(0.5)\,(0.5)} = \sqrt{8\,(0.25)} = 1.4,$$

we find that $ns = 8\,(1.4) = 11.2 > 5$ ($ns > 5$) is one "rule of thumb" for the applicability of the normal curve as an approximation to a discrete distribution like the binomial. We will find the area over an interval whose midpoint is 5. It is common practice to add and subtract $\frac{1}{2}$ from (to) the desired value of X (in this case 5) when calculating Z-scores for the standard normal curve. Thus,

$$Z_1 = \frac{5 - \frac{1}{2} - \mu}{1.4} \quad \text{and} \quad Z_2 = \frac{5 + \frac{1}{2} - \mu}{1.4}$$

Substitute $\mu = np = 8\,(0.5) = 4$:

$$Z_1 = \frac{5 - \frac{1}{2} - 4}{1.4} \quad \text{and} \quad Z_2 = \frac{5 + \frac{1}{2} - 4}{1.4}$$

$$Z_1 = \frac{4.5 - 4}{1.4} = \frac{0.5}{1.4} = 0.36 \quad \text{and}$$

141

$$Z_2 = \frac{5.5 - 4}{1.4} = \frac{1.5}{1.4} = 1.07$$

We are ready to compute

$$P\{X = 5\} = P\{0.36 < Z < 1.07\}$$
$$= P\{0 < Z < 1.07\} - P\{0 < Z < 0.36\}$$

[subtracting areas]

$$= 0.3577 - 0.1406 = 0.2171,$$

which is only 0.0017 less than the exact probability given by the binomial distribution. This is an approximation.

● **PROBLEM 5-53**

What is the probability that in 100 throws of an unbiased coin the number of heads obtained will be between 45 and 60, inclusive?

SOLUTION:

Let X be the number of heads obtained in $n = 100$ throws. We wish to find $P\{45 \leq X \leq 60\}$. This is a binomial probability and may be approximated by a normal probability.

If the coin is unbiased there is a probability $p = \dfrac{1}{2}$ of a head on any particular toss. Thus, the mean number of head is $E(X) = np = (100)\dfrac{1}{2} = 50$. The standard deviation is

$$\sqrt{\operatorname{Var} X} = \sqrt{np(1-p)} = \sqrt{100\frac{1}{2} \times \frac{1}{2}} = \sqrt{\frac{100}{4}} = \sqrt{25} = 5.$$

To correct for the approximation of a discrete random variable X by a continuous random variable Y, we extend the boundaries by adding $\dfrac{1}{2}$ to 60 and subtracting $\dfrac{1}{2}$ from 45. Thus,

$$P\{45 \leq X \leq 60\} \cong P\left\{45 - \frac{1}{2} \leq Y \leq 60 + \frac{1}{2}\right\}$$

where Y is normally distributed with mean $np = 50$ and standard deviation 5. To find $P(44.5 \le Y \le 60.5)$, we standardize Y by subtracting the mean and dividing by the standard deviation. Thus,

$P\{44.5 \le Y \le 60.5\}$

$$= P\left\{\frac{44.5-50}{5} \le Z \le \frac{60.5-50}{5}\right\}$$

$$= P\left\{\frac{-5.5}{5} \le Z \le \frac{10.5}{5}\right\}$$

$$= P\{-1.1 \le Z \le 2.1\}$$

where Z is normally distributed with mean 0 and standard deviation 1. From the table of the standard normal,

$$P\{-1.1 \le Z \le 2.1\} = P\{Z \le 2.1\} - P\{Z \le -1.1\}$$
$$= 0.982 - (1 - P\{Z \le -1.1\})$$
$$= 0.982 - 1 + 0.864$$
$$= 0.846$$

Thus, there is an approximate probability of 0.846 that the number of heads will be between 45 and 60.

● PROBLEM 5-54

Forty percent of all graduate students on a campus are married. If 100 graduate students are selected at random what is the probability that the proportion of married students in this particular sample will be between 32 percent and 47 percent?

SOLUTION:

Let X be the random variable denoting the number of married students in a random sample of size 100. Because 40 percent of the students are married, the probability of a randomly selected student being married is $p = 0.4$. The number of married graduate students is approximately binomially distributed.

The expected number of married students in the sample of size 100 is $np = (100)(0.4)$ and the standard deviation of X is

$$\sqrt{np(1-p)} = \sqrt{100\,(0.4)\,(1-0.4)}$$

$$= \sqrt{100\left(\frac{4}{10}\right)\left(\frac{6}{10}\right)}$$

Using the normal approximation to the binomial,

$$\frac{X-np}{\sqrt{\text{Var } X}} = \frac{X-np}{\sqrt{np(1-p)}}$$

is approximately normally distributed with mean 0 and standard deviation 1. But dividing the numerator and denominator by n,

$$\frac{X-np}{\sqrt{\text{Var } X}} = \frac{\dfrac{X}{n} - \dfrac{np}{n}}{\dfrac{1}{n}\sqrt{np(1-p)}} = \frac{\dfrac{X}{n} - p}{\sqrt{\dfrac{p(1-p)}{n}}}.$$

Thus, $\dfrac{\dfrac{X}{n} - p}{\sqrt{\dfrac{p(1-p)}{n}}}$ is also approximately normally distributed with mean 0

and standard deviation 1.

The quantity $\dfrac{X}{n}$ is the proportion of married students observed in the sample of size n.

We are interested in the probability that $\dfrac{X}{n}$, the sample proportion, is between the values 0.32 and 0.47, or

$$P\left\{0.32 < \frac{X}{n} < 0.47\right\}.$$

Substituting $n = 100$ and $p = 0.40$, we standardize $\dfrac{X}{n}$ and find that

$$P\left\{\frac{0.32-p}{\sqrt{\dfrac{p(1-p)}{n}}} < \frac{\dfrac{X}{n} - p}{\sqrt{\dfrac{p(1-p)}{n}}} < \frac{0.47-p}{\sqrt{\dfrac{p(1-p)}{n}}}\right\}$$

$$= P \left\{ \frac{0.32 - 0.04}{\sqrt{\dfrac{(0.04)(0.6)}{100}}} < \frac{\dfrac{X}{n} - p}{\sqrt{\dfrac{p(1-p)}{100}}} < \frac{0.47 - 0.04}{\sqrt{\dfrac{(0.04)(0.6)}{100}}} \right\}$$

But $Z = \dfrac{\dfrac{X}{n} - p}{\sqrt{\dfrac{p(1-p)}{100}}}$ is approximately a standard normal variable.

Thus,

$$P \left\{ 0.32 < \frac{X}{n} < 0.47 \right\} = P \left\{ \frac{-0.08}{0.49} < Z < \frac{0.07}{0.49} \right\}$$

where Z is standard normal.

From the table of the standard normal distribution

$$P \left\{ \frac{-0.08}{0.49} < Z < \frac{0.07}{0.49} \right\} = P \{-1.63 < Z < 1.43\}$$

$$= 0.8720$$

Thus, the probability that $\dfrac{X}{100}$, the sample proportion, is between 0.32 and 0.47 is .8720.

● PROBLEM 5-55

The probability that an electronic switch will operate successfully is 0.98. A random sample of 1,000 switches were tested and 30 were found to be defective. What is the probability of finding 30 or more defective switches in the sample?

SOLUTION:

The probability that a randomly selected switch is defective is $(1 - 0.98)$ = 0.02. Letting n = 1,000 and p = 0.02, we compute the expected number of defective switches, np = (1,000) (0.02) = 20 and the standard deviation is $\sqrt{np(1-p)}$ = $\sqrt{1,000(0.02)(0.98)}$ = $\sqrt{20(0.98)}$ = 4.43. Thinking of the number of defective switches as a random variable X, we can use the standard normal curve to find an approximate value of the binomial probability, $P\{X \geq 30\}$. Because a discrete random variable is being approximated by a continuous random variable, $P\{X \geq 30\}$ is approximated by the normal probability $P\{X > 29.5\}$. We must convert 29.5 to a Z-score in order to use the table:

$$\frac{29.5 - np}{\sqrt{np(1-p)}} = \frac{29.5 - 20}{4.43} = \frac{9.5}{4.43} = \frac{950}{443} \cong 2.14.$$

It follows that $P\{X > 29.5\} = P\{Z > 2.14\}$.
$$P\{Z > 2.14\} = 1 - P\{Z \leq 2.14\}$$
$$= 1 - \Phi\{2.14\} = 1 - 0.9838 = 0.0162$$
For tables that give probabilities from 0 to a positive K,
$$P\{Z > 2.14\} = 1 - P(Z \leq 2.14)$$

$$= 1 - \left(\frac{1}{2} + \Phi^*(2.14)\right) = 1 - (0.5 + 0.4838)$$

$$= 1 - 0.9838 = 0.0162$$
The probability that 30 or more switches will be defective is 0.0162.

● PROBLEM 5-56

In a random sample of 10,000 claims filed against an automobile insurance company, 75 percent exceeded $300. What is the probability that of the next 400 claims filed more than 72 percent will be above $300?

SOLUTION:

Let X be a random variable denoting the number of the claims exceeding $300 that are among the next 400 filed against this insurance company. We have a good idea that the probability of a claim exceeding $300 being filed is 0.75. We wish to find the probability that X is greater than 72 percent of 400. That is, we want the probability that of the next 400 claims, more than 72% will be above $300, or $P\{X > 72\% \text{ of } 400\} = P\{X > 288\}$.

Now X is a binomially distributed random variable with mean $np = (400)$ $(0.75) = 300$ and standard deviation $\sqrt{np(1-p)} = \sqrt{400(0.75)(0.25)} = \sqrt{75} = 8.66$. Using the normal approximation to the binomial, the binomial probability $P(X > 288)$ is closely approximated by $P\{Y > 287.5\}$ where Y is normally distributed with mean $E(Y) = np = 300$ and standard deviation of $\sqrt{np(1-p)} = 8.66$.

Thus, we standardize Y to find its probability

$$P\{Y > 287.5\} = P\left\{\frac{Y-\mu}{\sqrt{\text{Var } Y}} > \frac{287.5-\mu}{\sqrt{\text{Var } Y}}\right\}$$

$$= P\left\{Z > \frac{287.5-300}{8.66}\right\}$$

where Z is normally distributed with mean 0 and standard deviation 1.
$$P\{Z > -1.44\} = 0.9251.$$

Thus, the probability that there are more than 288 claims of $300 is 0.925.

● PROBLEM 5-57

A new car was designed on the assumption that 60 percent of its sales would be to female customers. If a random sample of 500 purchasers is selected, what is the probability that at least 275 of them are female?

SOLUTION:

Let X be the number of female purchasers observed in the random sample of 500 purchasers. Now X may be assumed to be binomially distribued with parameters $n = 500$ and $p = 0.60$.

We wish to estimate the binomial probability that $X > 275$. X has mean $E(X) = np = 500\,(0.60) = 300$ and standard deviation of $\sqrt{np(1-p)} = 10.9$. Using the normal approximation to the binomial,

$$P\{X > 275\} \cong P\left\{Y > 275 - \frac{1}{2}\right\}$$

where Y is normally distributed with mean $np = 300$ and standard deviation of $\sqrt{np(1-p)} = 10.9$.

The $\frac{1}{2}$ is subtracted from 275 to correct for a discrete random variable being approximated by a continuous random variable. To compute $P\{Y > 274.5\}$, we convert Y to a standard normal random variable by subtracting its mean and dividing by its standard deviation. Thus,

$$P\{Y > 274.5\} = P\left\{\frac{Y-p}{\sqrt{np\,(1-p)}} > \frac{274.5-np}{\sqrt{np\,(1-p)}}\right\}$$

$$= P\left\{Z > \frac{274.5-300}{10.9}\right\}$$

where Z is normally distributed with mean 0 and standard deviation 1. Thus,

$$P\{X > 275\} \cong P\{Z > -2.34\}$$

and from the table of the standard normal,

$$P\{Z > -2.34\} = P\{Z < 2.34\}$$
$$= 0.99$$

Thus, the probability that there are more than 275 female purchasers in a random sample of 500 purchasers given $p = 0.60$ is approximately 0.99.

● PROBLEM 5-58

A company produces light bulbs and knows that, on the average, 10 percent are defective and will not pass inspection. What is the probability that at least 15 percent of a random sample of 100 bulbs is defective?

SOLUTION:

Let X be the number of defective bulbs in a random sample of size 100. If, on the average, 10% of the bulbs are defective, and each bulb in the sample is selected independently from the entire population of bulbs, X may be assumed to be a binomially distributed random variable with parameters $n = 100$ and $p = 0.10$. The expected number of defective bulbs is $E(X) = np = 10$ and the standard deviation is $\sqrt{\mathrm{Var}\,X} = \sqrt{np\,(1-p)} = \sqrt{100\,(0.1)\,(1-0.9)} = \sqrt{9} = 3$.

We wish to find the probability that there are more than 15 defective light bulbs in the sample of size 100.

Using the normal approximation to the binomial,

$$P\{X \geq 15\} \cong P\{Y \geq 14.5\},$$

where Y is normally distributed with mean np and standard deviation $\sqrt{np\,(1-p)}$. To find $P\{Y \geq 14.5\}$, we standardize Y by subtracting the mean and dividing by the standard deviation. Thus,

$$P\{X \geq 15\} \cong P\{Y \geq 14.5\} = P\left\{Z > \frac{14.5 - 10}{3}\right\}$$

where $Z = \dfrac{Y - np}{\sqrt{np(1-p)}}$ is normally distributed with mean 0 and variance 1.

From the table of the standard normal,

$$P\{Z \geq 1.5\} = 1 - P\{Z < 1.5\}$$
$$= 1 - 0.9332 = 0.0668$$

Thus, the probability that there are at least 15 light bulbs in the sample is approximately 0.067.

● PROBLEM 5-59

The diameters of a large shipment of ball bearings are normally distributed with a mean of 2.0 cm and a standard deviation of 0.01 cm. If three ball bearings are selected at random from the shipment, what is the probability that exactly two of the selected ball bearings will have a diameter larger than 2.02 cm?

SOLUTION:

We will solve this problem in two steps. First, using the normal distribution, we will determine the probability that the diameter of any one ball bearing is greater than 2.02 cm. Second, using the binomial formula,

$$P\{X = x\} = \binom{n}{x} p^x (1 - p)^{n-x},$$

we determine the probability that exactly two diameters exceed 2.02 cm.

Step 1: Since X is normally distributed, we can standardize it by subtracting the mean and dividing by the standard deviation. Then

$$p = P\{X > 2.02\}$$

$$= P\left\{\frac{X - \mu}{\sigma} > \frac{2.02 - \mu}{\sigma}\right\}$$

$$= P\left\{\text{Standard Normal Quantity} > \frac{2.02 - \mu}{\sigma}\right\}$$

149

Substituting, $p = P \left\{ \text{Standard Normal Quantity} > \dfrac{2.02 - \mu}{0.01} \right\}$

$p = P$ (Standard Normal Quantity > 2) .

From the standard normal table, $p = 0.0228$.

Step 2: We want $P\{X = 2\} = \binom{n}{2} p^2 (1 - p)^{n-2}$.

p was found to be 0.0228 and $n = 3$. Hence,

$$P\{X = 2\} = \binom{3}{2} (0.0228)^2 (1 - 0.0228)$$

$$= \frac{3!}{2!1!} (0.0228)^2 (0.9772) = 3 \, (0.00051984) \, (0.9772)$$

$$= 0.00152$$

● PROBLEM 5-60

A poultry farmer wished to make a comparison between two feed mixtures. One flock of hens was fed from mixture 1 and another flock from mixture 2. In a six-week period, the flock being fed from mixture 1 increased egg production by 25 percent, while those fed from mixture 2 increased egg production by 20 percent. Random samples of 200 and 300 hens were selected from the respective flocks. Let $\hat{p}_1$ be the proportion of the sample from the first flock with increased egg production, and let $\hat{p}_2$ be the proportion of the sample from the second flock. Find

    (a) the expected difference between the two proportions,
    (b) the standard error of this difference, and
    (c) the probability that hens fed from mixture 1 increased their egg production more than those fed from mixture 2.

SOLUTION:

Let p_1 and p_2 denote the population proportions representing the percentage increase in egg production of hens who were fed mixtures 1 and 2, respectively. We are given that $p_1 = 0.25$ and $p_2 = 0.20$.

After the random samples of size 200 and 300 have been selected, $\hat{p}_1$ and $\hat{p}_2$ will denote the proportions representing the percentage increase in egg production observed in the two samples. Now

$$\hat{p}_1 = \frac{Y_1}{200}$$ will be the observed increase in egg production (Y_1) divided by the size of the first sample population.

$$\hat{p}_2 = \frac{Y_2}{300}$$ will be the observed increase in egg production (Y_2) divided by the size of the second sample population.

(a) The expected difference between $\hat{p}_1$ and $\hat{p}_2$ is

$$E(\hat{p}_1 - \hat{p}_2) = E(\hat{p}_1) - E(\hat{p}_2)$$

by the properties of expectation. To find the difference, we need to know that Y_1 and Y_2 may be assumed to be binomially distributed with parameters $n_1 = 200$ and $p_1 = 0.25$ and $n_2 = 300$ and $p_2 = 0.20$, respectively. Thus,

$$E(Y_1) = n_1 p_1 = (200)(0.25) = 50 \text{ and}$$
$$E(Y_2) = n_2 p_2 = (300)(0.20) = 60.$$
$$\text{Var } Y_1 = n_1 p_1 (1 - p_1) = 37.5 \text{ and}$$
$$\text{Var } Y_2 = n_2 p_2 (1 - p_2) = 48.$$

Substituting, we find the expected value of

$$\hat{p}_1 - \hat{p}_2 = \frac{Y_1}{n_1} - \frac{Y_2}{n_2} ;$$

$$E(\hat{p}_1 - \hat{p}_2) = E(\hat{p}_1) - E(\hat{p}_2)$$

$$= E\left(\frac{Y_1}{200}\right) - E\left(\frac{Y_2}{300}\right) = \frac{E(Y_1)}{200} - \frac{E(Y_2)}{300}$$

$$= \frac{50}{200} - \frac{60}{300} = 0.25 - 0.20 = 0.05$$

(b) To find the standard error or standard deviation of this difference, we first find Var ($\hat{p}_1 - \hat{p}_2$). Using the properties of variance we see that Var $(ax + by) = a^2$ Var $X + b^2$ Var Y when X and Y are independent. Therefore, Var $(\hat{p}_1 - \hat{p}_2) = $ Var $\hat{p}_1 + (-1)^2$ Var $\hat{p}_2$

$$= \text{Var } \frac{Y_1}{n_1} + \text{Var } \frac{Y_2}{n_2} = \frac{1}{n_1^2} \text{Var } Y_1 + \frac{1}{n_2^2} \text{Var } Y_2$$

$$= \frac{p_1(1 - p_1)}{n_1} + \frac{p_2(1 - p_2)}{n_2} = \frac{(0.25)(0.75)}{200} + \frac{(0.20)(0.80)}{300}$$

151

$$= 0.0009375 + 0.000533 = 0.00147$$

The standard error of $\hat{p}_1 - \hat{p}_2$ is

$$\sqrt{\mathrm{Var}\,(\hat{p}_1 - \hat{p}_2)} = \sqrt{0.00147} = 0.038.$$

(c) The probability that the sample of hens fed from mixture 1 increased their egg production more than the sample fed from mixture 2 is P $(\hat{p}_1 > \hat{p}_2)$ or

$$P\{\hat{p}_1 - \hat{p}_2 > 0\}.$$

To compute this probability we use the normal approximation to the binomial. Thus,

$$P\{\hat{p}_1 - \hat{p}_2 > 0\} \cong P\{Y > 0\}$$

where Y is distributed normally with mean $E(\hat{p}_1 - \hat{p}_2) = 0.05$ and standard deviation 0.038.

Standardizing, we see that

$$P\{Y > 0\} \cong P\left\{\frac{Y - 0.05}{.038} > \frac{0 - 0.05}{0.038}\right\}$$

$$= P\left\{Z > \frac{0 - 0.05}{0.038}\right\} = P\{Z \geq -1.31\}$$

$$= 1 - P\{Z > 1.31\} = 0.9049$$

Thus, the probability is 0.9049 as the sample of hens fed from mixture 1 increased their egg production more than the sample fed from mixture 2.

● PROBLEM 5-61

The receiving department of a television manufacturer uses the following rule in deciding whether to accept or reject a shipment of 100,000 small parts shipped every week by a supplier: select a sample of 400 parts from each lot received. If three percent or more of the selected parts are defective, reject the lot; if the proportion of defectives is less than three percent accept that lot. What is the probability of rejecting a lot that actually contains two percent defectives?

SOLUTION:

Let X be the number of defective parts in a sample of 400. If the probability of selecting a defective item is 0.02, we want to find the probability that three percent or more of the sample is defective.

Equivalently, we wish to find the probability that $X \geq 3\%$ of 400 or $X \geq (0.03)$ $(400) = 12$.

The expected number of defectives is $E(X) = (0.02)400 = 8$ and the standard deviation of the number of defectives is $\sqrt{\text{Var } X} = \sqrt{np(1-p)} = \sqrt{400(0.2)(0.98)} = 2.8$ since X is distributed binomially with parameters $n = 400$ and $p = 0.02$.

We now employ the normal approximation to the binomial to find the probability that $X \geq 12$. We obtain

$$P\{X \geq 12\} \cong P\{Y \geq 11.5\},$$

where Y is normally distributed with mean $np = 8$ and standard deviation 2.8. We standardize Y by subtracting the mean and dividing by the standard deviation. Thus,

$$P\{X \geq 12\} \cong P\{Y \geq 11.5\}$$

$$\cong P\left\{ \frac{Y - np}{\sqrt{np(1-p)}} \geq \frac{11.5 - np}{\sqrt{np(1-p)}} \right\}$$

where $Z = \dfrac{Y - np}{\sqrt{np(1-p)}}$ is normally distributed with mean 0 and standard deviation 1. From the table of the standard normal,

$$P\{Y \geq 11.5\} = P\left\{ Z > \frac{11.5 - 8}{2.8} \right\}$$

$$= P\{Z \geq 1.25\} = 1 - 0.8944 = 0.1056.$$

Thus, given that two percent of the population is defective, there is a probability of approximately 0.1056 of parts three percent defective in the sample of size 400.

● **PROBLEM 5-62**

Congressional candidate X will base his decision on whether or not to endorse the Educational Opportunity Act on the results of a poll of a random sample of 200 registered voters from his district. He will endorse the Educational Opportunity Act only if 100 or more voters are in favor of it.
  (a) What is the probability that candidate X will endorse the Act if 45% of all registered voters in his district are in favor of it?
  (b) What is the probability that candidate X will fail to endorse the Act if 52% of all voters in his district are in favor of it?

SOLUTION:

(a) We will regard the random selection of 200 voters from a district in which 45 percent of all voters are in favor of the Educational Opportunity Act as a binomial experiment with parameters $n = 100$ and $p = 0.45$. The expected value and the standard deviation of this experiment are computed below.

$$E(X) = np = 200\,(0.45) = 90 \text{ voters}$$

$$\sigma_x = \sqrt{np\,(1-p)} = \sqrt{49.5} = 7.04 \text{ voters}$$

Candidate X will endorse the Act only when 100 or more voters are in favor of it. Using the normal distribution as an approximation to the binomial, the probability that the Act will be endorsed by 100 or more voters is approximated by the area under the normal curve lying to the right of $x = 99.5$ (see shaded area below).

We want $P\,(X \ge 99.5)$.

Equivalently, we will find after standardizing

$$P\left\{\frac{X-\mu}{\sigma} \ge \frac{99.5-\mu}{\sigma}\right\}$$

or $\quad P\left\{Z \ge \dfrac{99.5-\mu}{\sigma}\right\}$.

Substituting, we obtain

$$P\left\{Z \ge \frac{99.5-90}{7.04}\right\} = P\,\{Z \ge 1.35\}.$$

Reading off the table, we see the probability that candidate X will endorse the Educational Opportunity Act is 0.0885.

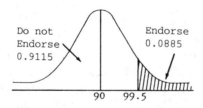

(b) The random selection of 200 voters from a district in which 52% of all voters endorse the Act can be regarded as a binomial experiment with $n = 200$ and $p = 0.52$. The expectation and standard deviation are computed as follows:

$$E(X) = np = 200\,(0.52) = 104 \text{ voters}$$

$$\sigma_x = \sqrt{np(1-p)} = \sqrt{200\,(0.52)\,(1-0.52)} = \sqrt{49.92} = 7.07$$

Candidate X will fail to endorse the Act if less than 100 voters are in favor of it.

$$P\{X \leq 99.5\}$$

We standardize and obtain $P\left\{\dfrac{X-\mu}{\sigma} \leq \dfrac{99.5-\mu}{\sigma}\right\}$.

We have $P\left\{\text{Standard Normal Quantity} \leq \dfrac{99.5-\mu}{\sigma}\right\}$.

Substituting, we have $P\left\{Z \leq \dfrac{99.5-104}{7.07}\right\}$ or $P\{Z \leq 0.636\}$. From the tables, this is about 0.26.

● PROBLEM 5–63

Find the expected value of a normally distributed random variable with parameters μ and σ^2.

SOLUTION:

Since a symmetric random variable is symmetric about its mean and a normal random variable is symmetric, it is symmetric about its mean. But it is also symmetric about μ, so the mean must be $/\mu$.

SHORT ANSWER QUESTIONS FOR REVIEW

Choose the correct answer.

1. The function $f(x) = 1 - \dfrac{1}{x^2}$ over the interval $0 < x < 1$ is (a) always equal to 1. (b) never equal to 1. (c) always positive. (d) always negative.

2. The limit of $\dfrac{1}{x^3}$ as $x \to -\infty$ is (a) ∞. (b) $-\infty$. (c) 0. (d) 1.

3. The correct integration of $f(x) = e^{2x}$ is (a) $2e^{2x}$. (b) $\dfrac{1}{2}e^{2x}$. (c) $\dfrac{1}{e^{2x}}$.

   (d) $\dfrac{2}{e^{2x}}$.

4. To convert a raw score to a Z-score (a) subtract the mean and divide by the standard deviation. (b) add the mean and divide by the standard deviation. (c) subtract the standard deviation and divide by the mean. (d) add the standard deviation and divide by the mean.

5. Since the probability of flipping a coin is $\dfrac{1}{2} = 0.5$, what is the probability of getting tails five times if you have the binomial distribution with $n = 8$?

   (a) $P\{x = 5\} = \left(\dfrac{5}{8}\right) (0.5)^5 (1 - 0.5)^{(8-5)}$

   (b) $P\{x = 8\} = \left(\dfrac{5}{8}\right) (0.5)^5 (1 - 0.5)^{(5-8)}$

   (c) $P\{x = 5\} = \left(\dfrac{8}{5}\right) (0.5)^5 (1 - 0.5)^{(8-5)}$

   (d) $P\{x = 8\} = \left(\dfrac{8}{5}\right) (0.5)^5 (1 - 0.5)^{(8-5)}$

156

6. What type of distribution would one use for $f(x) = 1 - e^{-2x}$? (a) Normal distribution (b) Exponential distribution (c) Natural logarithmic distribution (d) Uniform distribution

7. How many times would you have to flip a coin until you are guaranteed that it will come up heads at least once? (a) 1 (b) 2 (c) 4 (d) Unable to determine.

8. When the density function is complicated, in order to find the area you must (a) differentiate. (b) approximate. (c) integrate. (d) find a new curve.

9. In order to check that an area is a proper density function, it must be (a) as large as necessary. (b) equal to the root-mean-square. (c) equal to 1. (d) the difference of the mean and median.

10. When dealing with a polynomial function, $f(x)$ should be (a) integrable. (b) continuous. (c) positive for all x. (d) all of the above.

11. When dealing with a cumulative distribution, $F(x)$ should be the function which gives the probability that a single observation of the random variable will be (a) less than or equal to x. (b) greater than or equal to x. (c) equal to 1. (d) larger than the density distribution.

12. The normal distribution is similar to what type of curve? (a) Quadratic (b) Logarithmic (c) Linear (d) Bell-shaped

13. A normal distribution is symmetric about its (a) median. (b) mean. (c) mode. (d) largest value.

Fill in the blanks.

14. The simplest continuous random variable is one whose distribution is _____ over some interval (a, b) and zero everywhere else.

15. If a curve comes closer and closer to a line, but never touches it, the curve is said to be _____ .

16. $F(x) = \lambda e^{-\lambda x}$ is a(n) _____ distribution.

17. If we have already spent some time waiting, and if the distribution of further waiting time is the same as that of the initial waiting time, this implies that x has no _____ .

18. The assumptions made in using the binomial distribution are: the number of trials is _____ , the probability of success is _____ for each trial, and the trials are all _____ .

19. The probability of something happening and the probability of that same thing not happening _____ 1.

20. μ = _____ .

21. If $P\{a \le X \le b\}$ equals the area under the curve $f(x)$ from a to b with the conditions $f(x)$ must be _____ and the total _____ between $f(x)$ and the x-axis equals 1.

22. The probability of a standard normal variable being found in a particular interval can be determined with the help of _____ in the back of most statistic books.

23. $\_\_\_\_ = \dfrac{x - \bar{x}}{S}$ or $\dfrac{x - \mu}{\sigma}$

24. Z tells us how many _____ _____ a value lies above or below the mean of a set of data to which it belongs.

25. The median is a number such that half of the _____ _____ lies above or below it.

26. $\sigma = \sqrt{np(1 - p)}$ is the standard deviation of the _____ _____ .

Determine whether the following statements are true or false.

27. The probability that x is between a and b is always a rectangular area based on a and b.

28. Since the values of a probability distribution are probabilities, they must be numbers on the interval from 0 to 1.

29. The median is the number for which all of the probability distribution lies below it.

30. The sum of the deviations from the mean, $\sum(x - \bar{x})$, is always 1.

31. The binomial distribution cannot be used in the case of how many dresses a woman tries on before she buys one.

32. A graph of a distribution never helps in determining the type of distribution.

33. $s = \sqrt{\sum (x-\mu)^2 \times f(x)}$

34. A density function is the probabilies of a continuous random variable computed as a continuous function.

35. The probability of flipping a coin three times and getting heads each time is $\dfrac{1}{16}$.

36. A linear function could be determined using exponential distribution.

37. The probability of being dealt a royal flush is given by multiplying $\dfrac{1}{13} \times \dfrac{1}{51} \times \dfrac{1}{5} \times \dfrac{1}{49} \times \dfrac{1}{4}$.

38. Statistics cannot be used in application to other branches of mathematics.

39. There is only one way to calculate standard deviations.

40. An exponential distribution can be determined in several ways, even though some may be more difficult than others.

ANSWER KEY

1. d	2. c	3. b
4. a	5. c	6. b
7. d	8. c	9. c
10. d	11. a	12. d
13. b	14. constant	15. asymptotic
16. exponential	17. memory	18. fixed, the same, independent
19. equals	20. $\dfrac{\sum x}{n}$	21. non-negative, area
22. table	23. Z	24. standard deviations
25. probability distribution		26. binomial distribution
27. False	28. True	29. False
30. False	31. True	32. False
33. False	34. True	35. False
36. False	37. True	38. False
39. False	40. True	

CHAPTER 6

CONDITIONAL PROBABILITY

GENERAL CONCEPTS

Find the probability that a face card is drawn on the first draw and an ace on the second in two consecutive draws, without replacement, from a standard deck of cards.

SOLUTION:

This problem illustrates the notion of conditional probability. The conditional probability of an event, say event B, given the occurrence of a previous event, say event A, is written $P\{B \mid A\}$. This is the conditional probability of B given A and is defined to be $\dfrac{P\{AB\}}{P\{A)}$, where

$\quad\quad P\{AB\}$ =probability of the joint occurrence of events A and B.

$\quad\quad$ Let A =event that a face card is drawn on the first draw.

$\quad\quad\quad$ B =event that an ace is drawn on the second draw.

We wish to find the probability of the joint occurrence of these events, $P\{AB\}$, which is equal to $P\{A\}\ P\{B \mid A\}$.

The probability that a face card is drawn on the first draw is

$$\frac{12}{52} = \frac{3}{13} \ .$$

The probability that an ace is drawn on the second draw given that a face card is drawn on the first is the number of ways an ace can be drawn on the second draw given a face card is drawn on the first divided by the total number of possible outcomes of the second draw, or

$$\frac{4}{51}$$

since there will be only 51 cards left in the deck after the face card is drawn. Thus, $P\{AB\} = \frac{3}{13} \times \frac{4}{51} = \frac{4}{13 \times 17} = \frac{4}{221} \ .$

● PROBLEM 6-2

A survey was made of 100 customers in a department store. Sixty of the 100 indicated that they visited the store because of a newspaper advertisement. The remainder had not seen the ad. A total of 40 customers made purchases; of these customers, 30 had seen the ad. What is the probability that a person who did not see the ad made a purchase? What is the probability that a person who saw the ad made a purchase?

SOLUTION:

In the problem, we are told that only 40 customers made purchases. Of these 40, only 30 had seen the ad. Thus, 10 of 100 customers made purchases without seeing the ad. The probability of selecting such a customer at random is

$$\frac{10}{100} = \frac{1}{10} \ .$$

Let A represent the event of "a purchase," B the event of "having seen the ad," and $\overline{B}$ the event of "not having seen the ad."

Symbolically, $P\{A \cap \overline{B}\} = \frac{1}{10}$. We are told that 40 of the customers did not see the ad. Thus, $P\{\bar{B}\} = \dfrac{40}{100} = \dfrac{4}{10}$. Dividing, we obtain $\dfrac{1/10}{4/10} = \dfrac{1}{4}$, and,

by definition of conditional probability, $P\{A \mid \bar{B}\} = \dfrac{1}{4}$. Thus, the probability

that a customer made a purchase given that they did not see the ad is $\dfrac{1}{4}$.

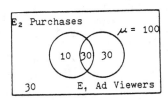

To solve the second problem, note that 30 purchasers saw the ad. The probability that a randomly selected customer saw the ad *and* made a pur-

chase is $\dfrac{30}{100} = \dfrac{3}{10}$. Since 60 of the 100 customers saw the ad, the probability

that a randomly picked customer saw the ad is $\dfrac{60}{100} = \dfrac{6}{10}$. Dividing, we

obtain

$$P\{A \mid B\} = \dfrac{P\{A \cap B\}}{P\{B\}} = \dfrac{3/10}{6/10} = \dfrac{3}{6} = \dfrac{1}{2}.$$

● **PROBLEM 6-3**

A coin is tossed three times, and two heads and one tail fall. What is the probability that the first toss was heads?

SOLUTION:

This problem is one of conditional probability. Given two events, p_1 and p_2, the probability that event p_2 will occur on the condition that we have event p_1 is

163

$$P\{p_1 \mid p_2\} = \frac{P\{p_1 \text{ and } p_2\}}{P\{p_1\}} = \frac{P\{p_1 p_2\}}{P\{p_1\}}.$$

Define

p_1: two heads and one tail fall,

p_2: the first toss is heads.

Then $P\{p_1\} = \dfrac{\text{number of ways to obtain two heads and one tail}}{\text{number of possibilities resulting from three tosses}}$

$$= \frac{\{H, H, T\}, \{H, T, H\}, \{T, H, H\}}{\{H, H, H\}, \{H, H, T\}, \{H, T, H\}, \{T, T, H\},}{\{T, H, T\}, \{T, H, H\}, \{T, T, T\}}$$

$$= \frac{3}{8}$$

Also $P\{p_1 p_2\} = P\{\text{two heads and one tail and the first toss is heads}\}$

$$= \frac{\text{number of ways to obtain } p_1 \text{ and } p_2}{\text{number of possibilities resulting from three tosses}}$$

$$= \frac{\{H, H, T\}, \{H, T, H\}}{8} = \frac{2}{8} = \frac{1}{4},$$

$$P\{p_2 \mid p_1\} = \frac{P\{p_1 p_2\}}{P\{p_1\}} = \frac{1/4}{3/8} = \frac{2}{3}$$

● PROBLEM 6-4

A coin is tossed three times. Find the probability that all three are heads if it is known that

    (a) the first is heads,

    (b) the first two are heads, and

    (c) two of them are heads.

SOLUTION:

This problem is one of conditional probability. If we have two events, A and B, the probability of event A given that event B has occurred is

$$P\{A|B\} = \frac{P\{AB\}}{P\{B\}}.$$

(a) We are asked to find the probability that all three tosses are heads given that the first toss is heads. The first event is A and the second is B. Then

$P\{AB\}$ = probability that all three tosses are heads given that the first toss is heads

$$= \frac{\text{the number of ways that all three tosses are heads}}{\text{given that the first toss is a head}}$$
$$\text{the number of possibilities resulting}$$
$$\text{from three tosses}$$

$$= \frac{\{H, H, T\}, \{H, T, H\}, \{T, H, H\}}{\{H, H, H\}, \{H, H, T\}, \{H, T, H\}, \{T, T, H\}, \{T, H, T\}, \{T, H, H\}, \{T, T, T\}}$$

$$= \frac{1}{8}$$

$P\{B\}$ = P (first toss is a head)

$$= \frac{\text{the number of ways to obtain a head}}{\text{on the first toss}}$$
$$\text{the number of ways to obtain a head}$$
$$\text{or a tail on the first of three tosses}$$

$$= \frac{\{H, H, H\}, \{H, H, T\}, \{H, T, H\}, \{H, T, T\}}{8}$$

$$= \frac{4}{8} = \frac{1}{2}$$

$$P\{A|B\} = \frac{P\{AB\}}{P\{B\}} = \frac{1/8}{1/2} = \frac{1}{8} \times \frac{1}{2} = \frac{1}{4}.$$

To see what happens, in detail, we note that if the first toss is head, the logical possibilities are *HHH, HHT, HTH, HTT*. There is only one of these for which the second and third are heads. Hence,

$$P\{A|\,B\} = \frac{1}{4}\ .$$

(b) The problem here is to find the probability that all three tosses are heads given that the first two tosses are heads. Then

$P\{AB\}$ = the probability that all three tosses are heads given that the first two are heads

$$= \frac{\text{the number of ways to obtain three heads}}{\text{given that the first two tosses are heads}}$$
$$\frac{}{\text{the number of possibilities resulting}}$$
$$\text{from three tosses}$$

$$= \frac{1}{8}. \text{ Now}$$

$P\{B\}$ = the probability that the first two are heads

$$= \frac{\text{the number of ways to obtain heads}}{\text{on the first two tosses}}$$
$$\frac{}{\text{the number of possibilities resulting}}$$
$$\text{from three tosses}$$

$$= \frac{\{H, H, H\}, \{H, H, T\}}{8} = \frac{2}{8} = \frac{1}{4}$$

Finally, $P\{A|\,B\} = \dfrac{P\{AB\}}{P\{B\}} = \dfrac{1/8}{1/4} = \dfrac{4}{8} = \dfrac{1}{4}.$

(c) In this last part, we are asked to find the probability that all three are heads on the condition that any two of them are heads.
Define:
A = the event that all three are heads
B = the event that two of them are heads
$P\{AB\}$ = the probability that all three tosses are heads knowing that two of them are heads

$$= \frac{1}{8}$$

Now $P\{B\}$ = the probability that two tosses are heads

$$= \frac{\text{the number of ways to obtain at least two heads}}{\text{the number of possibilities resulting}}$$
$$\text{out of three tosses}$$
$$\text{from three tosses}$$

$$= \frac{\{H, H, H\}, \{H, H, T\}, \{H, T, H\}, \{T, H, H\}}{8}$$

$$= \frac{4}{8} = \frac{1}{2} .$$

So $P\{A| B\} = \dfrac{P\{AB\}}{P\{B\}} = \dfrac{1/8}{1/4} = \dfrac{2}{8} = \dfrac{1}{4}.$

● **PROBLEM 6-5**

A committee is composed of six Democrats and five Republicans. Three Democrats are men, and three Republicans are men. If a man is chosen for chairman, what is the probability that he is a Republican?

SOLUTION:

Let E_1 be the event that a man is chosen, and E_2 the event that the man is a Republican.

We are looking for $P\{E_2 | E_1\}$. From the definition of conditional probability $P\{E_2| E_1\} = \dfrac{P\{E_1 \cap E_2\}}{P\{E_1\}}$.

Of the 11 committee members, three are both male and Republican, hence, $P\{E_1 \cap E_2\} = \dfrac{\text{number of male Republicans}}{\text{number of committee members}} = \dfrac{3}{11}$.

Of all the members, six are men, three are Democrats, and three are Republicans; therefore, $P\{E_1\} = \dfrac{6}{11}$.

Furthermore, $P\{E_2 | E_1\} = \dfrac{P\{E_1 \cap E_2\}}{P\{E_1\}} = \dfrac{3/11}{6/11} = \dfrac{3}{6} = \dfrac{1}{2}.$

A hand of five cards is to be dealt at random and without replacement from an ordinary deck of 52 playing cards. Find the conditional probability of an all-spade hand given that there will be at least four spades in the hand.

SOLUTION:

Let C_1 be the event that there are at least four spades in the hand and C_2 that there are five. We want $P\{C_2 \mid C_1\}$.

Now, $C_1 \cap C_2$ is the intersection of the events. Since C_2 is contained in C_1, $C_1 \cap C_2 = C_2$. Therefore,

$$P\{C_2 \mid C_1\} = \frac{P\{C_1 \cap C_2\}}{P\{C_1\}} = \frac{P\{C_2\}}{P\{C_1\}} \; ;$$

$$P\{C_2\} = P \text{ (five spades)} = \frac{\text{number of possible five spade hands}}{\text{number of total hands}} \; .$$

The denominator is $\binom{52}{5}$ since we can choose any five out of 52 cards.

For the numerator we can have only spades, of which there are 13. We must choose five; hence, we have $\binom{13}{5}$ and $P\{C_2\} = \binom{13}{5} \div \binom{52}{5}$.

$$P\{C_1\} = P \text{ (four or five spades)}$$

$$= \frac{\text{number of possible four or five spades}}{\text{number of total hands}} \; .$$

The denominator is still $\binom{52}{5}$. The numerator is $\binom{13}{5}$ + (number of four spade hands). To obtain a hand with four spades, we can choose any four of the 13, $\binom{13}{4}$. We must also choose one of the 39 other cards, $\binom{39}{1}$. By the Fundamental Principle of Counting, the number of four spade hands is $\binom{13}{4}\binom{39}{1}$. Hence, the numerator is $\binom{13}{5} + \binom{13}{4}\binom{39}{1}$ and

$$P\{C_1\} = \frac{\binom{13}{5} + \binom{13}{4}\binom{39}{1}}{\binom{52}{5}}.$$

Thus,

$$P\{C_2 \mid C_1\} = \frac{P\{C_1\}}{P\{C_1\}} = \frac{\dfrac{\binom{13}{5}}{\binom{52}{5}}}{\dfrac{\binom{13}{5} + \binom{13}{4}\binom{39}{1}}{\binom{52}{5}}}$$

$$= \frac{\binom{13}{5}}{\binom{13}{5} + \binom{13}{4}\binom{39}{1}} = 0.044$$

● PROBLEM 6-7

Find the probability of drawing a spade on a draw from a deck of cards and rolling a seven on a roll of a pair of dice.

SOLUTION:

Now $P\{\text{spade}\} = \dfrac{13}{52}$, and $P\{\text{rolling } 7\} = \dfrac{1}{6}$.

We must now somehow combine these two probabilities to compute the joint probability of the two events. To do this we assume independence. Because drawing a spade is physically unconnected to rolling a seven, the probabilities of these two events should be unrelated. This is reflected in the statement that $P\{A \mid B\} = P\{A\}$. By our rule for conditional probability this implies that $P\{AB\} = P\{B\}\ P\{A \mid B\} = P\{B\} \times P\{A\}$.

Two events with this property are called independent, and in general the probability of the joint occurrence of independent events is equal to the product of the probability that the events occur in isolation.

In our example,

$$P\{AB\} = P\{A\}\ P\{B\}$$

$$= \frac{13}{52} \times \frac{1}{6}$$

$$= \frac{1}{4} \times \frac{1}{6} = \frac{1}{24}$$

● **PROBLEM 6-8**

A bowl contains eight chips. Three of the chips are red and the remaining five are blue. If two chips are drawn successively, at random and without replacement, what is the probability that the first chip drawn is red and the second drawn is blue?

SOLUTION:

The probability that the first chip drawn is red is denoted $P\{R_1\}$. Since sampling is performed at random and without replacement, the classical probability model is applicable. Thus,

$$P\{R_1\} = \frac{\text{number of red chips}}{\text{total number of chips}}$$

$$= \frac{3}{8}$$

We now wish to calculate the conditional probability that a blue chip is drawn on the second draw given a red chip was drawn on the first. Denote this by $P\{B_2 \mid R_1\}$. The second chip is sampled without replacement. Thus,

$$P\{B_2 \mid R_1\} = \frac{\text{number of blue chips}}{\text{total of chips after one red chip is drawn}}$$

$$= \frac{5}{8-1} = \frac{5}{7}$$

The probability we wish to find is $P\{R_1 \text{ and } B_2\}$. By the multiplication rule,
$$P\{R_1 \text{ and } B_2\} = P\{R_1\} \, P\{B_2 \mid R_1\}$$

$$= \left(\frac{3}{8}\right)\left(\frac{5}{7}\right) = \frac{15}{56}$$

Thus, the probability that a red chip and then a blue chip are respectively

drawn is $\frac{15}{56}$.

● PROBLEM 6-9

From an ordinary deck of playing cards, cards are drawn successively at random and without replacement. Compute the probability that the third spade appears on the sixth draw.

SOLUTION:

Recall the following form of the multiplication rule: $P\{C_1 \cap C_2\} = P\{C_1\}$ $P\{C_2 \mid C_1\}$. Let $P\{C_1\}$ be the event of two spades in the first five draws and let C_2 be the event of a spade on the sixth draw. Thus the probability that we wish to compute is $P\{C_1 \cap C_2\}$.

After five cards have been picked there are $52 - 5 = 47$ cards left. We also have $13 - 2 = 11$ spades left after two spades have been picked in the first five cards. Thus, by the classical model of probability,

$$P\{C_2 \mid C_1\} = \frac{\text{favorable outcomes}}{\text{total possibilities}}$$

$$= \frac{11}{47}$$

Now $P\{C_1\} = \dfrac{\text{ways of drawing two spades in five}}{\text{all ways of drawing five}}.$

The number of ways to choose five cards from 52 is $\binom{52}{5}$. Now count how many ways one can select two spades in five draws. We can take any two of 13 spades, so there are $\binom{13}{2}$ ways to do this. The other three cards can be chosen from any of the 39 non-spades, so there are $\binom{39}{3}$ ways to choose three from 39. To determine the total number of ways of drawing two spades and three non-spades, we invoke the basic principle of counting and obtain $\binom{13}{2}\binom{39}{3}$. Hence,

$$P\{C_1\} = \frac{\binom{13}{2}\binom{39}{3}}{\binom{52}{5}}, \text{ and}$$

$$P\{C_1 \cap C_2\} = P\{C_1\} \, P\{C_2 \mid C_1\}$$

$$= \frac{\binom{13}{2}\binom{39}{3}}{\binom{52}{5}} \times \frac{11}{47} = 0.274$$

More generally, let X be the number of draws required to produce the third spade. Let C_1 be the event of two spades in the first $X - 1$ draws and let C_2 be the event that a spade is drawn on the Xth draw. We want to compute the probability $P\{C_1 \cap C_2\}$. To find $P\{C_2 \mid C_1\}$ note that after $X - 1$ cards have been picked, two of which were spades, 11 of the remaining $52 - (X - 1)$ cards are spades. The classical model of probability gives

$$P\{C_2 \mid C_1\} = \frac{11}{52 - (X - 1)}.$$

Again by the classical model,

$$P\{C_1\} = \frac{\text{ways of two spades in } x - 1}{\text{all ways of } x - 1 \text{ cards}}.$$

The denominator is the number of ways to choose $X - 1$ from 52 or $\binom{52}{X-1}$. Now determine the number of ways of choosing two spades in

$Z - 1$ cards.

There are still only 13 spades in the deck, two of which we must choose.

Hence, we still have a $\binom{13}{2}$ term. The other $(X - 1) - 2 = X - 3$ cards must

be non-spades. Thus, we must choose $X - 3$ out of 39 cards. There are

$\binom{39}{X-3}$ such possibilities. The basic principle of counting asserts that to

obtain the number of ways of choosing two spades and $X - 3$ non-spades

we must multiply the two terms, $\binom{13}{2} \times \binom{39}{X-3}$.

Therefore, $P\{C_1\} = \dfrac{\binom{13}{2}\binom{39}{X-3}}{\binom{52}{X-1}}$ and the probability of drawing the third

spade on the Xth card is

$$P\{C_1 \cap C_2\} = P\{C_1\} \times P\{C_2 \mid C_1\}$$

$$= \dfrac{\binom{13}{2}\binom{39}{X-3}}{\binom{52}{X-1}} \times \dfrac{11}{52 - (X-1)}$$

● PROBLEM 6-10

Find the probability that three face cards are drawn in three successive draws (without replacement) from a deck of cards.

SOLUTION:

Define Events A, B, and C as follows:

Event A: a face card is drawn on the first draw,

Event B: a face card is drawn on the second draw,

Event C: a face card is drawn on the third draw.

Let ABC = the event that three successive face cards are drawn on three successive draws.

Let $D = AB$ = the event that two successive face cards are drawn on the first two draws. Then $P\{ABC\} = P\{DC\} = P\{D\}\ P\{C \mid D\}$ by the properties of conditional probability. But

$$P\{D\} = P\{AB\} = P\{A\}\ P\{B \mid A\}.$$

We have shown that $P\{ABC\} = P\{A\}\ P\{B \mid A\}\ P\{C \mid AB\}$. Now

$$P\{A\} = \frac{\text{number of face cards}}{\text{total number of cards}} = \frac{12}{52}$$

$$P\{B \mid A\} = \frac{\text{number of face cards} - 1}{\text{total number of cards in the deck} - 1} = \frac{11}{51}$$

$$P\{C \mid AB\} = \frac{12 - 2}{52 - 2} = \frac{10}{50}$$

$$P\{ABC\} = \frac{12}{52} \times \frac{11}{51} \times \frac{10}{50} = \frac{11}{1,105} = 0.010.$$

The above is an example of sampling without replacement.

● PROBLEM 6–11

If four cards are drawn at random and without replacement from a deck of 52 playing cards, what is the probability of drawing all four aces?

SOLUTION:

We will do this problem in two ways. First,, we will use the classical model of probability, which tells us

$$\text{Probability} = \frac{\text{number of favorable outcomes}}{\text{all possible outcomes}}, \text{ assuming all outcomes are}$$

equally likely.

There is one of four aces we can draw first. Once that is done any one of three can be taken second. We have two choices for third and only one for fourth. Using the Fundamental Principle of Counting, we see that there are $4 \times 3 \times 2 \times 1$ possible favorable outcomes. Also, we can choose any one of 52 cards first. There are 51 possibilities for second, etc. The Fundamental Principle of Counting tells us that there are $52 \times 51 \times 50 \times 49$ possible outcomes in the drawing of four cards. Thus,

174

$$\text{Probability} = \frac{4 \times 3 \times 2 \times 1}{52 \times 51 \times 50 \times 49} = \frac{1}{270{,}725} = 0.0000037.$$

Our second method of solution involves the multiplication rule and shows some insights into its origin and its relation to conditional probability. The formula for conditional probability $P\{A \mid B\} = \dfrac{P\{A \cap B\}}{P\{B\}}$ can be extended as follows:

$$P\{A \mid B \cap C \cap D\} = \frac{P\{A \cap B \cap C \cap D\}}{P\{B \cap C \cap D\}}; \text{ thus,}$$

$P\{A \cap B \cap C \cap D\} = P\{A \mid B \cap C \cap D\}\, P\{B \cap C \cap D\}$, but

$P\{B \cap C \cap D\} = P\{B \mid C \cap D\}\, P\{C \cap D\}$; therefore,

$P\{A \cap B \cap C \cap D\} = P\{A \mid B \cap C \cap D\}\, P\{B \mid C \cap D\}\, P\{C \cap D\}$, but

$P\{C \cap D\} = P\{C \mid D\}\, P\{D\}$; hence,

$P\{A \cap B \cap C \cap D\} = P\{A \mid B \cap C \cap D\}\, P\{B \mid C \cap D\}\, P\{C \mid D\}\, P\{D\}$.

Let D be the event drawing an ace on the first card

   C = drawing an ace on the second card

   B = drawing an ace on the third draw

   A = drawing an ace on the fourth card

Our conditional probability extension becomes $P\{\text{four aces}\} = P\{\text{on fourth} \mid \text{first three}\} \times P\{\text{third} \mid \text{first two}\} \times P\{\text{second} \mid \text{on first}\} \times P\{\text{on first}\}$.

Assuming all outcomes are equally likely, $P\{\text{on first draw}\} = \dfrac{4}{52}$. There are four ways of success in 52 possibilities. Once we pick an ace there are 51 remaining cards, three of which are aces. This leaves a probability of $\dfrac{3}{51}$ for picking a second ace once we have chosen the first. Once we have two aces there are 50 remaining cards, two of which are aces, thus $P\{\text{on third} \mid \text{first two}\} = \dfrac{2}{50}$. Similarly, $P\{\text{fourth ace} \mid \text{first three}\} = \dfrac{1}{49}$. According to our formula above,

$$P\{\text{four aces}\} = \frac{1}{49} \times \frac{2}{50} \times \frac{3}{51} \times \frac{4}{52} = 0.000037.$$

Four cards are to be dealt successively, without replacement, from an ordinary deck of playing cards. Find the probability of receiving a spade, a heart, a diamond, and a club, in that order.

SOLUTION:

Let the events of drawing a spade, heart, diamond, or club be denoted by S, H, D, or C. We wish to find $P \{S, H, D, C\}$, where the order of the symbols indicates the order in which the cards are drawn. This can be rewritten as

$$P \{S, H, D, C\} = P \{S, H, D\} \, P \{C \mid S, H, D\}$$

by the multiplication rule.

Continuing to apply the multiplication rule yields

$$P \{S, H, D, C\} = P \{S\} \, P \{H \mid S\} \, P \{D \mid S, H\} \, P \{C \mid S, H, D\}.$$

The product of these conditional probabilities will yield the joint probability. Because each card is drawn at random, the classical model is an apt one. Now,

$P \{$drawing a spade on the first draw$\}$

$$= \frac{\text{number of spades}}{\text{number of cards in the deck}}$$

$$P \{S\} = \frac{13}{52}$$

$$P \{H \mid S\} = \frac{\text{number of hearts}}{\text{number of cards after a spade is drawn}}$$

$$= \frac{13}{52 - 1} = \frac{13}{51}$$

$$P \{D \mid S, H\} = \frac{\text{number of diamonds}}{\text{number of cards after a heart and a spade are drawn}}$$

$$= \frac{13}{52 - 2} = \frac{13}{50}$$

$$P \{C \mid S, H, D\} = \frac{\text{number of clubs}}{\text{number of cards after a heart , spade, and diamond are drawn}}$$

$$= \frac{13}{52 - 3} = \frac{13}{49}$$

Thus,

$$P\{S, H, D, C\} = \frac{13}{52} \times \frac{13}{51} \times \frac{13}{50} \times \frac{13}{49}.$$

Find the probability that on a single draw from a deck of playing cards we draw a spade or a face card or both.

SOLUTION:

We wish to find the probability of drawing a spade or a face card or both. Define Event A and B as follows:

      Event A: drawing a spade

      Event B: drawing a face card

Then $A \cup B$ = the event of drawing a spade or face card or both, and

$$P\{A\} + P\{B\} = \frac{\text{number of ways a spade can occur}}{\text{total number of possible outcomes}} +$$

$$\frac{\text{number of ways a face card can occur}}{\text{total number of possible outcomes}}.$$

But we have counted too much. Some cards are spades and face cards, so we must subtract from the above expression the

$$\frac{\text{number of ways a spade and a face card can occur}}{\text{total number of possible outcomes}}.$$

This can be rewritten as

$$P\{A \cup B\} = P\{A\} + P\{B\} - P\{AB\}.$$

$$P\{A\} = \frac{13}{52}, \; P\{B\} = \frac{12}{52}$$

$P\{AB\} = P\{B\}\,P\{A \mid B\}$, where

$P\{A \mid B\}$ = probability that a spade is drawn given that a face card is drawn.

$$= \frac{\text{number of spades that are face cards}}{\text{total number of face cards which could be drawn}}$$

$$= \frac{3}{12}$$

Now $P\{AB\} = \dfrac{12}{52} \times \dfrac{3}{12} = \dfrac{3}{52}$.

We could have found $P\{AB\}$ directly be counting the number of spades that are face cards and then dividing by the total possibilities. Thus

$$P\{A \cup B\} = P\{A\} + P\{B\} - P\{AB\}$$

$$= \frac{13}{52} + \frac{12}{52} - \frac{3}{52} = \frac{22}{52} = \frac{11}{26}$$

We could have found the answer more directly in the following way:

$$P\{A \cup B\} = \frac{\text{number of spades or face cards or both}}{\text{total number of cards}}$$

$$= \frac{22}{52} = \frac{11}{26}$$

● **PROBLEM 6-14**

Your company uses a pre-employment test to screen applicants for the job of repairman. The test is passed by 60 percent of the applicants. Among those who pass the test, 80 percent complete training successfully. In an experiment, a random sample of applicants who do not pass the test are also employed. Training is successfully completed by only 50 percent of this group. If no pre-employment test is used, what percentage of applicants would you expect to complete training successfully?

SOLUTION:

We can utilize a tree diagram:

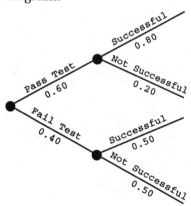

178

From the definition of conditional probability and the multiplication rule:

P {Successful ∩ Pass} = P {Successful | Pass} P {pass}

= {0.80} {0.60} = 0.48

Similarly, P {Successful ∩ Fail} = P {Successful | Fail} P {Fail}

= {0.50} {0.40} = 0.20

The event "an applicant is successful" is composed of two mutually exclusive events. These events are: "an applicant passed the test and was successful" {denoted by $S \cap P$} and "an applicant failed the test and was successful" {denoted $S \cap F$}. Thus,

P {Success} = P {$S \cap P$} + P ($S \cap F$)

= 0.48 + 0.20 = 0.68.

We expect 68 percent of the applicants to successfully complete the training.

● **PROBLEM 6-15**

An electronic device contains two easily removed subassemblies, A and B. If the device fails, the probability that it will be necessary to replace A is 0.50. Some failures of A will damage B. If A must be replaced, the probability that B will also have to be replaced is 0.70. If it is not necessary to replace A, the probability that B will have to be replaced is only 0.10. In what percentage of all failures will you require to replace both A and B?

SOLUTION:

This situation may be pictured by the following tree diagram. Each "branch" of the tree denotes a possible event which might occur if device A fails.

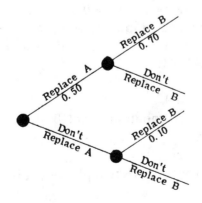

If device A fails, A will be replaced or not replaced. These first two outcomes are represented by the first two branches of the tree diagram. The branches are labeled with their respective probabilities.

Given that A is replaced, the behavior of B is described by the two secondary branches emanating from the primary branch denoting replacement of A.

If A is not replaced, B's possible behavior is described by the secondary branches emanating from the branch denoting non-replacement of A. The tree diagram, each branch labeled by its respective probability, is thus:

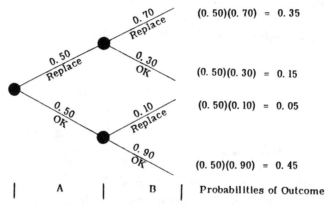

| | A | B | Probabilities of Outcome |

The Probability that both A and B must be replaced is 0.35.

The conditional probabilities that B is not replaced given A is replaced, and that B is not replaced given A is not replaced can also be found by $P\{B' \mid A\}$ and $P\{B' \mid A'\}$, respectively. Also let

$P\{B \mid A\}$ = probability B is replaced given A is replaced and

$P\{B \mid A'\}$ = probability B is replaced given A is not replaced.

If A is replaced, then B can be replaced or not replaced. These events are mutually exclusive and exhaustive; thus,

$P\{B' \mid A\} + P\{B \mid A\} = 1$

$P\{B \mid A\} = 0.7$

thus, $P\{B' \mid A\} = 1 - P\{B \mid A\} = 1 - 0.7 = 0.3$.

Similarly, if A is not replaced, B may be replaced or not replaced. Given that A is not replaced, these events are mutually exclusive and exhaustive, thus $P\{B' \mid A'\} + P\{B \mid A'\} = 1$.

But $P\{B \mid A'\} = 0.1$;

thus $P\{B' \mid A'\} = 1 - 0.1 = 0.9$.

The problem asks for the probability that both A and B are replaced. Using the multiplication rule,

$P\{A$ and B are replaced$\}$

$= P\{A$ is replaced$\}$ $P\{B$ is replaced $\mid A$ is replaced$\}$

$P \{A \text{ is replaced}\} \, P \{B \mid A\}$

$\qquad = (0.5)\,(0.7) = 0.35.$

The probability that both A and B are replaced is 0.35.

● PROBLEM 6-16

A bag contains one white ball and two red balls. A ball is drawn at random. If the ball is white then it is put back in the bag along with another white ball. If the ball is red then it is put back in the bag with two extra red balls. Find the probability that the second ball drawn is red. If the second ball drawn is red, what is the probability that the first ball drawn was red?

SOLUTION:

Let W_i or R_i be the event that the ball chosen on the ith draw is white or red, respectively. Assuming that each ball is chosen at random, a tree diagram of this problem can be drawn showing the possible outcomes.

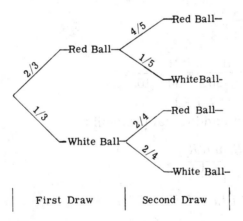

The probabilities of different outcomes are labeled on the "branches" of this tree. These probabilities depend on the number of balls of each color in the bag at the time of the draw. For example, before the first draw there are two red balls and one white ball. Thus, two of three balls on the average will result in a red ball being chosen or $P \{R_i\} = \dfrac{2}{3}$.

If a red ball is chosen on the first draw, then two more red balls are added to the bag. There are now four red balls and one white ball in the bag, so on the average four of five balls chosen will result in a red ball.

Thus, $P\{R_2$ given a red ball on the first draw$\} = P\{R_2 \mid R_1\} = \dfrac{4}{5}$. The other probabilities are computed in a similar fashion.

We wish to compute $P\{R_2\}$, the probability that the second ball drawn is red. As we see from the tree diagram, there are two ways this can happen; thus, $P\{R_2\} = P\{R_1$ and R_2 or W_1 and $R_2\}$. The events R_1 and R_2 and W_1 and R_2 and mutually exclusive.

Thus, $P\{R_2\} = P\{R_1$ and $R_2\} + P\{W_1$ and $R_2\}$.

But $P\{R_1$ and $R_2\} = P\{R_2 \mid R_1\} \times P\{R_1\}$

and $P\{W_1$ and $R_2\} = P\{R_2 \mid W_1\} \times P\{W_1\}$

by the definition of conditional probability.

From our diagram,

$$P\{R_2 \mid R_1\} = \frac{4}{5} \text{ and } P\{R_2 \mid W_1\} = \frac{2}{4}.$$

Also, $P\{R_1\} = \dfrac{2}{3}$ and $P\{W_1\} = \dfrac{1}{3}$.

Thus, $P\{R_2\} = P\{R_2 \mid R_1\} P\{R_1\} + P\{R_2 \mid W_1\} P\{W_1\}$

$$= \frac{4}{5} \times \frac{2}{3} + \frac{2}{4} \times \frac{1}{3}$$

$$= \frac{8}{15} + \frac{1}{6} = \frac{16+5}{30} = \frac{21}{30} = \frac{7}{10}$$

Now we wish to find $P\{R_1 \mid R_2\}$.

From the definition of conditional probability

$$P\{R_1 \mid R_2\} = \frac{P\{R_1 \text{ and } R_2\}}{P\{R_2\}} .$$

We also know that $P\{R_2\} = P\{R_2 \mid R_1\} P\{R_1\} + P\{R_2 \mid W_1\} P\{W_1\}$ by the previous problem.

We also know that

$P\{R_1$ and $R_2\} = P\{R_2 \mid R_1\} \times P\{R_1\}$

Putting these together we see that

$$P\{R_1 \mid R_2\} = \frac{P\{R_1 \mid R_2\} P\{R_1\}}{P\{R_1 \mid R_2\} P\{R_1\} + P\{R_2 \mid W_1\} P\{W_1\}}$$

$$= \cfrac{\dfrac{4}{5} \times \dfrac{2}{3}}{\dfrac{4}{5} \times \dfrac{2}{3} + \dfrac{2}{4} \times \dfrac{1}{3}}$$

$$= \cfrac{\dfrac{8}{15}}{\dfrac{7}{10}} = \dfrac{10 \times 8}{7 \times 15} = \dfrac{16}{21}$$

Note that in order to compute these probabilities, we needed to know the number of red and white balls in the bag at the beginning.

BAYES' THEOREM

Twenty percent of the employees of a company are college graduates. Of these, 75 percent are in a supervisory position. Of those who did not attend college, 20 percent are in supervisory positions. What is the probability that a randomly selected supervisor is a college graduate?

SOLUTION:

Let the events be as follows:

E: The person selected is a supervisor.

E_1: The person selected is a college graduate.

E_2: The person selected is not a college graduate.

We are searching for $P\{E_1 \mid E\}$.

By the definition of conditional probability

$$P\{E_1 \mid E\} = \frac{P\{E_1 \cap E\}}{P\{E\}}.$$

But also by the conditional probability $P\{E_1 \cap E\} = P\{E \mid E_1\} \times P\{E_1\}$. Since E is composed of mutually exclusive events, E_1 and E_2, $P\{E\} = P\{E_1 \cap E\} + P\{E_2 \cap E\}$. Furthermore, $P\{E_2 \cap E\} = P\{E \mid E_2\} P\{E_2\}$, by conditional probability. Inserting these expressions into $\frac{P\{E_1 \cap E\}}{P\{E\}}$, we obtain

$$P\{E_1 \mid E\} = \frac{P\{E_1\} P\{E_1 \mid E\}}{P\{E_1\} P\{E_1 \mid E\} + P\{E_2\} P\{E \mid E_2\}}.$$

This formula is a special case of the well-known Bayes' Theorem. The general formula is

$$P\{E_1 \mid E\} = \frac{P\{E_1\} P\{E \mid E_1\}}{\sum_{1}^{n} P\{E_n\} P\{E \mid E_n\}}.$$

In our problem,

$P\{E_1\} = P\{\text{College graduate}\} = 20\% = 0.20,$

$P\{E_2\} = P\{\text{Not a graduate}\} = 1 - P\{\text{Graduate}\} = 1 - 0.2 = 0.80,$

$P\{E \mid E_1\} = P\{\text{Supervisor} \mid \text{Graduate}\} = 75\% = 0.75,$ and

$P\{E \mid E_2\} = P\{\text{Supervisor} \mid \text{Not a graduate}\} = 20\% = 0.20.$

Substituting,

$$P\{E_1 \mid E\} = \frac{(0.20)(0.75)}{(0.20)(0.75) + (0.80)(0.20)} = \frac{0.15}{0.15 + 0.16}$$

$$= \frac{15}{31}$$

● PROBLEM 6-18

In a factory four machines produce the same product. Machine A produces 10 percent of the output; Machine B, 20 percent; Machine C, 30 percent; and Machine D, 40 percent. The proportion of defective items produced by these follows: Machine A: 0.001; Machine B: 0.0005; Machine C: 0.005; and Machine D: 0.002. An item selected at random is found to be defective. What is the probability that the item was produced by A? by B? by C? by D?

SOLUTION:

Each question requires us to find the probability that a defective item was produced by a particular machine. Bayes' Rule allows us to calculate this using known (given) probabilities. First, we define the necessary symbols: M_1 means the item was produced at A, M_2 means it was produced at B, and M_3 and M_4 refer to machines C and D, respectively. Let M mean that an item is defective. Using Bayes' Rule,

$$P\{M_1 \mid M\} = \frac{P\{M_1\}\,P\{M \mid M_1\}}{P\{M_1\}\,P\{M \mid M_1\} + P\{M_2\}\,P\{M \mid M_2\} + P\{M_3\}\,P\{M \mid M_3\}}{+P\{M_4\}\,P\{M \mid M_4\}}$$

we substitute the given proportions as follows:

$$P\{M_1 \mid M\} = \frac{(0.1)(0.001)}{(0.1)(0.001) + (0.2)(0.0005) + (0.3)(0.005) + (0.4)(0.002)}$$

$$= \frac{0.0001}{0.0001 + 0.0001 + 0.0015 + 0.0008} = \frac{0.0001}{0.0025}$$

$$= \frac{1}{25}$$

To compute $P\{M_2 \mid M\}$ we need only change the numerator to $P\{M_2\}$ $P\{M \mid M_2\}$. Substituting given proportions, we have $\{0.20\}\,\{0.0005\} = 0.0001$.

We see that $P\{M_2 \mid M\} = \dfrac{1}{25} = P\{M_1 \mid M\}$. By the same procedure we find

that $P\{M_3 \mid M\} = \dfrac{3}{25}$ and $P\{M_4 \mid M\} = \dfrac{8}{25}$.

To check our work, note that a defective item can be produced by any one of the four machines and that the four events "produced by machine i and defective" ($i = 1, 2, 3, 4$) are mutually exclusive. Thus,

$$P\{M\} = \sum_{i=1}^{4} P\{M \text{ and } M_i\} \text{ or } \sum_{i=1}^{4} \frac{P\{M \text{ and } M_i\}}{P\{M\}} = 1;$$

but $\qquad \dfrac{P\{M \text{ and } M_i\}}{P\{M\}} = P\{M_i \mid M\}$.

Thus, $\displaystyle\sum_{i=1}^{4} P\{M_i \mid M\} = 1$. Adding, we see that

$$\frac{1}{25} + \frac{1}{25} + \frac{15}{25} + \frac{8}{25} = \frac{25}{25} = 1 .$$

● PROBLEM 6-19

In the St. Petersburg Community College, 30 percent of the men and 20 percent of the women are studying mathematics. Further, 45 percent of the students are women. If a student selected at random is studying mathematics, what is the probability that the student is a woman?

SOLUTION:

This problem involves conditional probabilities. The first two percentages given can be thought of as conditional probabilities; "30 percent of the men are studying mathematics" means that the probability that a male student selected at random is studying mathematics is 0.3. Bayes' formula allows us to use the probabilities we know to compute the probability that a mathematics student is a woman. Using the symbols M (the student is studying mathematics); W (the student is a woman); and N (the student is not a woman), we write:

$$P\{W \mid M\} = \frac{P\{W\} P\{M \mid W\}}{P\{W\} P\{M \mid W\} + P\{N\} P\{M \mid N\}}, \text{ substituting}$$

$$= \frac{(0.45)(0.2)}{(0.45)(0.2)+(0.55)(0.3)} = \frac{0.09}{0.09+0.165}$$

$$= \frac{0.09}{0.255} = \frac{6}{17}$$

Thus, the probability that a randomly selected math student is a woman

equals $\frac{6}{17}$ = 0.353.

RANDOM SAMPLING

If four different balls are placed at random in three different cells, find the probability that no cell is empty. Assume that there is ample room in each cell for all four balls.

SOLUTION:

There are three ways to place each of the four balls into a cell. Thus, there are 3 × 3 × 3 × 3 = 3^4 ways to put the four balls into three cells. If each arrangement is equally likely, then any one arrangement will occur with the probability

$$\frac{1}{3^4} = \frac{1}{81} .$$

We now must count the number of ways the balls can be placed in the cells so that none of the cells are empty.

First, we know that one cell will have two balls in it. Choose these two

balls from the four; there are $\binom{4}{2}$ ways to do this. Now place these two balls

in a cell; there are three ways to do this. There are two ways and one way respectively to place the two remaining balls in the two remaining cells to insure that all the cells are filled. Together, by the Fundamental Counting

Principle, there are $\binom{4}{2} \times 3 \times 2 \times 1$ or 36 arrangements. Thus, the probability of observing an arrangement with no cells empty if the balls are dropped in at random is $\dfrac{36}{81} = \dfrac{4}{9}$.

● **PROBLEM 6-21**

A box contains four black marbles, three red marbles, and two white marbles. What is the probability that a black marble, then a red marble, then a white marble is drawn without replacement?

SOLUTION:

Here we have three dependent events. There is a total of nine marbles from which to draw. We assume on the first draw we will get a black marble. The probability of drawing a black marble is

$$\frac{\text{number of ways of drawing a black marble}}{\text{number of ways of drawing one out of } (4+3+2) \text{ marbles}}, \text{ so}$$

$$P\{A\} = \frac{4}{4+3+2} = \frac{4}{9}.$$

There are now eight marbles left in the box.

On the second draw, we get a red marble. The probability of drawing a red marble is

$$\frac{\text{number of ways of drawing a red marble}}{\text{number of ways of drawing one out of the eight remaining marbles}}, \text{ so}$$

$$P\{B\} = \frac{3}{8}.$$

There are now seven marbles remaining in the box.

On the last draw, we get a white marble. The probability of drawing a white marble is

$$\frac{\text{number of ways of drawing a white marble}}{\text{number of ways of drawing one out of the seven remaining marbles}}, \text{ so}$$

$$P\{C\} = \frac{2}{7}.$$

When dealing with two or more dependent events, if P_1 is the probability of a first event, P_2 the probability that, after the first has happened, the second will occur, P_3 the probability that, after the first and second have happened, the third will occur, etc., then the probability that all events will happen in the given order is the product $P_1 \times P_2 \times P_3 \ldots$

Thus, $P\{A \cap B \cap C\} = P\{A\} \times P\{B\} \times P\{C\}$

$$= \frac{4}{9} \times \frac{3}{8} \times \frac{2}{7} = \frac{1}{21}.$$

● **PROBLEM 6-22**

There is a box containing five white balls, four black balls, and seven red balls. If two balls are drawn one at a time from the box and neither is replaced, find the probability that

(a) both balls will be white.

(b) the first ball will be white and the second red.

(c) three balls will be drawn in the order white, black, red if a third ball is drawn.

SOLUTION:

(a) To find the probability that both balls will be white, we express it symbolically.

  P {both balls will be white}

  $= P$ {first ball will be white and the second ball will be white}

  $= P$ {first ball will be white} $\times P$ {second ball will be white given that the first one was}

$$= \frac{\text{number of ways to choose a white ball}}{\text{number of ways to choose a ball}} \times$$

$$\frac{\text{number of ways to choose a second white ball}}{\text{after removal of the first white ball}}{\text{number of ways to choose a ball after removal of the first ball}}$$

$$= \frac{5}{16} \times \frac{4}{15} = \frac{1}{12}$$

189

(b) P {first ball will be white and the second ball will be red}

    $= P$ {first ball will be white} × P {the second ball will be red given the first was white}

$$= \frac{\text{number of ways to choose a white ball}}{\text{number of ways to choose a ball}} \times$$

$$\frac{\text{number of ways to choose a red ball}}{\text{number of ways to choose a ball after removal of the first ball}}$$

$$= \frac{5}{16} \times \frac{7}{15} = \frac{7}{48} \ .$$

(c) P {three balls drawn in the order white, black, red}

    $= P$ {first ball is white} P {second ball is black given the first was white} P {third ball is red given the first was white and the second was black}

$$= \frac{\text{number of ways to choose that the first ball is white}}{\text{number of ways to choose the first ball}} \times$$

$$\frac{\text{number of ways to choose that the second one is black}}{\text{number of ways to choose the second one}} \times$$

$$\frac{\text{number of ways to choose that the third one is red}}{\text{number of ways to choose the third one}}$$

$$= \frac{5}{16} \times \frac{4}{15} \times \frac{7}{14} = \frac{1}{24} \ .$$

SHORT ANSWER QUESTIONS FOR REVIEW

Choose the correct answer.

1. Since tossing a coin is an independent event, it is (a) never a conditional probability problem. (b) always a conditional probability problem. (c) always a uniform probability problem. (d) dependent on the wording of the problem.

2. In order to determine the probability of dealing four cards from a well-shuffled deck and that those cards are the four 7's, you would have to multiply

   (a) $\dfrac{1}{52} \times \dfrac{1}{51} \times \dfrac{1}{50} \times \dfrac{1}{49}$.

   (b) $\dfrac{1}{13} \times \dfrac{1}{17} \times \dfrac{1}{25} \times \dfrac{1}{49}$.

   (c) $\dfrac{4}{52} \times \dfrac{3}{52} \times \dfrac{2}{52} \times \dfrac{1}{52}$.

   (d) $\dfrac{1}{13} \times \dfrac{1}{13} \times \dfrac{1}{13} \times \dfrac{1}{13}$.

3. In a bag containing six red marbles and six white marbles, what is the probability of choosing two marbles, without replacement, that are both red?

   (a) $\dfrac{6}{12} \times \dfrac{5}{11}$

   (b) $\dfrac{1}{12} \times \dfrac{1}{12}$

   (c) $\dfrac{1}{12} \times \dfrac{2}{12}$

   (d) $\dfrac{1}{6} \times \dfrac{2}{5}$

4. $P \{A \cap B\}$ is read (a) the probability of A or B occurring. (b) the probability of A and B occurring. (c) the probability of A but not B occurring. (d) the probability of A not occurring and B occurring.

5. The probability of drawing a diamond or a heart from a well-shuffled

deck of cards and rolling a 4 on a well-balanced die is

(a) $\dfrac{1}{52} \times \dfrac{4}{6}$.

(b) $\dfrac{4}{52} \times \dfrac{1}{6}$.

(c) $\dfrac{1}{2} \times \dfrac{1}{6}$.

(d) $\dfrac{1}{4} \times \dfrac{4}{6}$.

Fill in the blanks.

6. The conditional probability of drawing _____ kings from a deck of cards without replacement is $\dfrac{1}{221}$.

7. In the definition of conditional probability, it states that $P\{B\} > 0$; that is because you are _____ _____ $P\{B\}$.

8. If $P\{A \mid B\} = P\{A\}$, then we say that event A is _____ of event B.

9. $P\{A\} \times P\{A \mid B\} =$ _____ .

10. $P\{A' \cap B\}$ is read as the probability that A _____ occur and B _____ occur.

Determine whether the following statements are true or false.

11. $P\{A \cap B\}$ equals $P\{A\}\, P\{B \mid A\}$ as well as $P\{B\}\, P\{A \mid B\}$.

12. A coin is tossed three times and two heads and one tail fall. If the coin is tossed a fourth time, what is the probability of it landing tails? (This question is an example of conditional probability.)

13. When we speak of $P\{A \mid B\}$, A and B do not have to be independent events.

14. The probability of drawing two cards in succession and having both be aces is the same as having both be picture cards.

15. The probability of rolling two 7's in a row as a 3, 4 and a 5, 2 is the same as the reverse roll (e.g., 5, 2 then 3, 4).

ANSWER KEY

1. d	2. b	3. a
4. b	5. c	6. two
7. dividing by	8. independent	9. $P\{AB\}$ [or $P\{BA\}$]
10. does not, does	11. True	12. False
13. True	14. False	15. True

CHAPTER 7

EXPECTATION

FOR RANDOM VARIABLES

● **PROBLEM 7-1**

Let X be a random variable whose value is determined by the flip of a fair coin. If the coin lands heads up $X = 1$, if tails then $X = 0$. Find the expected value of X.

SOLUTION:

The expected value of X, written $E(X)$, is the theoretical average of X. If the coin were flipped many, many times and the random variable X was observed each time, the average of X would be considered the expected value. The expected value of a discrete variable such as X is defined as

$$E(X) = x_1 \, P\{X = x_1\} + x_2 \, P\{X = x_2\} \ldots + x_n \, P\{X = x_n\}$$

where x_1, x_2, x_3, ... x_n are the values X may take on and $P\{X = x_j\}$ is the probability that X actually equals the value x_j.

For our problem, the random variable X takes on only two values, 0 and 1. X assumes these values with

$$P\{X = 1\} = P\{X = 0\} = \frac{1}{2} .$$

Thus, according to our definition,

$$E(X) = 0 \times P \, (X = 0) + 1 \times P \, (X = 1)$$

$$= 0 \times \frac{1}{2} + 1 \times \frac{1}{2} = 0 + \frac{1}{2} = \frac{1}{2}$$

● **PROBLEM 7–2**

Let X be the random variable defined as the number of dots observed on the upturned face of a fair die after a single toss. Find the expected value of X.

SOLUTION:

The random variable X can take on the values 1, 2, 3, 4, 5, or 6. Since the die is fair, we assume that each value is observed with equal probability. Thus, $P \, \{X = 1\} = P \, \{X = 2\} = \ldots = P \, \{X = 6\}$

$$= \frac{1}{6}$$

The expected value of X is

$E(X) = \sum x \, P \, \{X = x\}$. Hence,

$$E(X) = 1 \times \frac{1}{6} + 2 \times \frac{1}{6} + 3 \times \frac{1}{6} + 4 \times \frac{1}{6} + 5 \times \frac{1}{6} + 6 \times \frac{1}{6}$$

$$= \frac{1}{6} \, (1 + 2 + 3 + 4 + 5 + 6)$$

$$= \frac{21}{6} = 3\frac{1}{2}$$

Suppose the earnings of a laborer denoted by X are given by the following probability function:

X	0	8	12	16
$P\{X = x\}$	0.3	0.2	0.3	0.2

Find the laborer's expected earnings.

SOLUTION:

The laborer's expected earnings are denoted by $E(X)$, the expected value of the random variable X.

The expected value of X is defined to be

$E(X)$ = (0) $P\{X = 0\}$ + (8) $P\{X = 8\}$ + (12) $P\{X = 12\}$ + (16) $P\{X = 16\}$

$\quad$ = (0) (0.3) + (8) (0.2) + (12) (0.3) + (16) (0.2)

$\quad$ = 0 + 1.6 + 3.6 + 3.2

$\quad$ = 8.4

Thus, the expected earnings are 8.4.

A brush salesman sells door-to-door. His products are short and long brushes. The profit on the long brush is $0.30 and on the short one it is $0.10. The chances of selling a long brush are one out of ten calls, and the chances of selling a short one are two out of ten calls. The chances of no sales are seven out of ten calls. Find the expected profit per call.

SOLUTION:

Let P be a random variable representing the profit per call. We wish to find $E(P)$. The probability distribution of P, given in the problem, is summarized in the following table:

	P	$P\{P = p\}$
long brush	0.30	0.1
short brush	0.10	0.2
no sale	0.00	0.7

Thus,

$$E(P) = (0.30)\ P\{P = 0.30\} + (0.10)\ P\{P = 0.10\} + (0.0)\ P\{P = 0.0\}$$
$$= (0.30)\ (0.1) + (0.10)\ (0.2) + (0)\ (0.7)$$
$$= 0.03 + 0.02 + 0.00 = 0.05$$

The expected profit per call is $0.05 or 5 cents.

● **PROBLEM 7–5**

The State of New Hampshire conducts an annual lottery to raise funds for the school districts in the state. Assume a million tickets are sold. One ticket is the winning ticket and the winner receives $10,000. If each ticket costs $0.25, find the expected value of a randomly purchased ticket and the revenue that the lottery generates for the school districts in the state.

SOLUTION:

Let X be the value of a randomly purchased lottery ticket. Then

$$X = -\$0.25 \text{ with probability } \frac{999,999}{1,000,000}.$$

This is because 999,999 of 1,000,000 lottery tickets have no value and the buyers of these tickets lose the $0.25 price.

However,

$$X = \$10,000 - \$0.25 \text{ with probability } \frac{1}{1,000,000}.$$

This reflects the fact that one of the million tickets wins $10,000 minus the purchase price of the ticket, thus the winner receives $10,000 – $0.25.

The expected value of the random variable X is the expected value of a

197

randomly purchased lottery ticket. By definition of expected value,

$$E(X) = \$[10{,}000 - 0.25] \times \frac{1}{1{,}000{,}000} + [-\$0.25] \times \frac{999{,}999}{1{,}000{,}000} \ .$$

Rearranging terms, we see that

$$E(X) = \$10{,}000 \times \left[\frac{1}{1{,}000{,}000}\right] + \left[\frac{-\$0.25 - (\$0.25)\ (999{,}999)}{1{,}000{,}000}\right]$$

$$= \$10{,}000 \left[\frac{1}{1{,}000{,}000}\right] - \$0.25\left[\frac{1{,}000{,}000}{1{,}000{,}000}\right]$$

$$= \$\frac{1}{100} - \$0.25$$

$$= \$0.01 - \$0.25 = -\$0.24$$

Thus, the expected value of an average lottery ticket is –$0.24. Each buyer loses an average of 24 cents on a lottery ticket.

The total revenue is the number of tickets sold times the price of each ticket or $(0.25)(1,000,000) = $250,000. The net revenue, after the prize is paid, is

$250,000 – 10,000 = $240,000.

Thus, the school districts receive $240,000.

● PROBLEM 7-6

Suppose a shipping company buys a new trailer truck for $10,000. If the truck is lost either through an accident or theft, it is regarded as a complete loss. The chance of loss is 0.001; hence, the chance of no loss is 0.999. Find the expected loss.

SOLUTION:

Let L be the random variable representing the loss that the shipping company takes in the course of a year, taking on the values 0 and 10,000. The probability distribution of L is $P\ \{L = 0\} = 0.999$ and $P\ \{L = 10{,}000\} = 0.001$. This information is summarized in the following table:

	l	$P\{L = l\}$
No loss	0	0.999
Loss	10,000	0.001

To find the expected loss, we calculate the expected value of the random variable L. This is,

$$E(L) = l_1 \, P\{L = l_1\} + l_2 \, P\{L = l_2\}$$
$$= 0 \, P\{L = 0\} + 10,000 \, P\{L = 10,000\}$$
$$= 0 \, (0.999) + (10,000) \, (0.001)$$
$$= 10$$

Thus, the expected loss is $10.

● **PROBLEM 7-7**

In the previous problem, suppose 1,000 shipping companies, each having a truck worth $10,000, form an industry association to protect themselves against the loss of a new truck. How much should the firms pay in total to the association to insure their trucks?

SOLUTION:

The expected loss for all the companies combined is

$$L_T = L_1 + L_2 + L_3 + \ldots + L_{1,000}$$

where L_i represents the loss of the ith company. The expected loss of all 1,000 companies is $E(L_T)$.

By the properties of expectation,

$$E(L_T) = E \, (L_1 + L_2 + \ldots + L_{1,000})$$
$$= E(L_1) + E(L_2) + \ldots + E(L_{1,000})$$

The expected loss of each company is $E(L_i) = \$10$. Thus,

$$E(L_T) = \underbrace{10 + 10 + \ldots + 10}_{1,000 \text{ terms}}$$

$$= (1000) \, 10 = 10,000$$

On the average, there will be a loss of 10,000 a year among the 1,000 companies. Some years the loss will be greater than $10,000, some years the loss will be less than \$10,000, but on the average the loss will be \$10,000 a year. Dividing this loss equally among all 1,000 companies gives the annual premium each company should pay. Thus,

$$\text{premium} = \frac{10,000}{1,000} = 10 \text{ dollars.}$$

Here X is an example of a binomially distributed random variable. We note that for a binomial random variable

$$E(X) \text{ also equals } 4 \times \frac{1}{2} = n \times p = 2.$$

This formula $E(X) = np$ is true for all binomial random variables.

Find the expected number of boys on a committee of three selected at random from four boys and three girls.

SOLUTION:

Let X represent the number of boys on the committee, which can be equal to 0, 1, 2, or 3. The probability that there are zero boys on the committee is

$$P\{X = 0\} = \frac{\text{number of ways zero boys can be picked}}{\text{number of ways a committee of three can be chosen}}.$$

The number of ways a committee of three can be chosen from the four boys and three girls is the number of ways three can be selected from seven

or $\binom{7}{3}$.

The number of ways a committee of three can be chosen that contains

zero boys is $\binom{4}{0} \times \binom{3}{3}$, the number of ways zero boys are chosen from four

multiplied by the number of ways three girls are chosen from the three available. Thus,

$$P\{X = 0\} = \frac{\binom{4}{0} \times \binom{3}{3}}{\binom{7}{3}}.$$

Similarly,

$$P\{X = 1\} = \frac{\binom{4}{1} \times \binom{3}{2}}{\binom{7}{3}},$$

$$P\{X = 2\} = \frac{\binom{4}{2} \times \binom{3}{1}}{\binom{7}{3}},$$

and

$$P\{X = 3\} = \frac{\binom{4}{3} \times \binom{3}{0}}{\binom{7}{3}}.$$

By definition, the expected number of boys is

$$E(X) = (0)\ P\{X = 0\} + (1)\ P\{X = 1\} + (2)\ P\{X = 2\} + (3)\ P\{X = 3\}$$

$$= (0)\frac{\binom{4}{0} \times \binom{3}{3}}{\binom{7}{3}} + (1)\frac{\binom{4}{1} \times \binom{3}{2}}{\binom{7}{3}} + (2)\frac{\binom{4}{2} \times \binom{3}{1}}{\binom{7}{3}} + (3)\frac{\binom{4}{3} \times \binom{3}{0}}{\binom{7}{3}}$$

$$= (1)\frac{\frac{4!}{3!\,1!} \times \frac{3!}{2!\,1!}}{\binom{7}{3}} + (2)\frac{\frac{4!}{2!\,2!} \times \frac{3!}{2!\,1!}}{\binom{7}{3}} + (3)\frac{\frac{4!}{3!\,1!} \times \frac{3!}{0!\,3!}}{\binom{7}{3}}$$

$$= \frac{1}{\binom{7}{3}}[(4)(3) + (2)(6)(3) + (3)(4)(1)]$$

$$= \frac{12 + 36 + 4}{\binom{7}{3}} = \frac{52}{\dfrac{7!}{3!\,4!}}$$

$$= \frac{52}{\dfrac{7 \times 6 \times 5}{3 \times 2 \times 1}} = \frac{52}{35} = 1.5$$

Thus, if a committee of three is selected at random repeatedly it would contain on the average 1.5 boys.

Let the random variable X represent the number of defective radios in a shipment of four radios to a local appliance store. Assume that each radio is equally likely to be defective or non-defective; hence, the probability that a radio is defective is $p = \dfrac{1}{2}$. Also assume that each radio is defective or non-defective independently of the other radios. Find the expected number of defective radios.

SOLUTION:

First we find the probability distribution of X, the number of defective radios in the shipment of four. This can assume the values 0, 1, 2, 3, or 4.

If X is 0, then zero radios are defective. This can only take place if each is non-defective. By the independence assumption,

$$P\{X = 0\} = \left(\frac{1}{2}\right)\left(\frac{1}{2}\right)\left(\frac{1}{2}\right)\left(\frac{1}{2}\right)$$

$$= \frac{1}{2^4} = \frac{1}{16}$$

Similarly, $P\{X = 1\} = P\{\text{one radio is defective, three are not}\}$

$$= \frac{\text{number of favorable outcomes}}{\text{number of possible outcomes}}$$

$$= \frac{4}{2^4} = \frac{4}{16} = \frac{1}{4}. \text{ Now}$$

$P\{X = 2\} = P\{\text{two radios are defective}\}$

$$= \frac{\text{number of ways two can be chosen from four}}{\text{number of ways to choose four radios}}$$

$$= \binom{4}{2}\left(\frac{1}{2}\right)^4 = \frac{6}{16}.$$

By symmetry,

$$P\{X = 1\} = P\{X = 3\} = \frac{4}{16} = \frac{1}{4} \text{ and}$$

$$P\{X = 0\} = P\{X = 4\} = \frac{1}{16}.$$

The expected number of defective radios is

$$E(X) = 0 \times \frac{1}{16} + 1 \times \frac{4}{16} + 2 \times \frac{6}{16} + 3 \times \frac{4}{16} + 4 \times \frac{1}{16}$$

$$= \frac{4}{16} + \frac{12}{16} + \frac{12}{16} + \frac{4}{16} = \frac{32}{16} = 2$$

● PROBLEM 7–10

A retailer has the opportunity to sell a portion of slow-moving stock to a liquidator for $1,800. Since the items in question are children's toys, he is also aware that he may do better financially by keeping them in stock through the approaching Christmas shopping season and selling them at a discount. The following table indicates the retailer's estimate of the consequences of his decision given that a certain percentage of stock is sold in the Christmas season.

Percentage of Stock Sold	Revenue if Stock is Kept	Revenue if Stock is Sold Now
70%	$1,400	$1,800
80%	$1,600	$1,800
90%	$1,800	$1,800
100%	$2,000	$1,800

The retailer has kept good records of previous experience over 25 Christmas seasons and has found that:

$$P \{70\% \text{ of stock is sold}\} = \frac{4}{25}$$

$$P \{80\% \text{ of stock is sold}\} = \frac{7}{25}$$

$$P \{90\% \text{ of stock is sold}\} = \frac{12}{25}$$

$$P \{100\% \text{ of stock is sold}\} = \frac{2}{25}$$

Evaluate the decisions using expected revenue as the criterion.

SOLUTION:

Let X_1 = the revenue in dollars received by the retailer if he sells his stock now to the liquidator. Let X_2 = the revenue in dollars received by the retailer if he keeps his stock and sells it through the Christmas shopping season. We wish to calculate $E(X_1)$ and $E(X_2)$. If $E(X_1) > E(X_2)$, he should sell now and if $E(X_2) > E(X_1)$, he should keep the stock and sell it through the Christmas shopping season. This exemplifies decision-making based on expected value or the expected value criterion.

The expected value of X_1 is computed to be

$$E(X_1) = 1,800 \left(\frac{4}{25}\right) + 1,800 \left(\frac{7}{25}\right) + 1,800 \left(\frac{12}{25}\right) + 1,800 \left(\frac{2}{25}\right)$$

$$= 1,800 \left(\frac{4+7+12+2}{25}\right) = 1,800 \left(\frac{25}{25}\right)$$

$$= 1,800$$

The expected value of X_2 is computed to be

$$E(X_2) = (1,400) \, P \, (X_2 = 1,400) + 1,600 \, P \, (X_2 = 1,600)$$
$$+ 1,800 \, P \, (X_2 = 1,800) + 2,000 \, P \, (X_2 = 2,000);$$

but

$P \{X_2 = 1,400\} = P \{70\% \text{ of the stock is sold}\}$
$P \{X_2 = 1,600\} = P \{80\% \text{ of the stock is sold}\}$
$P \{X_2 = 1,800\} = P \{90\% \text{ of the stock is sold}\}$
$P \{X_2 = 2,000\} = P \{100\% \text{ of the stock is sold}\}.$

From previous experience the retailer has estimated that

$$E(X_2) = 1,400 \left(\frac{4}{25}\right) + 1,600 \left(\frac{7}{25}\right) + 1,800 \left(\frac{12}{25}\right) + 2,000 \left(\frac{2}{25}\right)$$

$$= 224 + 448 + 864 + 160$$
$$= 1,696$$

Thus, $E(X_2) < E(X_1)$. The retailer should sell his stock to the liquidator.

Let Y be the Rockwell hardness of a particular alloy of steel. Assume that Y is a continuous uniformly distributed random variable that can take on any value between 50 and 70. Find the expected Rockwell hardness.

SOLUTION:

The random variable Y has a density function that is sketched below.

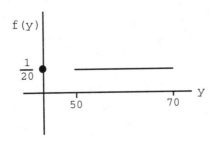

In order for Y to have a proper probability density function, the area under the density function must be 1. The area under the density function of Y is in the shape of a rectangle with length 20. Thus, the height of the rectangle, $f(y)$, must satisfy

$$f(y)(20) = 1 \qquad 50 < y < 70,$$

where the probability density function $f(y)$ represents the width of this rectangle. Solving for $f(y)$, we find the probability density function to be

$$f(y) = \frac{1}{20} \qquad 50 < y < 70.$$

To find the expected value of a continuous random variable, we use the fact that the random variable is symmetric about 60. Thus, the expected Rockwell hardness of this alloy is 60.

● PROBLEM 7-12

Suppose that the average income of those who work is \$30,000/year. If 10 percent of the population does not work, then find the average income of the entire population This random variable is partly discrete and partly continuous.

SOLUTION:

Since X has a mixed density, partly discrete and partly continuous,

$$E[X] = 0 \times P\{X = 0\} + E[X \mid x > 0] \, P\{x > 0\}$$
$$= 0 + (0.9)(\$30,000) = \$27,000 \text{ per year}$$

FUNCTIONS OF RANDOM VARIABLES

Find the expected value of the random variable $Y = f(X)$, when X is a discrete random variable with probability mass function $g(x)$. Let $f(X) = X^2 + X + 1$ and

$$P\{X = x\} = g(x) = \begin{cases} \dfrac{1}{2} & x = 1 \\[2mm] \dfrac{1}{3} & x = 2 \\[2mm] \dfrac{1}{6} & x = 3 \end{cases}$$

SOLUTION:

To find the expected value of a function of a random variable, we define

$$E(Y) = E(f(X)) = \sum_x f(X)\, g(x) = \sum_x f(X)\, P\{X = x\}.$$

As an example, we consider the above problem. Then

$$E(Y) = f(1)\, P\{X = 1\} + f(2)\, P\{X = 2\} + f(3)\, P\{X = 3\}.$$

But $f(1) = 1^2 + 1 + 1 = 3$,

$f(2) = 2^2 + 2 + 1 = 7$, and

$f(3) = 3^2 + 3 + 1 = 13$.

Substituting, we see that

$$E[Y] = 3\, P\{X = 1\} + 7\, P\{X = 2\} + 13\, P\{X = 3\}$$

$$= 3 \times \frac{1}{2} + 7 \times \frac{1}{3} + 13 \times \frac{1}{6}$$

$$= \frac{3}{2} + \frac{7}{3} + \frac{13}{6} = \frac{9}{6} + \frac{14}{6} + \frac{13}{6}$$

$$= \frac{36}{6} + \frac{1}{6} = 6 \, .$$

CONDITIONAL EXPECTATION

● PROBLEM 7-14

If $E[y|x = x] = 2x$ and $E[x] = 4$, then find $E[y]$.

SOLUTION:

We know that $E[y] = E\{E[y|x]\}$
$$= E[2x] = 2\, E[x]$$
$$= (2)\,(4) = 8$$

● PROBLEM 7-15

If $E[Y|X = x] = 2x + 3$ and $E[x] = 6$, then find $E[X + Y]$.

SOLUTION:

We know that $E[Y] = E\{E[Y|X]\} = E[2x + 3] = 2E[x] + 3$
$$= (2)\,(6) + 3 = 12 + 3 = 15$$

Then $\quad E[X + Y] = E[X] + E[Y]$
$$= 6 + 15$$
$$= 21$$

● PROBLEM 7-16

Conditional expectations may be used to find unconditional expectations. In particular,
$$E\{E[Y | X = x]\} = E[Y].$$
Let y be the amount in a randomly selected person's checking account on 1/1/95, and let x be the amount in this account on 1/1/94. If on average people had \$2,000 in checking accounts on 1/1/94, and on average checking accounts increased by \$500 from 1/1/94 to 1/1/95, then find the mean checking balance on 1/1/95.

SOLUTION:

We compute $E[y] = E\{E[y|x]\} = E\{x + \$500\}$
$$= E[x] + \$500 = \$2,000 + \$500$$
$$= \$2,500$$

Find the theoretical variance of the random variable with the following probability distribution:

x	$P\{X = x\}$
0	$\dfrac{1}{4}$
1	$\dfrac{1}{2}$
2	$\dfrac{1}{8}$
3	$\dfrac{1}{8}$

SOLUTION:

The theoretical variance is the expected mean square error, which represents an idealized measure of the spread or dispersion of a probability distribution about its mean. The variance of a random variable X is denoted σ_x^2, or var X. It is defined as var $X = E[(X - \mu^2)]$, where $\mu = E(X)$.

In this example,

$$E[X] = (0) \, P\{X = 0\} + (1) \, P\{X = 1\} + (2) \, P\{X = 2\} + (3) \, P\{X = 3\}$$

$$= 0 \times \frac{1}{4} + 1 \times \frac{1}{2} + 2 \times \frac{1}{8} + 3 \times \frac{1}{8}$$

$$= 0 + \frac{1}{2} + \frac{2}{8} + \frac{3}{8} = \frac{9}{8}$$

We now compute the variance of X as

var $X = E\,[(X - \mu^2)]$

$$= E\left[\left(X - \frac{9}{8}\right)^2\right]$$

$$= \left(0 - \frac{9}{8}\right)^2 P\,\{X = 0\} + \left(1 - \frac{9}{8}\right)^2 P\,\{X = 1\} + \left(2 - \frac{9}{8}\right)^2 P\,\{X = 2\} +$$

$$\left(3 - \frac{9}{8}\right)^2 P\,\{X = 3\}$$

$$= \left(\frac{81}{64} \times \frac{1}{4}\right) + \left(\frac{1}{64} \times \frac{1}{2}\right) + \left(\frac{49}{64} \times \frac{1}{8}\right) + \left(\frac{225}{64} \times \frac{1}{8}\right)$$

$$= \frac{2\,(81) + 4 + 49 + 225}{64\,(8)}$$

$$= \frac{440}{64\,(8)} = \frac{55}{64} = 0.859$$

A slightly less complicated formula for the theoretical variance is derived below as

$E\,[(X - \mu^2)] = E\,[X^2 - 2X\mu + \mu^2]$.

By the properties of expectation,

$E\,[(X - \mu^2)] = E\,(X^2) - 2\mu\,E\,(X) + E\,(\mu^2)$.

$E\,(\mu^2) = \mu^2$ because the expected value of a constant is a constant. Thus,

$E\,[(X - \mu^2)] = E\,(X^2) - 2\mu\,E\,(X) + \mu^2$

$E\,(X) = \mu$; thus,

$V\,X = E\,(X^2) - 2\mu \times \mu + \mu^2$

$\qquad = E\,(X^2) - 2\mu^2 + \mu^2 = E\,(X^2) - \mu^2$

or $\qquad V\,X = E\,(X^2) - [E\,(X)]^2$.

Recomputing var X, we see that

$V\,X = 0^2 \times P\,(X = 0) + 1^2\,P\,(X = 1) + 2^2\,P\,(X = 2) + 3^2\,P\,(X = 3) -$

$$\left(\frac{9}{8}\right)^2$$

$$= 0 + \frac{1}{2} + \frac{4}{8} + \frac{9}{8} - \left(\frac{9}{8}\right)^2$$

$$= \frac{(17)8 - 81}{64} = \frac{136 - 81}{64} = \frac{55}{64} = 0.859$$

VARIANCE OF RANDOM VARIABLES

PROBLEM 7-18

Given the probability distribution of the random variable X in the table below, compute $E[X]$ and var (X).

x_i	$P\{X = x_i\}$
0	$\dfrac{8}{27}$
1	$\dfrac{12}{27}$
2	$\dfrac{6}{27}$
3	$\dfrac{1}{27}$

SOLUTION:

First $E[X] = \sum_i x_i P\{X = x_i\}$ and var $(X) = E[(X - E[X])^2]$.

Thus, $E[X] = (0) P\{X = 0\} + (1) P\{X = 1\} + (2) P\{X = 2\} + (3) P\{X = 3\}$

$$= (0)\frac{8}{27} + (1)\frac{12}{27} + (2)\frac{6}{27} + (3)\frac{1}{27}$$

$$= 0 + \frac{12}{27} + \frac{12}{27} + \frac{3}{27} + \frac{27}{27} = 1. \text{ Also,}$$

$V(X) = (0 - 1)^2 P\{X = 0\} + (1 - 1)^2 P\{X = 1\} + (2 - 1)^2 P\{X = 2\} + (3 - 1)^2$
$P\{X = 3\}$

$$= (1^2)\frac{8}{27} + (0^2)\frac{12}{27} + (1^2)\frac{6}{27} + (2^2)\frac{1}{27}$$

$$= \frac{8}{27} + \frac{6}{27} + \frac{4}{27} = \frac{18}{27} = \frac{2}{3}$$

211

Given the following table of probabilities for values x_i of the random variable X, which represents the number of defective radios in a shipment of four, find the variance and standard deviation of X.

x_i	$P\{X = x_i\}$
0	$\dfrac{1}{16}$
1	$\dfrac{4}{16}$
2	$\dfrac{6}{16}$
3	$\dfrac{4}{16}$
4	$\dfrac{1}{16}$

SOLUTION:

The variance of a random variable X is defined to be
$$E\,[X - E\,(X)]^2 = \sigma^2.$$
Since we have a discrete set of data, the most efficient method of finding the variance is to construct a table which will extend the given one. First, compute the expected number of defective radios:

$$E\,[X] = \sum_{i=0}^{4} x_i\,P\{X = x_i\}$$

$$= 0 \times \left(\frac{1}{16}\right) + 1 \times \left(\frac{4}{16}\right) + 2 \times \left(\frac{6}{16}\right) + 3 \times \left(\frac{4}{16}\right) + 4 \times \left(\frac{1}{16}\right)$$

$$= \frac{4}{16} + \frac{12}{16} + \frac{12}{16} + \frac{4}{16} = \frac{32}{16} = 2$$

x_i	$P\{X = x_i\}$	$E(X) = (x_i - 2)$	$(x_i - 2)^2$	$(x_i - 2)^2 \, P\{X = x_i\}$
0	$\dfrac{1}{16}$	-2	4	$\dfrac{4}{16}$
1	$\dfrac{4}{16}$	-1	1	$\dfrac{4}{16}$
2	$\dfrac{6}{16}$	0	0	0
3	$\dfrac{4}{16}$	1	1	$\dfrac{4}{16}$
4	$\dfrac{1}{16}$	2	4	$\dfrac{4}{16}$

The variance of a discrete random variable X is defined to be

$$\sigma^2 = \sum_{i=1}^{n} (x_i - E[X])^2 \, P\{X = x_i\}.$$

Observe that in this problem σ^2 is the sum of the entries in the last column of the table, so

$$\sigma^2 = \frac{4}{16} + \frac{4}{16} + 0 + \frac{4}{16} + \frac{4}{16} = \frac{16}{16} = 1$$

The standard deviation of s of X is

$$\sigma = \sqrt{\sigma^2} = \sqrt{1} = 1.$$

● PROBLEM 7-20

The probability that a certain baseball player will get a hit on any given time at bat is $\dfrac{3}{10}$. If he is at bat 100 times during the next month, find the theoretical mean and variance of X, the number of hits. Assume that the binomial distribution is applicable.

SOLUTION:

The theoretical mean or expected value of X, the number of hits, is an idealized average. The expected value of X is the number of hits we would expect to see over the next 100 times at bat. The expected value of X, written as $E[X]$ or μ, is equal to

$$(0) \times P\{X = 0\} + (1) \times P\{X = 1\} + (2) \times P\{X = 2\} + \ldots + (100) \times P\{X = 100\}.$$

Since the binomial distribution is applicable,

$$P\{X = j\} = \binom{n}{j} p^j (1 - p)^{n - j} \quad j = 0, 1, \ldots \, n$$

and $n = 100$, $p = \dfrac{3}{10}$.

Writing $E[X]$ using summation notation, we see that

$$E[X] = \sum_{j=0}^{100} j \binom{100}{j} \left(\frac{3}{10}\right)^j \left(\frac{7}{10}\right)^{100-j}.$$

One way to simplify this expression is to decompose the event X hits in terms of other random variables.

Let $\; Z_i = \begin{cases} 1 & \text{if the } i\text{th trial results in a hit} \\ 0 & \text{if the } i\text{th trial does not result in a hit} \end{cases}$

Then $X = Z_1 + Z_2 + \ldots + Z_{100}$ or $X = \sum\limits_{i=1}^{100} Z_i$ and

$$E[X] = E\left[\sum_{i=1}^{100} Z_i\right] = \sum_{i=1}^{100} E[Z_i]$$

by the rules of expectation. Let

$$Z_j = \begin{cases} 1 & \text{with probability } p \text{ the batter hits} \\ 0 & \text{with probability } 1 - p \text{ the batter misses} \end{cases}$$

so $\quad E[Z_i] = 1 \times p + 0 \times (1 - p) = p$ and

$$E[X] = \sum_{i=1}^{100} E[Z_i] = \sum_{j=1}^{100} p = \underbrace{p + p + \ldots +}_{100 \text{ terms}}$$

$$= 100 \, p$$

Since $p = \dfrac{3}{10}$, $E[X] = 100 \left(\dfrac{3}{10}\right) = 30$. We would expect 30 hits in the next

214

100 times at bat.

The theoretical variance of X is an idealized measure of the dispersion or spread of X, the number of hits about the idealized average. This theoretical variance is denoted by σ^2 or $V(X)$ and is defined to be

$$V(X) = E([X - E[X]])^2 \, ;$$

from this definition follows the rules of variance, especially that if X and Y are independent random variables

$$V(X + Y) = VX + VY.$$

Returning to our problem, we see that

$$V(X) = \text{var}\left(\sum_{i=1}^{100} Z_i\right)$$

$$= \sum_{i=1}^{100} \text{var } Z_i \text{ because the } Z_j\text{'s are independent.}$$

Now
$$V(Z_i) = E([Z - E[Z_i]]^2)$$
$$= E([Z_i - p]^2) = E[Z_i^2] - p^2$$
$$E[Z_i^2] = 1^2 \times p + 0^2 \times (1 - p) = p; \text{ thus,}$$
$$V(Z_i) = p - p^2 = p(1 - p).$$

Thus,
$$V(X) = \sum_{i=1}^{100} \text{var } Z_i = \sum_{i=1}^{100} (p - p^2)$$

$$= \underbrace{p - p^2 + \ldots + p - p^2}_{100 \text{ terms}}$$

$$= 100 \, (p) \, (1 - p)$$

Since $p = \dfrac{3}{10}$, $V(X) = 100\left(\dfrac{3}{10}\right)\left(\dfrac{7}{10}\right) = 21.$

● **PROBLEM 7-21**

Suppose that 75 percent of the students taking statistics pass the course. In a class of 40 students, what is the expected number who will pass? Find the variance and standard deviation.

SOLUTION:

Let X be a random variable denoting the number of students in the class of 40 who will pass. If 75 percent of the students pass, then a randomly

215

chosen student will pass with probability 0.75 and fail with probability 0.25. It is reasonable to assume that a student passes or fails independently of what other students do.

With this assumption, it can be shown that X is a binomially distributed random variable with parameters $p = 0.75$ and $n = 40$. The parameter p indicates the probability of a student passing and n represents the number of students in the class.

In the previous problem, we have shown that the expected value of such a random variable is

$$E[X] = np.$$

In this case,

$$E[X] = (40)(0.75) = 30.$$

It has also been shown that the variance of X is

$$\sigma^2 = V(X) = np(1 - p)$$

and substituting we see that

$$\sigma^2 = V(X) = (40)(0.75)(1 - 0.75) = 7.5 .$$

The standard deviation is defined as $\sigma = \sqrt{\operatorname{var} X}$;

thus, $\sigma = \sqrt{np(1 - p)} = \sqrt{7.5} = 2.74$.

● PROBLEM 7-22

A new insecticide is advertised as being 90% effective in killing ants with one application. If 10,000 ants are treated with one application of the insecticide, find the expected value, variance, and standard deviation of the number of ants killed.

SOLUTION:

We find the theoretical mean, or expected value, of a random variable, X, by multiplying the outcomes of this random variable by the probability of its occurrence and adding the products.

Thus, $E[X] = \mu = x_1 P\{x_1\} + x_2 P\{x_2\} + \ldots + x_n P\{x_n\}$

$$= \sum_{i=1}^{n} x_i P(X = x_i).$$

Let X = the number of ants killed out of the 10,000 ants treated with the insecticide. Each ant is killed with probability $p = 0.90$ or survives with probability $1 - p = 1 - 0.90 = 0.10$. It is reasonable to assume that the effect of the insecticide on a single ant is independent of the insecticide's effect on any of the other ants. With these two assumptions, we see that X is the sum of $n = 10,000$ independent trials each with probability $p = 0.90$ of "success" and probability $1 - p = 0.10$ of "failure." Thus, X is by definition a binomially distributed random variable with parameters $p = 0.90$ and $n = 10,000$. To find the expected value of X, we use our previously derived results, namely, $E(X) = np$ and

$$\sigma^2 = \text{var } X = np(1 - p), \quad \sigma = \sqrt{\sigma^2} = \sqrt{np(1-p)}.$$

Substituting, we see that

$$E(X) = np = (10,000)(0.90) = 9,000$$
$$V(X) = np(1 - p) = (10,000)(0.90)(0.10) = 900$$

$$\sigma = \sqrt{V(X)} = \sqrt{900} = 30.$$

● PROBLEM 7-23

Use the properties of expectation to find the variance of the sum of two independent random variables.

SOLUTION:

The variance of the sum of two independent random variables is defined to be

$$V(X + Y) = E[(X + Y - E[X + Y])^2];$$

squaring inside the square brackets:

$$V(X + Y) = E[(X + Y)^2 - 2(X + Y)E[X + Y] - (E[X + Y])^2].$$

Squaring again yields:

$$V(X + Y) = E[X^2 + 2XY + Y^2 - 2(X + Y)E[X + Y] - (E[X + Y])^2].$$

But $(E[X + Y])^2 = (E[X] + E[Y])^2$

$$= [E[X]]^2 + 2E[X]E[Y] + [E[Y]]^2.$$

Substituting, we see that:

$$V(X + Y) = E[X^2 + 2XY + Y^2 - 2(X + Y)E[X + Y] + (E[X])^2 + 2E(X)E(Y) + [E(Y)]^2;$$

but $E[X + Y]$, $E[X^2]$, $E[X]E[Y]$, and $E[Y]^2$ are constants, and the expected value of a constant equals that constant; thus,

$$V(X + Y) = E[X^2 + 2XY + Y^2] - 2E[X + Y]E[X + Y] + [E[X + Y]]^2$$
$$= E[X^2 + 2XY + Y^2] - 2[E[X + Y]]^2 + [E[X + Y]]^2$$
$$= E[X^2 + 2XY + Y^2] - [E[X + Y]]^2$$
$$= E[X^2] + 2E[XY] + E[Y^2] - [E[X] + E[Y]]^2.$$

But since X and Y are independent,

$$E[XY] = E[X] \ E[Y].$$

Thus,

$$
\begin{aligned}
V(X + Y) &= E[X^2] + 2 \ E[X] \ E[Y] + E[Y^2] - [E[X]]^2 - \\
&\quad 2 \ E[X] \ E[Y] - [E[Y]]^2 \\
&= E[X^2] - (E[X])^2 + E[Y^2] - (E[Y])^2 \\
&= \text{var } X + \text{var } Y
\end{aligned}
$$

● PROBLEM 7-24

Find the variance of the random variable $X + b$ where X has variance var X and b is a constant.

SOLUTION:

$$
\begin{aligned}
V(X + b) &= E([X + b]^2) - (E[X + b])^2 \\
&= E[X^2 + 2 \ b \ X + b^2] - [E[X] + b]^2 \\
&= E[X^2] + 2 \ b \ E[X] + b^2 - (E[X])^2 - 2 \ E[X] b - b^2 ,
\end{aligned}
$$

thus $\quad V(X + b) = E[X^2] - (E[X])^2 = \text{var}(X).$

● PROBLEM 7-25

Find the variance of the random variable $Y = aX$ where a is a constant and X has variance var $X = \sigma^2$.

SOLUTION:

We wish to find var (Y) = var (aX). We know that var $Y = E[Y]^2 - (E[Y])^2$. But $Y^2 = a^2 X^2$ and $E[Y] = E[aX] = a \ E[X]$.

Now $V(aX) = E[a^2 X^2] - (a \ E[X])^2 = a^2 E[X^2] - a^2 (E[X])^2$
$\qquad = a^2 (E[X^2] - E[X]^2 = a^2 \text{ var } [X].$

● PROBLEM 7-26

A population consists of the measurements 2, 3, 3, 4, 4, 4, 5, 5, 5, 6, 6, 7. Compute: (a) μ, (b) σ^2.

SOLUTION:

Because the entire population is known, we may calculate μ and σ^2 directly. This is only possible when the entire population is known. If we have a sample from the entire population, we can only calculate estimates of μ and σ^2.

To find μ, we multiply each value in the population by its frequency of occurrence. Thus,

$$E[X] = \mu = 2\left(\frac{1}{12}\right) + 3\left(\frac{2}{12}\right) + 4\left(\frac{3}{12}\right) + 5\left(\frac{3}{12}\right) + 6\left(\frac{2}{12}\right) + 7\left(\frac{1}{12}\right)$$

$$\mu = \frac{2 + 6 + 12 + 15 + 12 + 7}{12} = \frac{54}{12} = 4.5$$

We also could have found μ by adding the population values and dividing by the number of values in the population.

By definition

$$E[X - \mu]^2 = \sum_i (X_i - \mu)^2 \, P(X_i)$$

$$= \sum_i (X_i - \mu)^2 \, \frac{1}{n}$$

$$= \frac{1}{n} \sum_i (X_i - \mu)^2$$

the average squared deviation from the mean μ.

Now

$$\sigma^2 = \frac{\sum_{i=1}^{n}(X_i - \mu)^2}{n}$$

$$= \frac{(2 - 4.5)^2 + 2(3 - 4.5)^2 + 3(4 - 4.5)^2 + 3(5 - 4.5)^2 + 2(6 - 4.5)^2 + (7 - 4.5)^2}{12}$$

$$= \frac{(-2.5)^2 + 2(-1.5)^2 + 3(-0.5)^2 + 3(0.5)^2 + 2(1.5)^2 + (2.5)^2}{12}$$

$$= \frac{2(2.5)^2 + 4(1.5)^2 + 6(0.5)^2}{12}$$

$$= \frac{12.5 + 4(2.25) + 1.5}{12}$$

$$= \frac{12.5 + 10.5}{12} = \frac{23}{12} = 1.9$$

219

If X and Y are independent random variables with variances $\sigma_x^2 = 1$ and $\sigma_y^2 = 2$, find the variance of the random variable $Z = 3X - 2Y + 5$.

SOLUTION:

Using the rules of variance,

$$\text{var}(Z) = \text{var}(3X - 2Y + 5) = \text{var}(3X) + \text{var}(-2Y) + \text{var}(5)$$

(because X and Y are independent)

$$= 3^2 \text{var}(X) + (-2)^2 \text{var}(Y) + 0$$

because $\text{var}(aX) = a^2 \text{var}(X)$ and the variance of a constant is zero. Now

$$\text{var}(Z) = 9\text{var}(X) + 4\text{var}(Y).$$

Since $\text{var}(X) = 1$ and $\text{var}(Y) = 2$,

$$\text{var}(Z) = 9 \times 1 + 4 \times 2 = 9 + 8 = 17.$$

Find the expected value and variance of a random variable

$$Y = a_1 X_1 + a_2 X_2 + \ldots + a_n X_n,$$

where the X_i are independent and each have mean μ and variance σ^2. The a_i are constants.

SOLUTION:

By a generalization of the property that the expected value of a sum is the sum of the expected values,

$$E[Y] = E[a_1 X_1 + \ldots + a_n X_n] = E[a_1 X_1] + \ldots + E[a_n X_n].$$

Also, the expected value of a constant multiplied by a random variable is the constant multiplied by the expected value of the random variable, or $E[ax] = aE[X]$. Thus,

$$E[a_i X_i] = a_i E[X_i] \text{ and}$$
$$E[Y] = a_1 E[X_1] + a_2 E[X_2] + \ldots + a_n E[X_n].$$

But $E[X_1] = E[X_2] = E[X_3] = \ldots = E[X_n] = \mu$;

hence, $E[Y] = a_1\mu + a_2\mu + a_3\mu + \ldots + a_n\mu$

$$= \mu(a_1 + a_2 + a_3 + \ldots + a_n).$$

To find the variance of Y, we generalize the properties of variance. Remember that if two variables, X_1 and X_2, are independent, then the variance of $X_1 + X_2$ is the sum of variance X_1 and the variance of X_2.

Because $X_1, X_2, \ldots, X_n$ are independent,

$$V(Y) = V(a_1X_1 + \ldots + a_nX_n)$$
$$= V(a_1X_1) + V(a_2X_2) + \ldots + V(a_nX_n).$$

Also, the variance of a constant multiplied by a random variable is the constant squared, times the variance of the random variable. Equivalently,

$$V(aX) = a^2 V(X).$$

Thus, $V(a_iX_i) = a_i^2 V(X_i)$.

But $V(X_i) = \sigma^2$ for all i, hence,

$$\text{var } Y = a_1^2 V(X_1) + a_2^2 V(X_2) + \ldots + a_n^2 V(X_n)$$

$$= a_1^2\sigma^2 + a_2^2\sigma^2 + \ldots + a_n^2\sigma^2$$

$$= \sigma^2 (a_1^2 + a_2^2 + \ldots + a_n^2).$$

COVARIANCE AND CORRELATION

● **PROBLEM 7–29**

Find the variance of the random variable $Z = X + Y$ in terms of the variance of X and of Y if X and Y are not independent.

SOLUTION:

$$V(Z) = V(X + Y) = E\{[(X + Y) - E[X + Y])^2\}$$
$$= E[(X - E[X] + Y - E[Y])^2]$$

(because $E[X + Y] = E[X] + E[Y]$),

$$= E[(X - E[X])^2 + 2(X - E[X])(Y - E[Y]) + (Y - E[Y])^2],$$

and by the properties of expectation,

$$= E[(X - E[X])^2] + 2E[(X - E[X])(Y - E[Y])] + E[Y - E[Y])^2].$$

Thus, var $(Z) = $ var $(X) + $ var $(Y) + 2E[(X - E[X])(Y - E[Y])]$.

If X and Y are independent, $E[(X - E[X])(Y - E[Y])] = 0$, but since X and Y are not independent, we may not assume that this cross-product is zero. The term

$$E[(X - E[X])(Y - E[Y])]$$

is called the covariance of X and Y and is a measure of the linear relation between X and Y. It is such a measure in the sense that if X is greater than

$E[X]$ at the same time that Y is greater than $E[Y]$ with high probability, then the covariance of X and Y will be positive. If X is below $E[X]$ at the same time Y is above $E[Y]$ with high probability, the covariance of X and Y will be negative.

Related to the covariance is the correlation coefficient defined as:

$$\rho = \frac{\text{cov}(X, Y)}{\sqrt{Var\ X}\sqrt{Var\ Y}}.$$

The correlation coefficient gives a clearer picture of the linear relation between X and Y because it takes into account the variation in the individual variables X and Y.

Also, cov $(X, Y) = 0$ if X and Y are independent. The converse is not true. Further, cov $(X, Y) = $ cov (Y, X).

● PROBLEM 7-30

Find a formula for the covariance of

$$Y = \sum_{i=1}^{m} a_i Y_i \text{ and } X = \sum_{j=1}^{n} b_j X_j$$

if Y_i and X_j are random variables and a_i and b_j are constants.

SOLUTION:

Write cov $(X, Y) = $ cov $\left(\sum_{j=1}^{n} b_j X_j, \sum_{i=1}^{m} a_i Y_i \right)$

$$= E\left[(X - E[X]) \right] (Y - E[Y]),$$

but $\quad E[X] = E\left[\sum_{j=1}^{n} b_j X_j \right] = \sum_{j=1}^{n} b_j E[X_j]$

and $\quad E[Y] = \sum_{i=1}^{m} a_i E[Y_i]$

by the linearity properties of expectation. Thus,

$$X - E[X] = \sum_{j=1}^{n} b_j X_j - \sum_{j=1}^{n} b_j E[X_j] = \sum_{j=1}^{n} b_j (X_j - E[X_j]),$$

and similarly,

222

$$Y - E[Y] = \sum_{j=1}^{m} a_i Y_i - \sum_{j=1}^{m} a_i E[Y_i] = \sum_{i=1}^{m} a_i (Y_i - E[Y_i]).$$

Thus,

$$\text{cov}(X, Y) = E\left[\left(\sum_{j=1}^{n} b_j(X_j - E[X_j])\right) \times \left(\sum_{i=1}^{m} a_i(Y_i - E[Y_i])\right)\right]$$

$$= E\left[\sum_{j=1}^{m} b_j(X_j - E[X_j])\right]\left[a_1(Y_1 - E[Y_1]) + \ldots + a_m(Y_m - E[Y_m])\right]$$

$$= \sum_{j=1}^{m} a_1 b_j(X_j - E[X_j])(Y_1 - E[Y_1]) +$$

$$\sum_{j=1}^{m} a_2 b_j(X_j - E[X_j])(Y_2 - E[Y_2]) + \ldots +$$

$$\sum_{j=1}^{m} a_n b_j(X_j - E[X_j])(Y_n - E[Y_n])$$

$$= E\left[\sum_{j=1}^{m} \sum_{i=1}^{n} a_i b_j(X_j - E[X_j])(Y_i - E[Y_i])\right]$$

$$= \sum_{j=1}^{m} \sum_{i=1}^{n} a_i b_j E\left[(X_j - E[X_j])(Y_i - E[Y_i])\right]$$

$$= \sum_{j=1}^{m} \sum_{i=1}^{n} a_i b_j \text{cov}(X_j, Y_i)$$

● PROBLEM 7-31

Find ρ for X and Y if cov $(x, y) = 3$, $V(x) = 4$, and $V(y) = 4$.

SOLUTION:

The correlation coefficient, ρ, is defined to be

$$\rho = \frac{\text{cov}(X, Y)}{\sqrt{V X} \sqrt{V Y}},$$

where cov $(X, Y) = E\left[(X - E\left[X\right])(Y - E\left[Y\right])\right]$,
$\quad\quad V\left(X\right) = E\left[X\right]^2 - \left[E\left[X\right]\right]^2,$
and $\quad V\left(Y\right) = E\left[Y\right]^2 - \left[E\left[Y\right]\right]^2.$

Now $\quad \rho = \dfrac{3}{\sqrt{(4)(4)}} = \dfrac{3}{\sqrt{16}} = \dfrac{3}{4} = 0.75$

● **PROBLEM 7-32**

Find the expected value of a random variable X that is uniformly distributed over the interval [0, 3].

SOLUTION:

The density function of X is $f(x) = \begin{cases} \dfrac{1}{3} & 0 < x < 3 \\ 0 & \text{otherwise} \end{cases}$

Now, $E\left[X\right] = \dfrac{3-0}{2} = \dfrac{3}{2}$

CHEBYSHEV'S INEQUALITY

● **PROBLEM 7-33**

Use Chebyshev's inequality to find a lower bound on $P\{-4 < X < 20\}$, where the random variable X has a mean $\mu = 8$ and variance $\sigma^2 = 9$.

SOLUTION:

Chebyshev's inequality gives

$$P\{\mu - k\sigma < X < \mu + k\sigma\} \geq 1 - \dfrac{1}{k^2}.$$

We wish to find k. Let $\mu - k\sigma = -4$ and $\mu + k\sigma = 20$ and $\mu = 8$ and $\sigma = \sqrt{\sigma^2} = \sqrt{9} = 3$. Thus, k satisfies either $8 - 3k = -4$ or $8 + 3k = 20$. Hence, $k = 4$. Then

$$P\{\mu - k\sigma < X < \mu + k\sigma\} \geq 1 - \frac{1}{k^2}$$

$$= P\{-4 < X < 20\} \geq 1 - \frac{1}{4^2}$$

$$= 1 - \frac{1}{4^2} = 1 - \frac{1}{16} = \frac{15}{16} .$$

Thus, a lower bound on $P\{-4 < X < 20\}$ is $\frac{15}{16}$.

● **PROBLEM 7-34**

Given that the discrete random variable X has density function $f(x)$ given by $f(-1) = \frac{1}{8}$, $f(0) = \frac{6}{8}$, $f(1) = \frac{1}{8}$, use Chebyshev's inequality,

$$P\{|X - \mu| \geq k\sigma\} \leq \frac{1}{k^2},$$

to find the upper bound when $k = 2$. What does this tell us about the possibility of improving the inequality to make the upper bound closer to the exact probability?

SOLUTION:

In order to use the inequality, we need to know the mean and variance of X. We compute

$$\mu = E[x] = \sum_x x\, f(x) = (-1)\left(\frac{1}{8}\right) + \left(0 \times \frac{6}{8}\right) + \left(1 \times \frac{1}{8}\right)$$

$$= \frac{1}{8} - \frac{1}{8} = 0, \text{ and}$$

$$\sigma^2 = E[(X - \mu)^2] = E[(X - 0)^2] = E[X]^2$$

$$= \sum_x x^2 f(x) = (-1)^2 \left(\frac{1}{8}\right) + 0 + (1)^2 \left(\frac{1}{8}\right) = \frac{1}{8} + \frac{1}{8} + \frac{1}{4} \ .$$

When $k = 2$, $P \{| X - \mu | \geq k\sigma\}$

$$= P \left\{|X| \geq 2\sqrt{\frac{1}{4}}\right\} = P \{| X | \geq 1\} \leq \frac{1}{2^2} = \frac{1}{4} \ .$$

The exact probability is $P \{| X | \geq 1\} = P \{X \leq -1 \text{ or } X \geq 1\}$, with $P \{X < 1\}$ $= 0 = P \{X > 1\}$ because the sum of the probabilities for $x = -1$, $x = 0$, and x

$= 1$ is $\dfrac{1}{8} + \dfrac{6}{8} + \dfrac{1}{8} = \dfrac{8}{8} = 1$. Therefore, we need to consider only

$$P \{X = -1\} = \frac{1}{8} \text{ and } P \{X = 1\} = \frac{1}{8} \ .$$

Since $x = -1$ and $x = 1$ are mutually exclusive events, we can add their probabilities:

$$\frac{1}{8} + \frac{1}{8} = \frac{2}{8} = \frac{1}{4} \ .$$

Therefore, the exact probability is $P \{| X | \geq 1\} = \dfrac{1}{4}$, which equals the upper bound given by Chebyshev's inequality, so that we cannot improve the inequality for the random variable in this example.

● PROBLEM 7-35

Given that the random variable X has density function $f(x) = \dfrac{1}{2\sqrt{3}}$ when $-\sqrt{3} < X < \sqrt{3}$ and $f(x) = 0$ when $X \leq -\sqrt{3}$ or $X \geq \sqrt{3}$, compute P $\left\{| X | \geq \dfrac{3}{2}\right\}$. Compare this with the upper bound given by Chebyshev's inequality.

SOLUTION:

Since X has a uniform distribution on $\left\{-\sqrt{3}, \sqrt{3}\right\}$,

$$P\left\{|x| \geq \frac{3}{2}\right\} = 1 - P\left\{|x| < \frac{3}{2}\right\} = 1 - \frac{\frac{3}{2} - \left(-\frac{3}{2}\right)}{\sqrt{3} - \left(-\sqrt{3}\right)}$$

$$= 1 - \frac{\frac{3}{2} + \frac{3}{2}}{\sqrt{3} + \sqrt{3}} = 1 - \frac{\frac{6}{2}}{2\sqrt{3}} = 1 - \frac{3}{2\sqrt{3}}$$

$$= 1 - \frac{\sqrt{3}}{2}.$$

Then, Chebyshev's inequality indicates that

$$P\left\{|X| \geq \frac{3}{2} \times 1\right\} \leq \frac{1}{\left(\frac{3}{2}\right)^2} = \frac{1}{\left(\frac{9}{4}\right)} = \frac{4}{9}. \text{ Hence,}$$

$$P\left\{|X| \geq \frac{3}{2}\right\} \leq \frac{4}{9}.$$

The exact probability $1 - \frac{\sqrt{3}}{2} \cong 0.134$ is much less than the upper bound given by Chebyshev's inequality.

● PROBLEM 7-36

Suppose that X assumes the values 1 and –1, each with probability 0.5. Find and compare the lower bound on $P\{-1 < X < 1\}$ given by Chebyshev's inequality and the actual probability that $-1 < X < 1$.

SOLUTION:

Chebyshev's inequality gives

$$P\{\mu - k\sigma < X < \mu + k\sigma\} \geq 1 - \frac{1}{k^2}.$$

For this random variable,

$$\mu = E[X] = P\{X = 1\} \times (1) + P\{X = -1\} \times (-1)$$
$$= 0.5 - 0.5 = 0, \text{ and } V X = E[X^2] - [E[X]]^2 = E[X^2]$$

$$= P\{X = 1\}\,(1)^2 + P\{X = -1\} \times (-1)^2 = 0.5 + 0.5 = 1.$$

Thus, $V(X) = \sigma^2 = 1$ and $\sigma = 1$.

Now $P\{0 - k < X < 0 + k\} \geq 1 - \dfrac{1}{k^2}$.

If $k = 1$, then $P\{-1 < X < 1\} \geq 1 - \dfrac{1}{1} = 0$

Thus $P\{-1 < X < 1\} \geq 0$.

The actual probability that X is between 1 and -1 is found by

$P\{-1 \leq X \leq 1\} = P\{X = 1\} + P\{-1 < X < 1\} + P\{X\} + P\{X = 1\}$.

But $P\{-1 \leq X \leq 1\} = 1$ because -1 and 1 are the only values that X assumes with positive probability. That is

$$1 = 0.5 + P\{-1 < X < 1\} + 0.5 \text{ or } P\{-1 < X < 1\} = 0,$$

so the lower bound on this probability equals the true probability.

● **PROBLEM 7–37**

Find a lower bound on $P\{-3 < X < 3\}$, where $\mu = E[X] = 0$ and var (X) $= \sigma^2 = 1$.

SOLUTION:

From Chebyshev's inequality,

$$P\{\mu - k\sigma < X < \mu + k\sigma\} \geq 1 - \frac{1}{k^2}.$$

We know that $\mu = 0$ and $\sigma = 1$. Thus, $\mu - k\sigma$ implies

$0 - k(1) = -3$ or $-k = -3k = 3$.

Thus, $P\{0 - 3 < X < 0 + 3\} \geq 1 - \dfrac{1}{3^2}$

$P\{-3 < X < 3\} > 1 - \dfrac{1}{9} = \dfrac{8}{9}$. The lower bound is thus $\dfrac{8}{9}$.

SHORT ANSWER QUESTIONS FOR REVIEW

Choose the correct answer.

1. An example of a continuous random variable is (a) potential heights of a child. (b) points scored in a football game. (c) number of congressional representatives from a state. (d) number of employees of a company.

2. The expected value for the quantity of televisions sold annually by a company is 240. This statement means that (a) the company sells 240 television sets every year. (b) 240 is the quantity that has the highest probability. (c) if the company sells 220 television sets this year, it must sell 260 next year. (d) the average annual company sales are 240 television sets, in the long run.

Use the following information to answer questions 3 and 4.

Let X be the number of music lessons taken before a young starting student can read and play several notes unassisted. The probability distribution of X is shown in the following table:

X	5	6	9
$P\{X\}$	0.5	0.3	0.2

3. The expected value of X is (a) 6.7 lessons. (b) 1.0 lesson. (c) 6.1 lessons. (d) 7.5 lessons.

4. The standard deviation, σ, of X is (a) 2.3 lessons. (b) 1.5 lessons. (c) 4.0 lessons. (d) 5.1 lessons.

5. An insurance company sells a life insurance policy with a face value of $1,000 and a yearly premium of $20. If 0.1 of the policyholders can be expected to die in a course of a year, the company's expected earnings per policyholder in any year would be (a) $20. (b) $10,000. (c) $19. (d) $81.

6. A shipment of 20 tape recorders contains five that are defective. If 10 of them are randomly selected for inspection, the probability that 2 of the 10 will be defective is (a) 0.348. (b) 0.438. (c) 0.843. (d) 0.200.

7. If a random variable x has the probability density function

$$f(x) = \begin{cases} 2e^{-2x} & \text{for } x > 0 \\ 0 & \text{for } x \le 0 \end{cases}$$

the probability that x will take on a value between 1 and 3 is (a) 0.331. (b) 0.313. (c) 0.133. (d) 0.662.

8. The value of k so that the following function can serve as the probability density function of a random variable x is

$$f(x) = \begin{cases} 0 & \text{for } x \le 0 \\ kxe^{-4x^2} & \text{for } x > 0 \end{cases}$$

(a) 4. (b) 8. (c) 2. (d) 6.

9. A card game consists of a single draw from a standard deck of cards. If the card is 10, you win $52 and if it is a face card (assume that aces are not face cards), you win $26. Otherwise, you lose $13. The expected value of this game is (a) $19. (b) $1. (c) $30.33. (d) $91.

Fill in the blanks.

10. A function whose domain is a sample space and whose range is a subset of the real numbers is called _____ _____ .

11. A _____ _____ _____ has a range consisting of a finite or countably infinite subset of the real numbers.

12. A _____ _____ _____ has a range consisting of an interval of real numbers.

13. If X is a continuous random variable, the probability of an individual value of X is _____ .

14. Assume that the time of birth of a New Year's baby of a city hospital will occur at some random time between midnight and 2:00 a.m. Let X be the number of minutes after midnight that the baby will be born so $0 \le X \le 120$. The probability distribution is shown below.

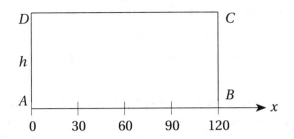

The probability that the New Year's baby will be born between 12:45 a.m. and 1:00 a.m. is equal to _____ .

15. The function F whose value for each real number x is given by $F(x) = P_x(X \le x)$ is called the _____ _____ _____ .

16. Let X be a random variable with possible values $S_x = \{x_1, x_2, x_3, \ldots x_n\}$ and probability point function $P\{x\}$. The mathematical expectation of X, denoted $E[X]$, is defined to be $E[X] = $ _____ .

Determine whether the following statements are true or false.

17. If X is a binomial random variable such that $S_x = \{0, 1\}$ and the probability of 1, $P\{1\}$, is given by $P\{1\} = p$, then the expected value of X, $E[X]$, is given by $E[X] = 1$.

18. If X is a finite random variable and a and b are arbitrary real numbers, then the expected value $E[aX + b]$, is given by $E[aX + b] = a\,E[X]$.

19. If the joint probability density function of two random variables is given by

$$f(x_1, x_2) = \begin{cases} 6e^{-2x_1 - 3x_2} & \text{for } x_1 > 0 \text{ and } x_2 > 0 \\ 0 & \text{elsewhere} \end{cases}$$

then the expected value of the product of the two random variables is given by $\dfrac{27}{2}$.

20. The mean, $\mu = E[X]$, of the binomial probability distribution where $n = 20$ and the probability of success in any single trial is $p = \dfrac{1}{5}$, is $\mu = E[X] = 4$.

231

21. If f is a probability density function and if $f(x) \geq 0$ for all values of x within the domain of f, then

$$\int_{-\infty}^{\infty} f(x)\, dx = 1.$$

22. The mean, μ (also called the expected value), and the variance, σ^2, of the binomial probability distribution, can be found using the following formulas: $\mu = np$ and $\sigma^2 = npq$, where p is the probability of success in any single trial, n is the number of trials, and $q = 1 - p$.

23. If a probability distribution has a mean $\mu = E[x]$, and a standard deviation σ, then the probability a value which deviates from μ by at least $k\sigma$ is at most $\dfrac{1}{k^2}$ for some constant k.

24. A high correlation between two variables, x and y, proves that x causes y.

25. The covariance of two variables, x and y, measures the strength of the linear correlation coefficient between the two variables, x and y, is a standard measure.

ANSWER KEY

1. a	2. d	3. c
4. b	5. a	6. a
7. c	8. b	9. b

10. random variable   11. discrete random variable

12. continuous random variable   13. zero

14. 0.125   15. cumulative distribution function

16. $\displaystyle\sum_{i=1}^{n} x_i\, P\{x_i\}$ 17. False   18. False

19. True   20. True   21. True

22. True   23. True   24. False

25. False

CHAPTER 8

JOINT DISTRIBUTIONS

DISCRETE DISTRIBUTIONS

● PROBLEM 8-1

Consider a bag containing two white and four black balls. If two balls are drawn at random without replacement from the bag, let X and Y be random variables representing the results of these two drawings. Let 0 correspond to drawing a black ball and 1 corresponding to drawing a white ball. Find the joint, marginal, and conditional distributions of X and Y.

SOLUTION:

We compute

$$P\{X = 0\} = P\{\text{a black ball is drawn first}\}$$

$$= \frac{\text{number of black balls}}{\text{total number of balls}} = \frac{4}{6} = \frac{2}{3}, \text{ and}$$

$$P\{X = 1\} = P\{\text{a white ball is drawn first}\}$$

$$= \frac{\text{number of white balls}}{\text{total number of balls}} = \frac{2}{6} = \frac{1}{3}.$$

We may use the notion of conditional probability to find the probability of a particular event on the second draw given a particular event on the first. We may talk about conditional distribution for the variable Y given X. A conditional distribution is defined in terms of conditional probability.

Now $P\{Y = y \mid X = x\} = f(y \mid x)$ is the conditional distribution of Y given X, $f(x, y) = P\{X = x, Y = y\}$ is the joint distribution of X and Y, and $f(x) = P\{X = x\}$ is the marginal distribution of X.

The conditional probabilities may be calculated directly from the problem. We then use the conditional probabilities and marginal distribution of X to find the joint distribution of X and Y.

Now $P\{Y = 0 \mid X = 0\} = P\{\text{black ball is second} \mid \text{black ball first}\}$

$$= \frac{\text{number of black balls} - 1}{\text{total number of balls} - 1} = \frac{4 - 1}{6 - 1} = \frac{3}{5},$$

$P\{Y = 1 \mid X = 0\} = P\{\text{white second} \mid \text{black first}\}$

$$= \frac{\text{number of white balls}}{\text{total number of balls} - 1} = \frac{2}{6 - 1} = \frac{2}{5},$$

$P\{Y = 0 \mid X = 1\} = P\{\text{black ball second} \mid \text{white ball first}\}$

$$= \frac{\text{number of black balls}}{\text{total number of balls} - 1} = \frac{4}{6 - 1} = \frac{4}{5}, \text{ and}$$

$P\{Y = 1 \mid X = 1\} = P\{\text{white ball second} \mid \text{white first}\}$

$$= \frac{\text{number of white balls} - 1}{\text{total number of balls} - 1} = \frac{2 - 1}{6 - 1} = \frac{1}{5}.$$

We now calculate the joint probabilities of X and Y as

$$\frac{P\{X = 0, Y = 0\}}{P\{X = 0\}} = P\{Y = 0 \mid X = 0\}, \text{ or,}$$

$$P\{X = 0 \mid Y = 0\} = P\{X = 0\}\, P\{Y = 0 \mid X = 0\} = \frac{2}{3} \times \frac{3}{5} = \frac{6}{15}.$$

Similarly,

$$P\{X = 1 \mid Y = 0\} = P\{Y = 0 \mid X = 1\}\, P\{X = 1\} = \frac{4}{5} \times \frac{1}{3} = \frac{4}{15},$$

$$P\{X = 0 \mid Y = 1\} = P\{Y = 1 \mid X = 0\}\, P\{X = 0\} = \frac{2}{5} \times \frac{2}{3} = \frac{4}{15}, \text{ and}$$

$$P\{X = 1 \mid Y = 1\} = P\{Y = 1 \mid X = 1\}\, P\{X = 1\} = \frac{1}{5} \times \frac{1}{3} = \frac{1}{15}.$$

Summarizing these results in the following table, we see:

	0	1	$P\{Y = y\}$
0	$\dfrac{6}{15}$	$\dfrac{4}{15}$	$\dfrac{10}{15}$
1	$\dfrac{4}{15}$	$\dfrac{1}{15}$	$\dfrac{5}{15}$
$P\{X = x\}$	$\dfrac{10}{15}$	$\dfrac{5}{15}$	

This is the joint distribution of X and Y, with the marginal distribution indicated. The conditional distribution of Y given X is

$$P\{Y = y | X = x\} = \frac{P\{Y = y, X = x\}}{P\{X = x\}} \begin{cases} \dfrac{6/15}{10/15} = \dfrac{3}{5} & x = y = 0 \\[2mm] \dfrac{4/15}{5/15} = \dfrac{4}{5} & x = 1; y = 0 \\[2mm] \dfrac{4/15}{10/15} = \dfrac{2}{5} & x = 0; y = 1 \\[2mm] \dfrac{1/15}{5/15} = \dfrac{1}{5} & x = y = 1 \end{cases}$$

For any fixed value of X, we see that $f(y \mid x) = P\{Y = y | X = x\}$ is a proper probability distribution for Y since

$$\sum_{y=0}^{1} P\{Y = y | X = 0\} = P\{Y = 0 \mid X = 0\} + P\{Y = 1 \mid X = 0\} = \frac{3}{5} + \frac{2}{5} = 1$$

and

$$\sum_{y=0}^{1} P\{Y = y | X = 1\} = P\{Y = 0 \mid X = 1\} + P\{Y = 1 \mid X = 1\} = \frac{1}{5} + \frac{4}{5} = 1.$$

Consider the joint distribution of X and Y given in the form of a table below. The cell (i, j) corresponds to the joint probability that X = i, Y = j, for i = 1, 2, 3, j = 1, 2, 3.

	1	2	3
1	0	$\frac{1}{6}$	$\frac{1}{6}$
2	$\frac{1}{6}$	0	$\frac{1}{6}$
3	$\frac{1}{6}$	$\frac{1}{6}$	0

Check that this is a proper probability distribution. What are the marginal distributions of X and Y?

SOLUTION:

A joint probability mass function gives the probabilities of events. These events are composed of the results of two (or more) experiments. An example might be the toss of two dice. In this case, each event of outcome has two numbers associated with it. The numbers are the outcomes from the toss of each die. The probability distribution of the pair (X, Y) is

$$P\{X = i, Y = j\} = \frac{1}{36} \qquad i = 1, 2, 3, 4, 5, 6 \qquad j = 1, 2, 3, 4, 5, 6$$

Another example is the toss of two dice where X = number observed on first die; Y = the larger of the two numbers.

In order for f(x, y) = P {X = x, Y = y} to be a proper joint probability, the sum of P {X = x, Y = y} over all points in the sample space must equal 1. Also, each probability must be nonnegative.

In the case of the pair of tossed dice,

$$\sum_x \sum_y P\{X = x, Y = y\} = \sum_{i=1}^{6} \sum_{j=1}^{6} \frac{1}{36} = \frac{6}{36} \cdot \frac{6}{36} = \frac{6 \cdot 6}{36} = 1.$$

Thus, this is a proper probability distribution. In our original example, it is clear that each probability is nonnegative. Also,

237

$$\sum_{i=1}^{3} \sum_{j=1}^{3} P\{X = i, Y = j\}$$

$$= \sum_{i=1}^{3} [P\{X = i, Y = 1\} + P\{X = i, Y = 2\} + P\{X = i, Y = 3\}]$$

$$= \sum_{i=1}^{3} P\{X = i, Y = 1\} + \sum_{i=1}^{3} P\{X = i, Y = 2\} + \sum_{i=1}^{3} P\{X = i, Y = 3\}$$

$$= \left(0 + \frac{1}{6} + \frac{1}{6}\right) + \left(\frac{1}{6} + 0 + \frac{1}{6}\right) + \left(\frac{1}{6} + \frac{1}{6} + 0\right)$$

$$= \frac{1}{3} + \frac{1}{3} + \frac{1}{3} = 1$$

Thus, the probability distribution specified in the table is a proper distribution. We can compute the individual probability distributions of X and Y. These are called the marginal distributions of X and Y and are calculated in the following way.

We wish to find the probability that $X = 1, 2, 3$. For example,
$$P\{X = 1\} = P\{X = 1, Y = 1, 2, \text{ or } 3\}.$$

Because the events "$X = 1, Y = 1$," "$X = 1, Y = 2$," "$X = 1, Y = 3$" are mutually exclusive,
$$P\{X = 1\} = P\{X = 1, Y = 1\} + P\{X = 1, Y = 2\} + P\{X = 1, Y = 3\}$$

$$= \sum_{i=1}^{3} P\{X = 1, Y = i\}$$

Thus, $P\{X = 1\} = 0 + \dfrac{1}{6} + \dfrac{1}{6} = \dfrac{1}{3}.$

Similarly, $P\{X = 2\} = \displaystyle\sum_{i=1}^{3} P\{X = 2, Y = i\} = \dfrac{1}{6} + 0 + \dfrac{1}{6} = \dfrac{1}{3},$

and $\quad P\{X = 3\} = \displaystyle\sum_{i=1}^{3} P\{X = 3, Y = i\} = \dfrac{1}{6} + \dfrac{1}{6} + 0 = \dfrac{1}{3}.$

We similarly compute the marginal probabilities of Y as
$$P\{Y = 1\} = P\{X = 1, Y = 1\} + P\{X = 2, Y = 1\} + P\{X = 3, Y = 1\}$$

$$= 0 + \frac{1}{6} + \frac{1}{6} = \frac{2}{6} = \frac{1}{3},$$

$$P\{Y = 2\} = \sum_{j=1}^{3} P\{X = j, Y = 2\} = \frac{1}{6} + 0 + \frac{1}{6} = \frac{1}{3}, \text{ and}$$

$$P\{Y = 3\} = \sum_{j=1}^{3} P\{X = j,\ Y = 3\} = \frac{1}{6} + \frac{1}{6} + 0 = \frac{1}{3}.$$

To see why these are called marginal probabilities we examine the way they were computed. The marginal probabilities of X were found by summing along the rows of the table of the joint distribution. The marginal probabilities of Y were found by summing along the columns of the table of the joint distribution. The probabilities resulting from these summations are often placed in the margins as in the table below, hence the name marginal probabilities.

Consider the table representing the joint distribution between X' and Y'.

	1	2	3
1	$\frac{1}{9}$	$\frac{1}{9}$	$\frac{1}{9}$
2	$\frac{1}{9}$	$\frac{1}{9}$	$\frac{1}{9}$
3	$\frac{1}{9}$	$\frac{1}{9}$	$\frac{1}{9}$

Find the marginal distributions of X' and Y'. Are X' and Y' independent? In the previous problem, were X and Y independent?

SOLUTION:

The marginal distributions of X' and Y' are found by summing across the rows and columns of the table above. That is,

$$P\{X' = 1\} = \sum_{i=1}^{3} P\{X' = 1,\ Y' = i\} = \frac{1}{9} + \frac{1}{9} + \frac{1}{9} = \frac{1}{3},$$

$$P\{X' = 2\} = \sum_{i=1}^{3} P\{X' = 2,\ Y' = i\} = \frac{1}{9} + \frac{1}{9} + \frac{1}{9} = \frac{1}{3},\ \text{and}$$

239

$$P\{X' = 3\} = \sum_{i=1}^{3} P\{X' = 3, Y' = i\} = \frac{1}{9} + \frac{1}{9} + \frac{1}{9} = \frac{1}{3}.$$

Similarly, $P\{Y' = 1\} = \sum_{j=1}^{3} P\{X' = j, Y' = i\} = \frac{1}{9} + \frac{1}{9} + \frac{1}{9} = \frac{1}{3},$

$$P\{X' = 2\} = \sum_{j=1}^{3} P\{X' = j, Y' = 2\} = \frac{1}{9} + \frac{1}{9} + \frac{1}{9} = \frac{1}{3}, \text{ and}$$

$$P\{X' = 3\} = \sum_{j=1}^{3} P\{X' = j, Y' = 3\} = \frac{1}{9} + \frac{1}{9} + \frac{1}{9} = \frac{1}{3}.$$

The marginal distributions are hence

$$P\{X' = x\} = \begin{cases} \dfrac{1}{3} & x = 1, 2, 3 \\ 0 & \text{otherwise} \end{cases}$$

and

$$P\{Y' = y\} = \begin{cases} \dfrac{1}{3} & y = 1, 2, 3 \\ 0 & \text{otherwise} \end{cases}.$$

Two random variables, X and Y, will be independent if and only if
$P\{X = x, Y = y\} = P\{X = x\} P\{Y = y\}$, for all x and y.
Checking X' and Y', we see that for all x and y,

$$P\{X' = x, Y' = y\} = \frac{1}{9} = P\{X' = x\} P\{Y' = y\} = \frac{1}{3} \times \frac{1}{3} = \frac{1}{9}.$$

In the previous problem, consider $P\{X = i, Y = i\}$ for $i = 1, 2, 3$. Now

$$P\{X = i\} P\{Y = i\} = \frac{1}{3} \times \frac{1}{3} = \frac{1}{9}$$

for $i = 1, 2, 3$, but the joint probability function specifies that
$P\{X = i, Y = i\} = 0$ for $i = 1, 2, 3$. Thus,
$P\{X = i\} P\{Y = i\} \neq P\{X = i, Y = i\}$
and X and Y are not independent.

Consider the experiment of tossing two tetrahedra (regular four-sided polyhedron) each with sides labeled 1 to 4.

Let X denote the number on the downturned face of the first tetrahedron and Y the larger of the two downturned numbers. Find the joint density of X and Y.

SOLUTION:

The values that a pair (X, Y) may assume are:

    (1, 1) (1, 2) (1, 3) (1, 4)

    (2, 2) (2, 3) (2, 4)

    (3, 3) (3, 4)

    (4, 4)

The probability that two numbers are observed as the downturned faces of the tetrahedra is $P\{X_1 = x, X_2 = t\}$ for $x = 1, 2, 3, 4$

$$t = 1, 2, 3, 4 \, .$$

Let X_1 = the result of the toss of the first tetrahedron,

        X_2 = the result of the toss of the second tetrahedron.

If all outcomes of X_1 and X_2 are equally likely, then

$$P\{X_1 = x, X_2 = t\} = \frac{1}{16} \text{ for } x = 1, 2, 3, 4$$

$$t = 1, 2, 3, 4 \, .$$

We calculate the probabilities of X and Y in terms of the probabilities for X_1 and X_2 as

$$P\{X = 1, Y = 1\} = P\{X_1 = 1, X_2 = 1\} = \frac{1}{16} \text{ and}$$

$$P\{X = 1, Y = 2\} = P\{1 \text{ die is } 1 \text{ and } Y = \max\{X_1, X_2\} = 2\}$$

$$= P\{X_1 = 1, X_2 = 2\} = \frac{1}{16} \, .$$

Similarly, $P\{X = 1, Y = 3\} = P\{1 \text{ die is } 1 \text{ and } Y = \max\{X_1, X_2\} = 3\}$

$$= P\{X_1 = 1, X_2 = 3\} = \frac{1}{16}$$

and $P\{X = 1, Y = 4\} = P\{1 \text{ die is } 1 \text{ and } Y = \max\{X_1, X_2\} = 4\}$

$$= P\{X_1 = 1, X_2 = 4\} = \frac{1}{16} \, .$$

But $P\{X = 2, Y = 1\} = 0$; it is impossible for 1 toss to be 2 and the larger of the two tosses to be 1.

For the same reasons $P\{X = 3, Y = 1\} = 0$ and $P\{X = 4, Y = 1\} = 0$. Also
$$P\{X = 3, Y = 2\} = P\{X = 4, Y = 3\} = P\{X = 4, Y = 2\} = 0.$$
Continuing,
$$P\{X = 2, Y = 2\} = P\{X_1 = 2, \max\{X_1, X_2\} = 2\} = P\{X_1 = 2, X_2 = 1 \text{ or } 2\}$$

$$= P\{X_1 = 2, X_2 = 1\} + P\{X_1 = 2, X_2 = 2\} = \frac{1}{16} + \frac{1}{16} = \frac{1}{8},$$

$$P\{X = 2, Y = 3\} = P\{X_1 = 2, \max\{X_1, X_2\} = 3\} = P\{X_1 = 2, X_2 = 3\} = \frac{1}{16},$$

$$P\{X = 2, Y = 4\} = P\{X_1 = 2, \max\{X_1, X_2\} = 4\} = P\{X_1 = 2, X_2 = 4\} = \frac{1}{16},$$

$P\{X = 3, Y = 3\} = P\{X_1 = 3, \max\{X_1, X_2\} = 3\} = P\{X_1 = 3, X_2 = 1, 2,$
    or 3$\}$
$$= P\{X_1 = 3, X_2 = 1\} + P\{X_1 = 3, X_2 = 2\} + P\{X_1 = 3, X_2 = 3\}$$

$$= \frac{1}{16} + \frac{1}{16} + \frac{1}{16} = \frac{3}{16},$$

$P\{X_1 = 3, Y = 4\} = P\{X_1 = 3, \max\{X_1, X_2\} = 4\} = P\{X_1 = 3, X_2 = 4\} =$

$$\frac{1}{16}, \text{ and}$$

$P\{X_1 = 4, X_2 = 4\} = P\{X_1 = 4, \max\{X_1, X_2\} = 4\} = P\{X_1 = 4, X_2 = 1, 2,$
    3, or 4$\}$

$P\{X_1 = 4, X_2 = 1\} + P\{X_1 = 4, X_2 = 2\} + P\{X_1 = 4, X_2 = 3\} + P\{X_1 = 4,$
    $X_2 = 4\}$

$$= \frac{4}{16} = \frac{1}{4}.$$

Thus, the distribution for X and Y is:

	1	2	3	4	$P\{Y = y\}$
1	$\dfrac{1}{16}$	0	0	0	$\dfrac{1}{16}$
2	$\dfrac{1}{16}$	$\dfrac{2}{16}$	0	0	$\dfrac{1}{16}$
3	$\dfrac{1}{16}$	$\dfrac{1}{16}$	$\dfrac{3}{16}$	0	$\dfrac{5}{16}$
4	$\dfrac{1}{16}$	$\dfrac{1}{16}$	$\dfrac{1}{16}$	$\dfrac{4}{16}$	$\dfrac{7}{16}$
$P\{X = x\}$	$\dfrac{4}{16}$	$\dfrac{4}{16}$	$\dfrac{4}{16}$	$\dfrac{4}{16}$	

The marginal probabilities of X and Y are given and we see that they are dependent random variables because
$$P\{X = x, \, Y = y\} \neq P\{X = x\} \, P\{Y = y\}.$$

Show, by altering the joint density of X and Y in the previous problem, that it is not always possible to construct a unique joint distribution from a pair of given marginal distributions.

SOLUTION:

The joint density of X and Y with its marginal distributions is given by the table below:

		1	2	3	4
	1	$\frac{1}{16}$	0	0	0
	2	$\frac{1}{16}$	$\frac{2}{16}$	0	0
	3	$\frac{1}{16}$	$\frac{1}{16}$	$\frac{3}{16}$	0
	4	$\frac{1}{16}$	$\frac{1}{16}$	$\frac{1}{16}$	$\frac{4}{16}$
$P\{X = x\}$		$\frac{4}{16}$	$\frac{4}{16}$	$\frac{4}{16}$	$\frac{4}{16}$

Imagine that we are given the marginal distributions of X and Y above and asked to construct the joint distribution of X and Y. There are an infinite number of possibilities for this distribution, as seen by the table below. For any ε, $0 < \varepsilon < \dfrac{1}{16}$, this joint distribution will yield the given marginal distributions. Thus, these marginal distributions do not specify a unique joint distribution.

243

	1	2	3	4
1	$\frac{1}{16} - \varepsilon$	ε	0	0
2	$\frac{1}{16} + \varepsilon$	$\frac{2}{16} - \varepsilon$	0	0
3	$\frac{1}{16}$	$\frac{1}{16}$	$\frac{3}{16}$	0
4	$\frac{1}{16}$	$\frac{1}{16}$	$\frac{1}{16}$	$\frac{4}{16}$
$P\{X = x\}$	$\frac{4}{16}$	$\frac{4}{16}$	$\frac{4}{16}$	$\frac{4}{16}$

● **PROBLEM 8-6**

Two individuals agree to meet at a certain spot sometime between 5:00 and 6:00 P.M. They will each wait 10 minutes starting from when they arrive. If the other person does not show up during that 10-minute interval, they will leave. Assume the arrival times of the two individuals are independent and uniformly distributed over the hour-long interval. Find the probability that the two will actually meet.

SOLUTION:

Let X be the arrive time of the first individual and Y be the arrive time of the second individual. Then X and Y have uniform distributions over any hour-long period, thus in minutes the densities are:

$$f(x) = \frac{1}{60} \qquad 0 < x < 60$$

$$g(y) = \frac{1}{60} \qquad 0 < y < 60$$

Furthermore, X and Y are independent. Thus, the joint density of X and Y will be the product of the individual density functions.

$$h(x, y) = f(x)\, g(y) = \begin{cases} \dfrac{1}{60} \times \dfrac{1}{60} & 0 < x < 60 \text{ and } 0 < y < 60 \\ 0 & \text{otherwise} \end{cases}$$

We now try to formulate the event "a meeting takes place" in terms of X and Y.

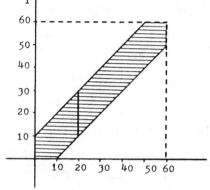

Consider the shaded region above. If the point (x, y) lies within this shaded region, a meeting will take place. To see that this is true, we arbitrarily test the point $X = 20$. If $X = 20$, the first individual arrives at 5:20. If the second individual arrived at any time between 5:10 and 5:30 there will be a meeting. Thus, Y may take on a value between 10 and 30. This region is described mathematically by $|X - Y| < 10$. The absolute value signs reflect the fact that the order of arrival is unimportant in assuring a meeting, only the proximity or closeness of the arrival times is important. Thus, $P\{\text{a meeting}\} = P\{|X - Y| < 10\}$ equals the volume over the shaded region in the x–y plane under $f(x, y)$.

This volume can be divided into three regions, A_1, A_2, A_3.

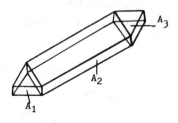

The volume of A_2 is the volume of a rectangular parellelapiped (box-shaped region), and A_1 and A_3 are right prisms of equal volume.

The volume of A_2 is length × width × height

$$= \left(10\sqrt{2}\right)\left(50\sqrt{2}\right)\left(\frac{1}{3,600}\right)$$

$$= 2 \ (500) \ \left(\frac{1}{3,600}\right)$$

And the volume of A_3 and A_1 each is (area of base) × height

$$= \frac{1}{2} (10) \, (10) \left(\frac{1}{3,600}\right)$$

$$= \frac{50}{3,600}$$

Thus, $P \, \{| \, X - Y \, | < 10\} = $ Volume of A_2 + Volume of A_1 + Volume of A_3

$$= \frac{1,000}{3,600} + \frac{50}{3,600} + \frac{50}{3,600} = \frac{1,100}{3,600} = \frac{11}{36}.$$

● PROBLEM 8-7

Two continuous random variables, X and Y, may also be jointly distributed. Suppose (X, Y) has a distribution which is uniform over a unit circle centered at (0, 0). Are X and Y independent?

SOLUTION:

The pairs of points (X, Y) lie in the unit circle with center at (0, 0).

The probability that a random point (X, Y) lies in a particular region of this circle is given by the volume over the region, A, and under a joint density function $f(x, y)$.

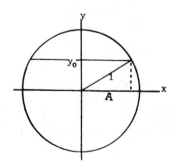

In the case of the uniform joint density function, the density function is a constant such that the total volume over some area in the (x, y) plane and under $f(x, y) = c > 0$ is 1.

The total area of the unit circle is πr^2, where $r = 1$. Thus, the area is π. In order for the total volume to equal 1,

$$c\pi = 1 \text{ or } c = \frac{1}{\pi} .$$

Thus, $f(x, y) = \begin{cases} \dfrac{1}{\pi} & \text{for } x^2 + y^2 < 1 \\ 0 & \text{otherwise} \end{cases}$.

Now X and Y will be independent if and only if the joint density is the product of the marginal densities or $f(x, y) = g(x) \, h(y)$ for each (x, y) pair. But this is impossible, since the range of y depends on the value of x. Thus, x and y are not independent.

● **PROBLEM 8-8**

Given that

$$f(x, y) = \begin{cases} 2 & x + y < 1, \ x \geq 0, \ y > 0 \\ 0 & \text{otherwise} \end{cases} .$$

Are x and y independent?

SOLUTION:

For x and y to be independent, it would need to be true that the range of y does not depend upon the value of x. But when x is 0, the range of y is $(0, 1)$, and when x is 1, y must be 0. Thus, x and y are not independent.

Let X and Y be jointly distributed with density function

$$f(x, y) = \begin{cases} \dfrac{1}{1-x} & 0 < x < 1, \; 0 < y < 1 \\ 0 & \text{otherwise} \end{cases}.$$

Find $F(\lambda \mid X > Y) = P\{X \le \lambda \mid X > Y\}$.

SOLUTION:

By the definition of conditional probability,

$$P\{A \mid B\} = \frac{P\{A \text{ and } B\}}{P\{B\}}.$$

Thus, $F(\lambda \mid X > Y) = P\{X \le \lambda \mid X > Y\}$

$$= \frac{P\{X \le \lambda \text{ and } X > Y\}}{P\{X > Y\}}.$$

The shaded region represents the area where $X \le \lambda$ and $X > Y$. Thus, $P\{X \le \lambda$ and $X > Y\}$ is the volume over the shaded region under the curve

$$f(x, y) = \frac{1}{1-x}.$$

This volume is that of a right prism. Thus, $P\{X \le \lambda$ and $X > Y\}$ = volume of the right prism whose base is the shaded region in the figure and whose height is 1.

Thus, $P\{X \le \lambda$ and $X > Y\}$ = (area of base) × height = $\dfrac{1}{2}\lambda \times \lambda \times 1 = ZZ$,

and $P\{X > Y\}$ equals the volume over the triangle with vertices $(0, 0)$, $(1, 1)$, and $(1, 0)$ and under $f(x, y) = 1$.

This solid is in the shape of a right prism with a base of area $\frac{1}{2}$ and a height of 1. The volume of this region is thus $\frac{1}{2} \times 1 = \frac{1}{2}$ and $P\{X > Y\} = \frac{1}{2}$. Thus,

$$\frac{P\{X \le \lambda \text{ and } X > y\}}{P\{X > Y\}} = \frac{\lambda^2/2}{1/2} = \lambda^2 .$$

The conditional CDF for X given $X > Y$ is therefore

$$P\{X \le \lambda \mid X > Y\} = \begin{cases} \lambda^2 & 0 < \lambda < 1 \\ 0 & \lambda < 0 \\ 1 & \lambda > 1 \end{cases}$$

● PROBLEM 8–10

Let a random variable Y represent the diameter of a shaft and a random variable X represent the inside diameter of the housing that is intended to support the shaft. By design the shaft is to have diameter 99.5 units and the housing inside diameter 100 units. If the manufacturing process of each of the items is imperfect, so that in fact Y is uniformly distributed over the interval (98.5, 100.5) and X is uniformly distributed over (99, 101), what is the probability that a particular shaft can be successfully paired with a particular housing, when "successfully paired" is taken to mean that $X - h < Y < X$ for some small positive quantity h? Assume that X and Y are independent, and $h < 0.5$.

SOLUTION:

Consider the following diagram.

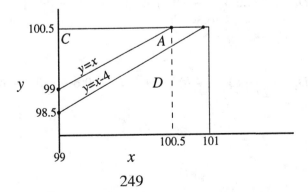

249

The shaft can be successfully paired with the housing if $x - h < y < x$. This occurs, for a given value of X, when Y falls between the lines $Y = X - h$ and $Y = X$. Since we are dealing with a bivariate uniform distribution, the probability is the ratio of the area between these two lines to the area between (99, 101) and (98.5, 100.5). Thus, P {successful pairing} = $^A/_B$, where A is the area between the lines and B is the total area. Now $B = (101 - 99)$ $(100.5 - 98.5) = (2)(2) = 4$. To find A, we notice that $A = B - C - D$, where C is the area of the upper-left triangle and D is the area of the lower-right region. Now

$$C = \left(\frac{1}{2}\right)(100.5 - 99.0)(100.5 - 99.0)$$

$$= \left(\frac{1}{2}\right)(1.5)(1.5)$$

$$= \frac{2.25}{2} = 1.125$$

and D can be further subdivided as in the following diagram:

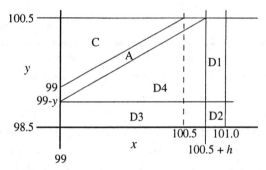

Now, $D_1 = [101.0 - (100.5 + h)] \times [100.5 - (99.0 - h)]$
$= [0.5 - h][1.5 + h]$
$= [0.75 - h - h^2],$

$D_2 = [(99.0 - h) - 98.5] \times [101.0 - (100.5 + h)]$
$= [0.5 - h][0.5 - h]$
$= 0.25 + h^2 - h,$

$D_3 = [(100.5 + h) - 99.0] \times [(99.0 - h) - 98.5]$
$= [1.5 + h][0.5 - h]$
$= 0.75 - h - h^2$

$D_4 = \left(\frac{1}{2}\right)[(100.5 + h) - 99.0] \times [100.5 - (99.0 - h)]$

250

$$= \frac{1}{2} \, [1.5 + h] \, [1.5 + h]$$

$$= \frac{1}{2} \, [2.25 + h^2 + 3h].$$

Thus

$$D = D_1 + D_2 + D_3 + D_4$$

$$= (0.75 - h - h^2) + (0.25 + h^2 - h) + (0.75 - h - h^2)$$

$$+ \, (1.125 + \frac{1}{2} h^2 + 1.5h)$$

$$= 2.875 - \frac{1}{2} h^2 - 1.5h$$

Finally

$$A = B - C - D = 4 - 1.125 - (2.875 - \frac{1}{2} h^2 - 1.5h)$$

$$= \frac{h^2}{2} + \frac{3h}{4} = \frac{h^2 + 3h}{2},$$

and

$$P \, \{\text{successful pairing}\} = \frac{A}{B} = \frac{\left[\dfrac{h^2 + 3h}{2} \right]}{4}$$

$$= \frac{h^2 + 3h}{8}$$

SHORT ANSWER QUESTIONS FOR REVIEW

Choose the correct answer.

1. From $\dfrac{P\{X=0, Y=0\}}{P\{X=0\}} = P\{Y=0, X=0\}$, we can obtain

    (a) $P\{X=0, Y=0\} = P\{Y=0\}\ P\{X=0\}$.

    (b) $P\{Y=0\} = P\{Y=0\}\ P\{Y=0, X=0\}$.

    (c) $P\{X=0, Y=0\} = P\{X=0\}\ P\{Y=0, X=0\}$.

    (d) $P\{Y=0\} = P\{X=0\}\ P\{Y=0, X=0\}$.

2. The individual probability distributions of X and Y are called (a) joint distributions. (b) marginal distributions. (c) discrete distributions. (d) uniform distributions.

    For problems 3 and 4 below, use the following information.

    If there is a bag of nine marbles, three of which are black and six of which are white, and if black corresponds to m and white corresponds to n, then:

3. $P\{Y=n \mid X=m\}$ means (a) the probability that the first marble is not black and the second marble is not black. (b) the probability that the first marble is not white and the second marble is not black. (c) the probability that the first marble is white and the second marble is black. (d) the probability that the first marble is black and the second marble is white.

4. $P\{Y=m \mid X=m\}$ means (a) the probability that the first marble is white and the second marble is white. (b) the probability that the first marble is black and the second marble is white. (c) the probability that the first marble is black and the second marble is black. (d) the probability that the first marble is white and the second marble is black.

Fill in the blanks.

5. A multivariate probability function with two discrete random variables involved is called the ____ probability function.

For problems 6–8 refer to the joint distribution table below.

		X		
		1	2	3
Y	1	$\dfrac{1}{12}$		$\dfrac{1}{6}$ · $\dfrac{1}{3}$
	2		$\dfrac{1}{4}$	$\dfrac{1}{12}$
		$\dfrac{5}{12}$		$\dfrac{1}{4}$

6. The missing values in the second column are ____ (top), $\dfrac{1}{4}$, and ____ (bottom).

7. The missing values in the second row are ____ , $\dfrac{1}{4}$, $\dfrac{1}{12}$, and ____ .

8. The marginal distribution of X is ____ , ____ , ____ .

Determine whether the following statements are true or false.

9. In the above joint distribution table, X and Y are independent.

10. A discrete distribution is a distribution with a finite number of set members.

11. Two random variables, X and Y, will be independent if, and only if, P {X = x, Y = y} = P {X = x} P {Y = y} for all x and y.

12. In order for $f(x, y) = $ P {X = x, Y = y} to be a proper joint probability, the sum of P {X = x, Y = y} over all points in the sample space must equal 0.

ANSWER KEY

1. c

2. b

3. d

4. c

5. joint (bivariate also acceptable)

6. $\dfrac{1}{12}, \dfrac{1}{3}$

7. $\dfrac{1}{3}, \dfrac{2}{3}$

8. $\dfrac{5}{12}, \dfrac{1}{3}, \dfrac{1}{4}$

9. False

10. True

11. True

12. False

CHAPTER 9

FUNCTIONS OF RANDOM VARIABLES

CHANGE OF VARIABLE TECHNIQUE

● PROBLEM 9-1

Let X be a discrete random variable with probability mass function $f(x)$ $= \dfrac{1}{n}$, $x = 1, 2, 3, ..., n;$ $= 0$ otherwise. If $Y = X^2$, find the probability mass function of Y.

SOLUTION:

Since $Y = X^2$ as x takes the values 1, 2, 3, ..., n, y takes the values 1, 4, 9, ..., n^2. Thus,

$$P\{Y = r^2\} = P\{X = r\} = \frac{1}{n}, r = 1, 2, ..., n$$

and so $h(y) = \begin{cases} \dfrac{1}{n} & y = 1, 4, ..., n^2 \\ 0 & \text{otherwise} \end{cases}$.

If X is a discrete random variable with probability mass function

$$f(x) = \begin{cases} \dfrac{1}{2n} & x = \pm 1, \pm 2, \ldots, \pm n \\ 0 & \text{otherwise} \end{cases}$$

and $Y = X^2$, then find the probability mass function of Y.

SOLUTION:

Since $Y = X^2$,

$$P\{Y = r^2\} = P\{X^2 = r^2\} = P\{X = r \text{ or } X = -r\}$$
$$= P\{X = r\} + P\{X = -r\}$$

$$= \frac{1}{2n} + \frac{1}{2n} = \frac{1}{n} \qquad r = 1, 2, \ldots,$$

Thus, $h(y) = \dfrac{1}{n}, \begin{cases} y = 1, 4, 9, \ldots, n^2 \\ 0 \text{ otherwise} \end{cases}$.

Suppose X takes on the values 0, 1, 2, 3, 4, 5 with probabilities P_0, P_1, P_2, P_3, P_4, and P_5. If $Y = g(X) = (X - 2)^2$, what is the distribution of Y?

SOLUTION:

First, examine the values that the random variable Y may assume. If $X = 0$ or 4,

$$Y = (0 - 2)^2 = (4 - 2)^2 = 2^2 = 4.$$

If $\qquad X = 1$ or 3,

$$Y = (1 - 2)^2 = (3 - 2)^2 = 1^2 = 1.$$

If $\qquad X = 2$,

$$Y = (2 - 2)^2 = 0^2 = 0.$$

and if $X = 5$,

$$Y = (5 - 2)^2 = 3^2 = 9.$$

Thus, Y assumes the values 0, 1, 4, and 9. We now find the probability distribution of Y.

We calculate

$$P\{Y = 0\} = P\,[\{X - 2\}^2 = 0]$$
$$= P\{X = 2\} = P_2,$$
$$P\{Y = 1\} = P\,[\{X - 2\}^2 = 1] = P\{X = 1 \text{ or } X = 3\}$$
$$= P\{X = 1\} + P\{X = 3\} = P_1 + P_3,$$
$$P\{Y = 4\} = P\,[\{X - 2\}^2 = 4] = P\{X = 0 \text{ or } X = 4\}$$
$$= P\{X = 0\} + P\{X = 4\} = P_0 + P_4,$$

and

$$P\{Y = 9\} = P\,[\{X - 2\}^2 = 9]$$
$$= P\{X = 5\} = P_5 .$$

Therefore, the distribution of Y can be written

$$h(y) = \begin{cases} P_2 & y = 0 \\ P_1 + P_3 & y = 1 \\ P_0 + P_4 & y = 4 \\ P_5 & y = 9 \\ 0 & \text{otherwise} \end{cases}.$$

MOMENT GENERATING FUNCTION TECHNIQUE

● **PROBLEM 9-4**

Let X_i be 1 if the ith member of a litter survives one year, and 0 otherwise. Suppose X_1, ..., X_n are independent Bernoulli random variables, that is, $P\{X_i = 0\} = 1 - p$ and $P\{X_i = 1\} = p$ for $i = 1$, ..., n.

What is the distribution of $Y = \sum_{i=1}^{n} X_i$, the number of offspring which survive one year?

SOLUTION:

We have a sum of independent and identically distributed random variables. We find

$$P \{y = k\} = \binom{n}{k} p^k (1-p)^{n-k}$$

Thus, Y has a binomial distribution with parameters n and p.

● **PROBLEM 9-5**

Suppose that $X_1, \ldots, X_n$ are as in the last problem, but now $Z_i = 1$ if the ith member of the litter is male, and $Z_i = 0$ if the ith member of the litter is female. Find the distribution of the number of males which survive beyond one year, assuming that gender and survival are independent.

SOLUTION:

Let $W_i = X_i Z_i$, which is 1 for a male surviving one year and 0 otherwise. By independence,

$$P \{W_i = 1\} = P \{X_i Z_i = 1\} = P \{X_i = 1\} P \{Z_i = 1\} = (P)(0.5) = \frac{P}{2}$$

Thus, $\{W_i\}$ is a sequence of independent Bernoulli random variables with

parameter $\frac{P}{2}$. By the last problem, then, $Y = \sum_{i=1}^{n} W_i$ has a binomial

distribution with parameters n and $\frac{P}{2}$.

● **PROBLEM 9-6**

Assume $X_1, \ldots, X_n$ are independent and identically distributed exponential random variables each with parameter λ. For example, there may be n light bulbs with each being replaced by the next when it burns out. What is the total expected time of illumination? That is, what is the

expected value of $Y = \sum_{i=1}^{n} X_i$.

SOLUTION:

Since the expected value of the lifetime of each bulb is $\frac{1}{\lambda}$, we compute

$$E[y] = E\left[\sum_{i=1}^{n} X_i\right] = \sum_{i=1}^{n} E[X_i] = \sum_{i=1}^{n} \frac{1}{\lambda} = \frac{n}{\lambda}$$

● **PROBLEM 9-7**

Suppose that X has a normal distribution with mean zero and variance one. Let $Y = X^2$. Find the distribution of Y.

SOLUTION:

For any value k, $Fy (k) = P\{y < k\} = P\{x^2 < k\} = P\{-k < x < k\}$.

Now, this last expression can be evaluated, for any value k, by checking the normal table. It turns out that y has a chi-square distribution with one degree of freedom.

DISTRIBUTION FUNCTION TECHNIQUE

● **PROBLEM 9-8**

Two points, A and B, are chosen on the circumference of a circle so that the angle at the center is uniformly distributed over $(0, \pi)$. What is the probability that the length of AB exceeds the radius of the circle?

SOLUTION:

Let a be the radius of the circle, $\varnothing$ the central angle formed by the chord, and O the center of the circle. Note that line segment OA will equal OB in every random chord. Both of these segments are radii of the circle and

259

equal to a. Thus, triangle AOB is an isoceles triangle with angle $AOB = \emptyset$. Bisecting angle AOB produces two congruent right triangles with angles of $\frac{\pi}{2}, \frac{\emptyset}{2}$, and $\frac{\pi}{2} - \frac{\emptyset}{2}$. Thus,

$$\sin \frac{\emptyset}{2} = \frac{\frac{1}{2}AB}{a} \text{ or } AB = 2a \sin \frac{\emptyset}{2}.$$

We wish to find

$$P \{AB \geq a\} = P \{2a \sin \frac{\emptyset}{2} \geq a\}$$

$$= P \left\{\sin \frac{\emptyset}{2} \geq \frac{1}{2}\right\}$$

In the interval $(0, \pi)$ over which $\emptyset$ varies, $\sin \frac{\emptyset}{2}$ is strictly increasing and is thus invertible in this interval.

Therefore,

$$P \left\{\sin \frac{\emptyset}{2} \geq \frac{1}{2}\right\} = P \left\{\frac{\emptyset}{2} \geq \sin^{-1}\frac{1}{2}\right\} = P \left\{\frac{\emptyset}{2} \geq \frac{\pi}{6}\right\}$$

and

$$P \{AB \geq a\} = P \left\{\emptyset \geq \frac{\pi}{3}\right\}.$$

The probability density function for $\emptyset$ is given as

$$f(x) = \begin{cases} \dfrac{1}{\pi} & 0 \leq x \leq \pi \\ 0 & \text{otherwise} \end{cases}.$$

This is the uniform distribution over $(0, \pi)$. Thus,

$$P \left\{\emptyset \geq \frac{\pi}{3}\right\} = \frac{1}{\pi}\left(\pi - \frac{\pi}{3}\right)$$

$$= 1 - \frac{1}{3} = \frac{2}{3}$$

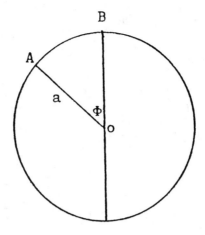

A certain river floods every year. Suppose the low watermark is set at one and the high mark, Y, has the distribution function

$$F(y) = P \{Y \le y\} = 1 - \frac{1}{y^2} \qquad 1 \le y < \infty.$$

What happens to the distribution if the low watermark is set at zero and the unit of measuring the height is $\frac{1}{10}$ of that used previously?

SOLUTION:

If the low watermark is set at zero and the unit of measuring the water height is $\frac{1}{10}$ of that previously used, then a conversion formula between the two systems of measurement may be devised. Let Z be a height measured under the new system and Y the height under the old system.

Then $Y = \frac{Z}{10} + 1$ will be an appropriate conversion formula. If the old system measures a height of one, then we wish a height of zero. Under the new system, if $Y = 1$, then $Z = 0$. If $Y = 2$, $Z = 10$.

We now use the cumulative distribution function technique to find the distribution Z from the distribution of Y. Thus,

$$P \{Z \le x\} = P \{10 \, (Y - 1) \le x\} = P \{Y \le \frac{x}{10} + 1\}$$

$$= 1 - \frac{1}{\left(\dfrac{x}{10}+1\right)^2} \quad \text{for } 1 \le \frac{x}{10} < \infty,$$

and

$$P\{Z \le x\} = 1 - \frac{100}{\left(10+x\right)^2} \quad 10 \le x < \infty.$$

An earlier example of a function of a random variable was the transformation between a random variable X that is distributed normally with mean μ and standard deviation σ and a random variable Z which is distributed normally with mean 0 and variance 1. Describe this transformation as a special case of the cumulative distribution technique for finding distributions of functions of random variables.

SOLUTION:

We wish to find $P\{X \le a\}$, given that we know $P\{Z \le c\}$ for most c. The distributions of X and Z are described above. Recall that to standardize a random variable, we subtracted the mean and divided by the standard deviation. Thus,

$$Z = \frac{X-\mu}{\sigma}.$$

Now $\quad P\{X \le a\} = P\left\{\dfrac{X-\mu}{\sigma} \le \dfrac{a-\mu}{\sigma}\right\} = P\{Z \le c\}$

where $c = \dfrac{a-\mu}{\sigma}$.

Let X be a random variable with an absolutely continuous cumulative distribution function $F(x) = P\{X \leq x\}$. Find the distribution of the random variable $U = F(X)$.

SOLUTION:

The distribution of the random variable U is found in the following way. An actual X value is observed, say $X = c$. Then the observed value of U is
$$u = P\{X \leq c\}.$$
To find the distribution of U, we wish to find the range of values that u may assume. Note that $F(x) = P(X \leq x)$ is between zero and one because it is a probability; hence, U ranges between zero and one.

Thus,

$$G(u) = P\{U \leq u\} = \begin{cases} 0 & u < 0 \\ P\{F(X) \leq u\} & 0 \leq u < 1. \\ 1 & 1 < u \end{cases}$$

But $P\{F(X) \leq u\} = P\{X \leq F^{-1}(u)\}$ where $F^{-1}(u) = x$ is the inverse function of F and is the smallest x such that $F(x) \geq u$.

Also,
$$P\{X \leq F^{-1}(u)\} = F\{F^{-1}(u)\} = u$$
for $0 < u < 1$ and

$$G(u) = \begin{cases} u & 0 < u < 1 \\ 0 & \text{otherwise} \end{cases}$$

and the density function of U is

$$G'(u) = g(u) = \begin{cases} 1 & 0 < u < 1 \\ 0 & \text{otherwise} \end{cases}.$$

Thus, U is uniformly distributed over the interval $[0,1]$. This transformation is known as the Probability Integral Transform.

Let $X_1, \ldots, X_n$ be independent random variables uniformly distributed over the interval $(0, 1)$. Find the distribution of $Y_n = \text{maximum}\ \{X_1, X_2, \ldots, X_n\}$.

SOLUTION:

We wish to find $P\{Y_n < y\}$. But if the maximum of X_1, ..., X_n is less than y, then it must be true that $X_1 < y$, $X_2 < y$, ..., $X_n < y$. Thus,
$$P\{Y_n < y\} = P\{X_1 < y, X_2 < y, ..., X_n < y\}.$$
By the independence of X_1, X_2, X_3, ..., X_n,
$$P\{X_1 < y, X_2 < y, ..., X_n < y\} = P\{X_1 < y\} P\{X_2 < y\} ... P\{X_n < y\}.$$
For $i = 1, ..., n$

$$P\{X_i < y\} = \begin{cases} y & 0 < y < 1 \\ 0 & \text{otherwise} \end{cases}.$$

This is the cumulative distribution of a uniformly distributed random variable with range $(0, 1)$. Thus,

$$P\{Y_n < y\} = \begin{cases} \underbrace{y \times y \times ... \times y}_{n \text{ terms}} & 0 < y < 1 \\ 0 & \text{otherwise} \end{cases}$$

or

$$P\{Y_n < y\} = \begin{cases} y^n & 0 < y < 1 \\ 0 & \text{otherwise} \end{cases}.$$

The density function of Y_n is

$$f(y) = \begin{cases} ny^{n-1} & 0 < y < 1 \\ 0 & \text{otherwise} \end{cases}.$$

● PROBLEM 9-13

Let X_1, ..., X_n represent the incomes of n randomly selected taxpayers. Assume that each observation is independent and has probability density function

$$f(x) = \begin{cases} \dfrac{\theta(x_0)^\theta}{x^{\theta+1}} & \text{for } x \geq x_0 \\ 0 & \text{otherwise} \end{cases}.$$

This is the Pareto distribution. Assume $\theta = 100$ and $x_0 = \$4,000$. Find the CDF of the minimum of the n observations. Note that the CDF is

$$F(x) = 1 - \left(\frac{x_0}{x}\right)$$

SOLUTION:

We first find $P\{Y_1 \le y\}$ where $Y_1 = \min\{X_1, X_2, \ldots, X_n\}$. Thus,

$$P\{Y_1 \le y\} = \begin{cases} 1 - P(Y_1 \ge y) & y > x_0 \\ 0 & y < x_0 \end{cases}.$$

But $Y_1 \ge y$ only if $X_1 \ge y, X_2 \ge y, \ldots, X_n \ge y$. Thus,

$$P\{Y_1 \ge y\} = P\{X_1 \ge y, X_2 \ge y, \ldots, X_n \ge y\}.$$

By the independence of the X_i,

$$P\{X_1 \ge y, X_2 \ge y, \ldots, X_n \ge y\} = P\{X_1 \ge y\} P\{X_2 \ge y\}, \ldots, P\{X_n \ge y\}.$$

For $i = 1, 2, 3, \ldots, n$,

$$P\{X_i \ge y\} = 1 - P\{X_i \le y\}, \text{ and}$$

$$P\{X_i \le y\} = 1 - \left(\frac{x_0}{y}\right)^\theta \text{ for } y > x_0$$

is the cumulative distribution function of each of the observations. Also,

$$P\{X_i \ge y\} = 1 - P\{X_i \le y\}$$

$$= 1 - \left[1 - \left(\frac{x_0}{y}\right)^\theta\right]$$

$$= \left(\frac{x_0}{y}\right)^\theta$$

Finally,

$$P\{Y_1 \ge y\} = P\{X_1 \ge y\} P\{X_2 \ge y\} \ldots P\{X_n \ge y\} \text{ for } y > x_0$$

$$= \underbrace{\left(\frac{x_0}{y}\right)^\theta \times \left(\frac{x_0}{y}\right)^\theta \times \ldots \times \left(\frac{x_0}{y}\right)^\theta}_{n \text{ terms}}$$

or

$$P\{Y_1 \le y\} = 1 - P\{Y_1 \ge y\}$$

$$= 1 - \left(\frac{x_0}{y}\right)^{n\theta} \quad y > x_0$$

265

Suppose X is uniformly distributed over the interval $(-\pi, \pi)$. Then the cumulative distribution of X is

$$F(x) = P\{X \le x\} = \int_{-\pi}^{x} \frac{1}{2\pi} dt = \frac{t}{2\pi}\Big|_{-\pi}^{x} = \begin{cases} 0 & x < -\pi \\ \dfrac{x+\pi}{2\pi} & -\pi < x < \pi \\ x \ge \pi \end{cases}$$

Find the distribution of
   a) $y = \cos X$ b) $Y = \sin X$ c) $Y = |X|$.

SOLUTION:

a)   We find the probability that $Y \le y$ as $P\{Y \le y\} = P\{\cos X \le y\}$. Over the interval $(-\pi, \pi)$ the cosine function is not one-to-one. For a single value of $y = \cos x$, there are two values of $x = \cos^{-1} y$. We also note that $\cos X \le y$ if and only if $\pi > X \ge \cos^{-1} y$ or $-\pi < X \le -\cos^{-1} y$. Thus, $P\{Y \le y\} = P\{\cos X \le y\}$

$$= \begin{cases} 0 & y < -1 \\ P\{\pi > X \ge \cos^{-1} y \text{ or } -\pi < X \le -\cos^{-1} y\} & -1 < y < 1 \\ 1 & y > 1 \end{cases}$$

For $-1 < y < 1$,
$$\begin{aligned} P\{Y \le y\} &= P\{\pi > X \ge \cos^{-1} y \text{ or } -\pi < X \le -\cos^{-1} y\} \\ &= P\{\pi > X \ge \cos^{-1} y\} + P\{-\pi < X \le -\cos^{-1} y\} \\ &= F(\pi) - F(\cos^{-1} y) + [F(-\cos^{-1} y) - F(-\pi)] \\ &= 1 - F(\cos^{-1} y) + F(-\cos^{-1} y) - 0 \\ &= 1 - \frac{\cos^{-1} y + \pi}{2\pi} + \frac{-\cos^{-1} y + \pi}{2\pi} \\ &= \frac{2\pi - \cos^{-1} y - \pi - \cos^{-1} y + \pi}{2\pi} \\ &= \frac{2\pi - 2\cos^{-1} y}{2\pi} = \frac{\pi - \cos^{-1} y}{\pi} \end{aligned}$$

Thus,

$$P\{Y \le y\} = \begin{cases} 0 & y < -1 \\ 1 - \dfrac{\cos^{-1} y}{\pi} & -1 < y < 1 \\ 1 & y > 1 \end{cases}$$

b) Let $G(u) = P\{Y = \sin X \le u\}$. Then

$$G(u) = P\{\sin X \le u\} = \begin{cases} 0 & u < -1 \\ ? & -1 < u < 1 \\ 1 & u > 1 \end{cases}$$

If $-1 < u < 1$, there are two possibilities, $-1 < u < 0$, or $0 \le u < 1$. From the graph of the sine function, we see that if $-1 \le u < 0$, then the values of x for which $\sin x \le u$ are $-\pi - \sin^{-1} u \le X \le \sin^{-1} u$. If $0 \le u \le 1$, then the values of X for which $\sin X \le u$ are $\pi \ge X \ge \pi - \sin^{-1} u$ and $-\pi \le X \le \sin^{-1} u$. Thus,

$$P\{\sin X \le u\} = P\{-\pi - \sin^{-1} u \le X \le \sin^{-1} u\}$$

for $-1 \le u < 0$ and

$$P\{\sin X \le u\} = P\{\pi \ge X \ge \pi - \sin^{-1} u \text{ or } -\pi \le X \le \sin^{-1} u\}$$

for $0 \le u < 1$. Now,

$$G(u) = F(\pi) - F(\pi - \sin^{-1} u) + [F(\sin^{-1} u) - F(-\pi)]$$

for $0 \le u < 1$ and

$$G(u) = F(\sin^{-1} u) - F(-\pi - \sin^{-1} u) \text{ for } -1 \le u < 0.$$

For $0 \le u \le 1$,

$$G(u) = 1 - \left[\frac{\pi - \sin^{-1} u + \pi}{2\pi} \right] + \left[\frac{\sin^{-1} u + \pi}{2\pi} - 0 \right]$$

$$= \frac{2\pi - (2\pi - \sin^{-1} u)}{2\pi} + \frac{\sin^{-1} u + \pi}{2\pi}$$

$$= \frac{\sin^{-1} u}{2\pi} + \frac{\sin^{-1} u + \pi}{2\pi} = \frac{2\sin^{-1} u + \pi}{2\pi}$$

and for $-1 \le u < 0$

$$G(u) = \frac{\sin^{-1} u + \pi}{2\pi} - \left[\frac{\pi - \sin^{-1} u + \pi}{2\pi} \right] = \frac{2\sin^{-1} u + \pi}{2\pi}.$$

Thus,

$$G(u) = \begin{cases} 0 & u < -1 \\ \dfrac{2\sin^{-1}u + \pi}{2\pi} & -1 < u < 1 \\ 1 & u > 1 \end{cases}.$$

c) To find the distribution of $Y = |X|$, we find

$$H(y) = P\{Y \le y\} = \begin{cases} 0 & y < 0 \\ P\{|X| \le y\} & \pi > y > 0 \\ 1 & y > \pi \end{cases}$$

But $|X| \le y$ only if $-y \le X \le y$. Thus for $\pi > y > 0$,
$$P\{|X| \le y\} = P\{-y \le X \le y\} = P\{X \le y\} - P\{X \le -y\}$$

$$= F(y) - F(-y) = \frac{y+\pi}{2\pi} - \left[\frac{-y+\pi}{2\pi}\right] = \frac{2y+\pi-\pi}{2\pi} = \frac{y}{\pi}.$$

Finally,

$$H(y) = P\{Y = |X| \le y\} = \begin{cases} 0 & y < 0 \\ \dfrac{y}{\pi} & \pi > y > 0 \\ 1 & y > \pi \end{cases}.$$

● **PROBLEM 9-15**

Let X and Y be independent, standard normal random variables, and let $R = \sqrt{X^2 + Y^2}$ be the distance of (X, Y) from $(0, 0)$. Find the distribution of R.

SOLUTION:

We shall find the distribution of R by quoting some of the previous results from problems in this chapter.

The random variables X^2 and Y^2 are independent and both are distributed with a chi-square distribution with one degree of freedom.

Then $X^2 + Y^2$ must be chi-square distributed with two degrees of freedom.

Then $X^2 + Y^2$ is exponentially distributed with parameter $\beta = \dfrac{1}{2}$.

Now $R = \sqrt{X^2 + Y^2}$ is the square root of an exponentially distributed random variable. We have shown that such a random variable is distributed with a Weibull distribution with parameters $\alpha = 1$, $\beta = 2$.

MULTIVARIATE FUNCTIONS

● PROBLEM 9-16

Suppose X and Y are independent random variables with densities $f(x)$ and $g(y)$. If $Z = XY$, graph the region $\{Z < k\}$.

SOLUTION:

This region is $\{Z < k\} = \{xy < k\}$, which is shown below.

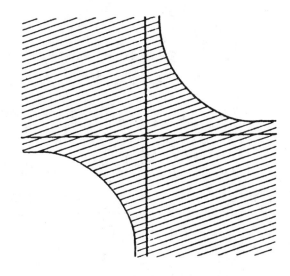

Let X_1, X_2, and X_3 be independent standard normal random variables. Define

$$Y_1 = X_1$$

$$Y_2 = \frac{X_1 + X_2}{2}$$

$$Y_3 = \frac{X_1 + X_2 + X_3}{3}$$

Among the Ys, which has the smallest variance? What is the practical application of this result?

SOLUTION:

Since $V(Y_1) = 1$, $V(Y_2) = \frac{1}{2}$, and $V(Y_3) = \frac{1}{3}$, Y_3 has the smallest variance.

This is important for experimenters, because it often turns out that a larger experiment will reduce the variance sufficiently to allow for the demonstration of the conclusions which the experimenter is looking for.

SHORT ANSWER QUESTIONS FOR REVIEW

Choose the correct answer.

1. Let X have a normal distribution with mean -2 and variance 9. Let $Y = 2X + 4$. Then the variance of Y is (a) 18. (b) 11. (c) 36. (d) 13.

2. Let X have a normal distribution with mean -2 and variance 9. Let $Y = 2X + 4$. Then the mean of Y is (a) 0. (b) 8. (c) -4. (d) -2.

3. Let X have a Poisson distribution with mean 2. Let $Y = 3X - 5$. Then the mean of Y is (a) 0. (b) 1. (c) 2. (d) 3.

4. Let X and Y each have a Bernoulli distribution with parameter 0.7. If X and Y are independent and $Z = X + Y$, then the distribution of Z is (a) Bernoulli. (b) Poisson. (c) binomial. (d) normal.

5. Let X and Y each have a normal distribution. If X and Y are independent and $Z = X + Y$, then the distribution of Z is (a) Bernoulli. (b) Poisson. (c) binomial. (d) normal.

6. Let X and Y each have a Poisson distribution. If X and Y are independent and $Z = X + Y$, then the distribution of Z is (a) Bernoulli. (b) Poisson. (c) binomial. (d) normal.

Fill in the blanks.

7. If X_i has a Poisson distribution with mean $\frac{1}{i}$, for $i = 1, 2, \ldots,$ and if these random variables are independent, the distribution of the sum of these random variables is _____ with mean _____ .

8. If X_i has a Bernoulli distribution with mean 0.3, for $i = 1, 2, \ldots, 10$, and if all these random variables are independent, then the distribution of $Y + \sum_{i=1 \text{ to } 10} X_i$ is _____ with parameters $n =$ _____ and $p =$ _____ .

9. If X_i has a normal distribution with mean 0 and variance 1 for $i = 1, 2, \ldots, 100$, and if all of these random variables are independent, then the distribution of $Y + \sum_{i=1 \text{ to } 100} X_i$ is _____ with mean _____ and variance _____ .

271

10. If X is a standard normal random variable, then the distribution of $Y = 10X - 7$ is _____ with mean _____ and variance _____ .

11. If X has a discrete uniform distribution with range $\{-1, 1\}$, then the distribution of $Y = \dfrac{X+1}{2}$ is _____ with parameter _____ .

Determine whether the following statements are true or false.

12. A function of a continuous random variable can be discrete.

13. A function of a discrete random variable can be continuous.

14. There is a one-to-one correspondence between distribution functions and moment generating functions.

15. If X is normally distributed with mean 5 and variance 4, then $Y = \dfrac{X-5}{2}$ has a standard normal distribution.

16. If $X_1, \ldots, X_n$ are independent and each has a Bernoulli distribution with parameter $\dfrac{1}{2}$, then $Y = \sum_{i=1 \text{ to } n} X_i$ has a Poisson distribution.

17. If X has a Poisson distribution with mean 4, then $Y = X - 4$ has a standard Poisson distribution with mean 0.

ANSWER KEY

1. c	2. a	3. b
4. c	5. d	6. b
7. Poisson, 2	8. binomial, 10, 0.3	9. normal, 0, 100
10. normal, −7, 100	11. Bernoulli, 0.5	12. True
13. False	14. True	15. True
16. False	17. False	

CHAPTER 10

SAMPLING THEORY

WEAK LAW OF LARGE NUMBERS

● PROBLEM 10-1

Suppose that some distribution with an unknown mean has variance equal to one. How large a sample must be taken in order that the probability will be at least 0.95 that the sample mean $\overline{X}_n$ will lie within 0.5 of the population mean?

SOLUTION:

This problem involves the Weak Law of Large Numbers. In order to establish the law, we must first verify the following lemma.

Lemma: Let X be a random variable and $g(X)$ a nonnegative function with the real line as a domain; then

$$P\{g(X) \geq K\} \leq \frac{E[g(X)]}{K} \text{ for all } K > 0.$$

This is the Weak Law of Large Numbers.
In the present problem, we want

$$P\{|\overline{X}_n - \mu| < 0.5\} \geq 0.95 = 1 - 0.05.$$

Comparing this with the general statement of the Weak Law of Large

Numbers, we set $e = 0.5$, and $\dfrac{\sigma^2}{n\varepsilon^2} = 0.05$. Multiplying through by $\dfrac{n}{0.05}$, we

see that we would need $n \geq \dfrac{\sigma^2}{0.05\varepsilon^2}$. Here

$$n \geq \frac{1}{(0.5)(0.05)^2} = \frac{1}{(0.05)(0.25)} = \frac{1}{0.0125}, \text{ or}$$

$$n \geq 80$$

We must therefore choose a sample of at least 80.

● **PROBLEM 10–2**

How large a sample must be taken in order that you are 99 percent certain that $\overline{X}_n$ is within $0.5\,\sigma$ of μ?

SOLUTION:

The general statement of the Weak Law of Large Numbers is

$$P\{|\,\overline{X}_n - \mu\,| < \varepsilon\} \geq 1 - \frac{\sigma^2}{n\varepsilon^2} .$$

We want

$$P\{|\,\overline{X}_n - \mu\,| < 0.5\sigma\} \geq 1 - 0.01 = 0.99.$$

We set $\varepsilon = 0.5\sigma$ and $\dfrac{\sigma^2}{n\varepsilon^2} = 0.01$. Multiplying through by $\dfrac{n}{0.01}$, we see

$$n = \frac{\sigma^2}{0.01\varepsilon^2} = \frac{\sigma^2}{0.01(0.05\sigma)^2} = \frac{\sigma^2}{0.01(0.25\sigma)^2} = \frac{1}{0.0025} = 400 .$$

THE CENTRAL LIMIT THEOREM

Briefly discuss the Central Limit Theorem.

SOLUTION:

The theorem has to do with the means of large (greater than 30) samples. As the sample size increases, the distribution of the sample mean, $\bar{X}$, has a distribution which is approximately normal. This distribution has a mean equal to the population mean and a standard deviation equal to the population standard deviation divided by the square root of the sample size.

Since $\bar{X}$ is approximately normal,

$$\frac{\bar{X} - E[\bar{X}]}{\sigma_{\bar{X}}} = \frac{\bar{X} - \mu}{\sigma/\sqrt{n}} = \frac{\sqrt{n}\,(\bar{X} - \mu)}{\sigma}$$

will have a standard normal distribution. Note that we require finite mean and variance.

For a large sample, the distribution of $\bar{X}$ is approximately normal if we are randomly sampling from a population with finite population mean and variance. Find the probability that the sample mean lies within
    a)   one standard error of the population mean.
    b)   two standard errors of the population mean.

SOLUTION:

    a)   The question asks what is $P\left\{\mu_{\bar{X}} - \sigma_{\bar{X}} < \bar{X} < \mu_{\bar{X}} + \sigma_{\bar{X}}\right\}$?
        If $\bar{X}$ is approximately normally distributed,

$$\frac{\bar{X} - \mu_{\bar{X}}}{\sigma_{\bar{X}}}$$

        will be approximately standard normal. Let $\mu_{\bar{X}} = \mu, \sigma_{\bar{X}} = \sigma$.

Note $P\{\mu - \sigma < \overline{X} < \mu + \sigma\}$

$$= P\left\{\frac{(\mu - \sigma) - \mu}{\sigma} < \frac{\overline{X} - \mu}{\sigma} < \frac{(\mu + \sigma) - \mu}{\sigma}\right\}$$

$= P\{-1 < \text{standard normal quantity} < 1\}$
$= 0.6826$ from the tables

b) We now want $P\{\mu_{\overline{X}} - 2\sigma_{\overline{X}} < \overline{X} < \mu_{\overline{X}} + 2\sigma_{\overline{X}}\}$.

Again assuming that $\overline{X}$ is approximately normally distributed,

$\dfrac{\overline{X} - \mu_{\overline{X}}}{\sigma_{\overline{X}}}$ will be approximately standard normal. Again, for ease of reading, let $\mu_{\overline{X}} = \mu, \sigma_{\overline{X}} = \sigma$.

Using a similar procedure,

$$P\{\mu_{\overline{X}} - 2\sigma_{\overline{X}} < \overline{X} < \mu_{\overline{X}} + 2\sigma_{\overline{X}}\} = P\left\{\frac{\mu - 2\sigma - \mu}{\sigma} < \frac{\overline{X} - \mu}{\sigma} < \frac{\mu + 2\sigma - \mu}{\sigma}\right\}$$

$= P\{-2 < \text{standard normal quantity} < 2\}$
$= 0.9544$ from the table

These problems can be completely generalized. Any normal distribution has 68.26 percent of the probability within one standard deviation of the mean and 95.44 percent within two.

● PROBLEM 10–5

A population of Australian Koala bears has a mean height of 20 inches and a standard deviation of 4 inches. You plan to choose a sample of 64 bears at random. What is the probability of a sample mean between 20 and 21?

SOLUTION:

Our method of attack will be to transform 20 and 21 into standard normal statistics. The sample is large enough, 64, so that the Central Limit Theorem will apply and $\dfrac{\sqrt{n}(\overline{X} - \mu)}{\sigma}$ will approximate a standard normal statistic. We want to know $P\{20 < \overline{X} < 21\}$. Equivalently, we want to know

$$P\left\{\frac{\sqrt{n}(20-\mu)}{\sigma} < \frac{\sqrt{n}(\overline{X}-\mu)}{\sigma} < \sqrt{n}(21-\mu)\right\}$$

or

$$P\left\{\frac{\sqrt{n}(20-\mu)}{\sigma} < Z < \frac{\sqrt{n}(21-\mu)}{\sigma}\right\}.$$

Substituting the values $n = 64$, $\mu = 20$, and $\sigma = 4$, we obtain

$$P\left\{\frac{\sqrt{64}(20-20)}{4} < Z < \frac{\sqrt{64}(21-20)}{4}\right\} = P\{0 < Z < 2\}.$$

From the standard normal table, this is 0.4772.

● PROBLEM 10-6

The mean diameter of marbles manufactured at a particular toy factory is 0.850 cm with a standard deviation of 0.010 cm. What is the probability of selecting a random sample of 100 marbles that has a mean diameter greater than 0.851 cm?

SOLUTION:

Our sample is of size 100, certainly large enough for the Central Limit Theorem to apply. We will use this theorem to assume that $\dfrac{\sqrt{n}(\overline{X}-\mu)}{\sigma}$ is a standard normal statistic.

We want to know $P\{\overline{X} > 0.851\}$. This is equivalent to

$$P\left\{\frac{\sqrt{n}(\overline{X}-\mu)}{\sigma} > \frac{\sqrt{n}(0.851-\mu)}{\sigma}\right\},$$

or, by the Central Limit Theorem,

$$P\left\{Z > \frac{\sqrt{n}(0.851-\mu)}{\sigma}\right\}.$$

Make the substitutions $\mu = 0.850$, $\sigma = 0.01$, and $n = 100$ to obtain

$$P\left\{Z > \frac{\sqrt{100}\,(0.851-0.850)}{0.01}\right\} = P\left\{Z > \frac{10(0.001)}{0.01}\right\} = P\{Z>1\}$$

$$= 1 - P\{Z < 1\} = 1 - 0.841 = 0.159,$$

from the standard normal tables.

An electrical firm manufactures a certain type of light bulb that has a mean life of 1,800 hours and a standard deviation of 200 hours.
  (a) Find the probability that a random sample of 100 bulbs will have an average life of more than 1,825 hours.
  (b) Find the probability that a random sample of 100 bulbs will have an average life of not more than 1,775 hours and not less than 1,760 hours.

SOLUTION:

(a) We have a large sample of 100. The Central Limit Theorem can therefore be used. The quantity $\dfrac{\sqrt{n}\,(X-\mu)}{\sigma}$ will be approximately standard normal. We are here asked for

$P\{\overline{X} > 1,825\}$.

This is equivalent to

$$P\left\{\frac{\sqrt{n}\,(X-\mu)}{\sigma} > \frac{\sqrt{n}\,(1,825-\mu)}{\sigma}\right\}.$$

Substituting $n = 100$, $\mu = 1,800$, and $\sigma = 200$, we obtain

$$P\left\{\frac{\sqrt{n}\,(X-\mu)}{\sigma} > \frac{\sqrt{100}\,(1,825-1,800)}{200}\right\}$$

$$= P\left\{\text{Standard Normal Quantity} > \frac{10(25)}{200}\right\}$$

$$= P\{Z > 1.25\} = 1 - 0.8944 = 0.1056,$$

from the standard normal tables.

(b) We now want $P\{1,760 < \overline{X} < 1,775\}$. We transform into standard normal quantities as follows:

$$P\left\{\frac{\sqrt{n}(1{,}760-\mu)}{\sigma}<\frac{\sqrt{n}(\overline{X}-\mu)}{\sigma}<\frac{\sqrt{n}(1{,}775-\mu)}{\sigma}\right\},$$

which is equal to

$$P\left\{\frac{\sqrt{n}(1{,}760-\mu)}{\sigma}<\text{Standard Normal Quantity}<\frac{\sqrt{n}(1{,}775-\mu)}{\sigma}\right\}.$$

Substituting $n = 100$, $\mu = 1{,}800$, and $\sigma = 200$, we obtain

$$P\left\{\frac{\sqrt{100}(1{,}760-1{,}800)}{200}<z<\frac{\sqrt{100}(1{,}775-1{,}800)}{200}\right\}$$

$$= P\left\{\frac{10(-40)}{200}<z<\frac{10(-25)}{200}\right\}$$

$$= P\{-2 < z < -1.25\} = P\{1.25 < z < 2\}$$

by the symmetry of the normal curve. Using the standard normal table, this is found to be 0.0828.

● PROBLEM 10-8

A manufacturing company receives a shipment of ball bearings each month from a supplier. The inspectors apply the following rule in deciding whether to accept or reject each shipment. A random sample of 36 bearings is selected and measured. If the mean diameter of the sample is between 0.245 and 0.255, the shipment is accepted; otherwise, it is rejected. What is the probability of accepting a shipment

(a) that has a mean diameter of 0.24 inches and a standard deviation of 0.015 inches?

(b) that has a mean diameter of 0.2515 inches and a standard deviation of 0.005 inches?

SOLUTION:

(a) The question rephrased is: for a sample of size 36 ($n = 36$) from a shipment that has $\mu = 0.24$ and $\sigma = 0.015$, what is $P\,(0.245 < \overline{X} < 0.255)$? This is equivalent to

$$P\left\{\frac{\sqrt{n}(0.245-\mu)}{\sigma}<\frac{\sqrt{n}(\overline{X}-\mu)}{\sigma}<\frac{\sqrt{n}(0.255-\mu)}{\sigma}\right\}$$

$$= P \left\{ \frac{\sqrt{36}(0.245 - 0.24)}{0.015} < \frac{\sqrt{n}(\overline{X} - \mu)}{\sigma} < \frac{\sqrt{36}(0.255 - 0.24)}{0.015} \right\}$$

$$= P \left\{ \frac{\sqrt{6}\,(0.005)}{0.015} < \frac{\sqrt{n}\,(\overline{X} - \mu)}{\sigma} < \frac{\sqrt{6}\,(0.015)}{0.015} \right\}$$

$$= P \left\{ 2 < \frac{\sqrt{n}(\overline{X} - \mu)}{\sigma} < 6 \right\}$$

A sample of size 36 is large enough for the Central Limit Theorem to apply. Hence, $\dfrac{\sqrt{n}(\overline{X} - \mu)}{\sigma}$ is approximately a standard normal quantity. We now have

$P\{2 < Z < 6\} \cong P\{Z > 2\}$,

since $P\{Z > 6\}$ is negligibly small; $P\{Z > 2\} = 0.0228$ from the table.

(b) We still want $P\{0.245 < \overline{X} < 0.255\}$, but now $n = 36$, $\mu = 0.2515$, and $\sigma = 0.005$. We perform the same series of operations,

$P\{0.245 < \overline{X} < 0.255\}$

$$= P \left\{ \frac{\sqrt{n}(0.245 - \mu)}{\sigma} < \overline{X} < \frac{\sqrt{n}(0.255 - \mu)}{\sigma} \right\}$$

$$= P \left\{ \frac{\sqrt{36}(0.245 - 0.2515)}{0.005} < \frac{\sqrt{n}(\overline{X} - \mu)}{\sigma} < \frac{\sqrt{36}(0.255 - 0.2515)}{0.005} \right\}$$

$$= P \left\{ \frac{6(-0.0065)}{0.005} > \text{Standard Normal Quantity} > \frac{6(0.0035)}{0.005} \right\}$$

$= P\{-7.8 < Z < 4.2\}$

$=$ virtually 1, from the standard normal table.

Suppose that light bulbs made by a standard process have an average life of 2,000 hours, with a standard deviation of 250 hours, and suppose that it is worthwhile to change the process if the mean life can be increased by at least 10 percent. An engineer wishes to test a proposed new process, and he is willing to assume that the standard deviation of the distribution of lives is about the same as for the standard process. How large a sample should he examine if he wishes the probability to be about 0.01 that he will fail to adopt the new process if in fact it produces bulbs with a mean life of 2,250 hours?

SOLUTION:

For the engineer to adopt the process the new mean must be a 10 percent increase over the old. Since 10 percent of 2,000 is 200, the new sample mean would have to be at least 2,200. Since we know that the true mean is 2,250, then $\overline{X} - \mu$ would have to be less than -50 in order to reject it. We want $P\{\overline{X} - \mu < -50\} = 0.01$. Divide by $\dfrac{\sigma}{\sqrt{n}}$ to obtain

$$P\left\{\frac{\overline{X}-\mu}{\sigma/\sqrt{n}} < -\frac{50}{\sigma/\sqrt{n}}\right\} = 0.01.$$

By the Central Limit Theorem, $\dfrac{\overline{X}-\mu}{\sigma/\sqrt{n}}$ is approximately a standard normal quantity. Hence, we have $P\left\{Z < \dfrac{50}{\sigma/\sqrt{n}}\right\} = 0.01$. The standard normal table tells us $P\{Z < -2.33\} = 0.01$; as a result set $-\dfrac{50}{\sigma/\sqrt{n}} = -2.33$. But since $\sigma = 250$, we have $\left(\dfrac{50}{250}\right)\sqrt{n} = 2.33$, $\sqrt{n} = 11.65$, $n = 135.7275$.

The sample should include at least 136 observations.

A research worker wishes to estimate the mean of a population using a sample large enough that the probability will be 0.95 that the sample mean will not differ from the population mean by more than 25 percent of the standard deviation. How large a sample should he take?

SOLUTION:

We want

$$P\left\{|\overline{X}-\mu|<\frac{\sigma}{4}\right\}=0.95.$$

Equivalently,

$$P\left\{-\frac{\sigma}{4}<\overline{X}-\mu<\frac{\sigma}{4}\right\}=0.95.$$

Divide through by $\dfrac{\sigma}{\sqrt{n}}$:

$$P\left\{\frac{\overline{X}-\mu}{\sigma/\sqrt{n}}<\frac{\sigma/4}{\sigma/\sqrt{n}}\right\}=0.95$$

or

$$P\left\{\frac{\overline{X}-\mu}{\sigma/\sqrt{n}}<\frac{\sqrt{n}}{4}\right\}=0.95.$$

By the Central Limit Theorem, $\dfrac{\overline{X}-\mu}{\sigma/\sqrt{n}}$ has approximately a standard normal distribution. Therefore, $P\left\{\text{Standard Normal Quantity}<\dfrac{\sqrt{n}}{4}\right\}=0.95.$

From the standard normal tables, we know

$$P\left\{-1.96<\text{Standard Normal Quantity}<1.96\right\}=0.95.$$

Now set

$$1.96=\frac{\sqrt{n}}{4},\ 4\,(1.96)=\sqrt{n},\ \sqrt{n}=7.84,\ n=61.4656.$$

The research worker would have to take a sample of at least 62 observations.

Car batteries produced by company A have a mean life of 3.5 years with a standard deviation of 0.4 years. A similar battery produced by company B has a mean life of 3.3 years and a standard deviation of 0.3 years. What is the probability that a random sample of 25 batteries from company A will have a mean life of at least 0.4 years more than the mean life of a sample of 36 batteries from company B?

SOLUTION:

The problem supplies us with the following data:

Population A: $\mu_1 = 3.5$ $\sigma_1 = 0.4$ $n_1 = 25$

Population B: $\mu_2 = 3.3$ $\sigma_2 = 0.3$ $n_2 = 36$

We are dealing with samples large enough to assume that the sample means, $\overline{X}_1$ and $\overline{X}_2$, are approximately normally distributed. Their difference $\overline{X}_1 - \overline{X}_2$ will then also be approximately normally distributed.

By the linearity properties of expectation,

$$E[X_1 - X_2] = E[X_1] + E[-X_2] = E[X_1] - E[X_2] = \mu_1 - \mu_2.$$

By the property $V(aX + bY) = a^2 V(X) + b^2 V(Y)$, for X and Y independent, $V(X_1 - X_2) = V[\overline{X}_1 + (-\overline{X}_2)] = V(\overline{X}_1) + (-1)^2 V(\overline{X}_2) = V(\overline{X}_1)$

$$+ V(\overline{X}_2) = \frac{\sigma_1^2}{n_1} + \frac{\sigma_2^2}{n_2}, \text{ so}$$

$$\sigma_{X_1-X_2} = \sqrt{V(X_1 - X_2)} = \sqrt{\frac{\sigma_1^2}{n_2} + \frac{\sigma_2^2}{n_2}}.$$

Applying these general results, we see $X_1 - X_2$ is approximately normally distributed with mean $\mu_1 - \mu_2 = 3.5 - 3.3 = 0.2$, and standard deviation

$$\sqrt{\frac{\sigma_1^2}{n_1} + \frac{\sigma_2^2}{n_2}} = \sqrt{\frac{0.16}{25} + \frac{0.09}{36}} = 0.094.$$

We are asked for $P\{(\overline{X}_1 - \overline{X}_2) > 0.4\}$. Subtracting $\mu_1 - \mu_2$ and dividing

by $\sqrt{\frac{\sigma_1^2}{n_1} + \frac{\sigma_2^2}{n_2}}$, we obtain

$$P\left\{\frac{(\overline{X}_1 - \overline{X}_2) - (\mu_1 - \mu_2)}{\sqrt{\dfrac{\sigma_1^2}{n_1} + \dfrac{\sigma_2^2}{n_2}}} > \frac{(0.4) - (\mu_1 - \mu_2)}{\sqrt{\dfrac{\sigma_1^2}{n_1} + \dfrac{\sigma_2^2}{n_2}}}\right\}.$$

The Central Limit Theorem tells us

$$\frac{(\overline{X}_1 - \overline{X}_2) - (\mu_1 - \mu_2)}{\sqrt{\dfrac{\sigma_1^2}{n_1} + \dfrac{\sigma_2^2}{n_2}}} = \frac{(\overline{X}_1 - \overline{X}_2) - E[\overline{X}_1 - \overline{X}_2]}{\sigma_{(\overline{X}_1 - \overline{X}_2)}}$$

is approximately standard normal. We now only want

$$P\left\{\text{Standard Normal Quantity} > \frac{(0.4) - (\mu_1 - \mu_2)}{\sqrt{\dfrac{\sigma_1^2}{n_1} + \dfrac{\sigma_2^2}{n_2}}}\right\}$$

$$= P\left(Z > \frac{0.4 - 0.2}{0.094}\right) = P(Z > 2.13) = 1 - P(Z < 2.13)$$

$$= 1 - 0.9834$$

$$= 0.0166 \text{ using standard normal tables}$$

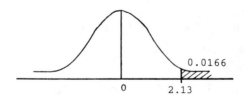

Random samples of size 100 are drawn, with replacement, from two populations, P_1 and P_2, and their means, X_1 and X_2, computed. If μ_1 = 10, σ_1 = 2, μ_2 = 8, and σ_2 = 1, find
  (a) $E[\overline{X}_1 - \overline{X}_2]$;

  (b) $\sigma_{\overline{X}_1 - \overline{X}_2}$;

  (c) the probability that the difference between a given pair of sample means is less than 1.5; and

  (d) the probability that the difference between a given pair of sample means is greater than 1.75 but less than 2.5.

SOLUTION:

a) By the linearity properties of the expectation operator

$$E[\overline{X}_1 - \overline{X}_1] = E[\overline{X}_1] - E[\overline{X}_2] = \mu_1 - \mu_2 = 10 - 8 = 2.$$

b) In light of the fact that we can say X_1 and X_2 are independent,

$$V(a\overline{X}_1 + b\overline{X}_2) = a^2 V(\overline{X}_1) + b^2 V(\overline{X}_2).$$

In our case $a = 1$ and $b = -1$, so $V(\overline{X}_1 - \overline{X}_2) = 1^2 V(\overline{X}_1) + (-1)^2$

$$V(\overline{X}_2) = V(\overline{X}_1) + V(\overline{X}_2) = \frac{\sigma_1^2}{n_1} + \frac{\sigma_2^2}{n_2}. \text{ Finally,}$$

$$\sigma_{\overline{X}_1 - \overline{X}_2} = \sqrt{V(\overline{X}_1 - \overline{X}_2)} = \sqrt{\frac{\sigma_1^2}{n_1} + \frac{\sigma_1^2}{n_1}}$$

$$= \sqrt{\frac{2^2}{100} + \frac{1^2}{100}} = \sqrt{\frac{5}{100}} = \frac{\sqrt{5}}{10}$$

c) We want $P\{|\overline{X}_1 - \overline{X}_2| < 1.5\}$, or equivalently,

$$P\{-1.5 < \overline{X}_1 - \overline{X}_2 < 1.5\}.$$

Subtract $E[\overline{X}_1 - \overline{X}_2] = 2$ and divide by $\sigma_{\overline{X}_1 - \overline{X}_2} = \dfrac{\sqrt{5}}{10}$ to obtain

$$P\left\{\frac{-1.5-2}{\sqrt{5}/10} < \frac{(\overline{X}_1 - \overline{X}_2) - E(\overline{X}_1 - \overline{X}_2)}{\sigma_{\overline{X}_1 - \overline{X}_2}} < \frac{-1.5-2}{\sqrt{5}/10}\right\}$$

$$= P\left\{-15.652 < \frac{(\overline{X}_1 - \overline{X}_2) - E(\overline{X}_1 - \overline{X}_2)}{\sigma_{\overline{X}_1 - \overline{X}_2}} < -2.236\right\}.$$

The Central Limit Theorem tells us that since we have large samples $\dfrac{(\overline{X}_1 - \overline{X}_2) - E[\overline{X}_1 - \overline{X}_2]}{\sigma_{\overline{X}_1 - \overline{X}_2}}$ is approximately standard normal.

We then have

$P\{-15.652 < \text{Standard Normal} < -2.236\}$

$\cong P\{\text{Standard Normal} < -2.236\}$,

since the area under the standard normal curve to the left of -15.652 is negligible. From the standard normal tables

$P\{Z \leq -2.236\} \cong 0.0127$.

d) To solve this, we will follow exactly the method of part c). We want $P\{-1.75 < \overline{X}_1 - \overline{X}_2 < 2.5\}$. As in c), this is equivalent to

$$P\left\{\frac{1.75 - 2}{5/10} < \frac{(\overline{X}_1 - \overline{X}_2) - E(\overline{X}_1 - \overline{X}_2)}{\sigma_{\overline{X}_1 - \overline{X}_2}} < \frac{2.5 - 2}{5/10}\right\}$$

$= P\{-1.118 < \text{Standard Normal} < 2.236\}$

$= P\{-1.12 < z < 0) + P(0 < z < 2.24\}$

(by the symmetry of the standard normal curve)

$= 0.3686 + 0.4875 = 0.8561$

● **PROBLEM 10-13**

A seed company advertises that it has developed an early tomato that will produce ripe tomatoes in 54 days with a standard deviation of four days. Another seed company advertises that they have developed an early tomato that will produce ripe tomatoes in 60 days with a standard deviation of six days. A gardener plants 400 seeds. The mean number of days $\overline{X}_1$ before ripe tomatoes for each planting from the first seed company was found. The average number of days $\overline{X}_2$ for each planting from the second company was found. Assume that the conditions were identical for each planting and find the probability that the difference between any one sample mean taken from seeds produced by the first company and any one sample mean taken from seeds developed by the second company is less than five days.

SOLUTION:

We begin with some preliminary observations: $\mu_1 = 54$, $\sigma_1 = 4$, $\mu_2 = 60$, $\sigma_2 = 6$, $E[\overline{X}_1 - \overline{X}_2] = \mu_1 - \mu_2 = 60 - 54 = 6$, and

$$\sigma_{\overline{X}_1 - \overline{X}_2} = \sqrt{\frac{\sigma_1^2}{n_1} + \frac{\sigma_2^2}{n_2}} = \sqrt{\frac{4^2}{400} + \frac{6^2}{400}} = \sqrt{\frac{52}{400}} = 0.36.$$

The problem asks for $P\{|\overline{X}_1 - \overline{X}_2| < 5\}$ or equivalently, what is $P\{-5 < \overline{X}_1 - \overline{X}_2 < 5\}$? We subtract $E[\overline{X}_1 - \overline{X}_2]$ and divide by σ_{X-Y} and the result is

$$P\left\{ \frac{-5 - E[\overline{X}_1 - \overline{X}_2]}{\sigma_{\overline{X}_1 - \overline{X}_2}} < \frac{(\overline{X}_1 - \overline{X}_2) - E[\overline{X}_1 - \overline{X}_2]}{\sigma_{\overline{X}_1 - \overline{X}_2}} < \frac{-5 - E[\overline{X}_1 - \overline{X}_2]}{\sigma_{\overline{X}_1 - \overline{X}_2}} \right\}.$$

By the Central Limit Theorem,

$$\frac{(\overline{X}_1 - \overline{X}_2) - E[\overline{X}_1 - \overline{X}_2]}{\sigma_{\overline{X}_1 - \overline{X}_2}}$$

is distributed approximately as standard normal. Using this and substituting our preliminary values, we obtain

$$P\left\{ \frac{-5 - 6}{0.36} < \text{Standard Normal Quantity} < \frac{5 - 6}{0.36} \right\}$$

$$= P\{-30.56 < Z < -2.78\} \approx P\{Z < -2.78\}$$

since the area under the standard normal curve to the left of -30.56 is negligible. From the standard normal tables, $P\{Z < -2.78\} \approx 0.0027$.

THE CHI-SQUARE, t, AND F-DISTRIBUTIONS

● **PROBLEM 10-14**

Find the expected value of the random variable $S_*^2 = \dfrac{1}{n} \sum_{i=1}^{n} (X_i - \overline{X})^2$,

where $\overline{X} = \sum_{i=1}^{n} \dfrac{X_i}{n}$ and the X_i are independent and identically distributed

with $E[X_i] = \mu$ and var $(X_i) = \sigma^2$ for $i = 1, 2, \ldots, n$.

SOLUTION:

By definition $E[S_*^2] = E\left[\dfrac{1}{n}\sum_{i=1}^{n}(X_i - \overline{X})^2\right]$. We will use the common math-

ematical trick of adding and subtracting the same quantity, thereby leaving everything unchanged. Hence,

$$E[S_*^2] = E\left[\frac{1}{n}\sum_{i=1}^{n}[(X_i - \mu) - (\overline{X} - \mu)]^2\right]$$

$$= E\left[\frac{1}{n}\sum_{i=1}^{n}[(X_i - \mu)^2 - 2(\overline{X} - \mu)(X_i - \mu) + (\overline{X} - \mu)^2]\right]$$

$$= E\left[\frac{1}{n}\sum_{i=1}^{n}(X_i - \mu)^2 - \frac{2}{n}\sum_{i=1}^{n}(\overline{X} - \mu)(X_i - \mu) + \frac{1}{n}\sum_{i=1}^{n}(\overline{X} - \mu)^2\right].$$

Since $(\overline{X} - \mu)$ is constant with respect to i, we have

$$E[S_*^2] = E\left[\frac{1}{n}\sum_{i=1}^{n}(X_i - \mu)^2 - \frac{2}{n}(\overline{X} - \mu)\sum_{i=1}^{n}(X_i - \mu) + \frac{1}{n}(\overline{X} - \mu)^2\sum_{i=1}^{n}1\right].$$

Since $\Sigma X_i = n\overline{X}$, we have

$$E[S_*^2] = E\left[\frac{1}{n}\sum_{i=1}^{n}(X_i - \mu)^2 - \frac{2}{n}(\overline{X} - \mu)(n\overline{X} - n\mu) + \frac{1}{n}(\overline{X} - \mu)^2 n\right]$$

$$= E\left[\frac{1}{n}\sum_{i=1}^{n}(X_i - \mu)^2 - 2(\overline{X} - \mu)^2 + (\overline{X} - \mu)^2\right]$$

$$= E\left[\frac{1}{n}\sum_{i=1}^{n}(X_i - \mu)^2 - (\overline{X} - \mu)^2\right]$$

$$= \frac{1}{n}\sum_{i=1}^{n}E\left[(X_i - \mu)^2\right] - E\left[(\overline{X} - \mu)^2\right],$$

by the linearity properties of the expectation operator; then,

$$E[S_*^2] = \frac{1}{n}\sum_{i=1}^{n}\sigma^2 - \sigma_{\overline{X}}^2 ;$$

$\sigma_{\overline{X}}$ = standard deviation of the sample mean,

$$= \frac{1}{n}(n\sigma^2) - \frac{\sigma^2}{n} = \sigma^2 - \frac{\sigma^2}{n} = \frac{n-1}{n}\sigma^2 .$$

If we estimate σ^2 by $\frac{1}{n}\sum_{i=1}^{n}(X_i - \overline{X})^2$, we see that $E[S_*^2] \neq \sigma^2$. The word given to this type of estimator is biased.

Let X_1, X_2, ..., X_n be a random sample from a density $F(\cdot)$ and let

$$S^2 = \frac{1}{n-1}\sum_{i=1}^{n}(X_i - \overline{X})^2 .$$

Show $E[S^2] = \sigma^2$.

SOLUTION:

We know from the last problem that

$$E\left[\frac{1}{n}\sum_{i=1}^{n}(X_i - \overline{X})^2\right] = \frac{n-1}{n}\sigma^2 .$$

But $\quad S^2 = \frac{n}{n-1}\left[\frac{1}{n}\sum_{i=1}^{n}(X_i - \overline{X})^2\right] .$

Hence, $E[S^2] = E\left[\frac{n}{n-1} \times \frac{1}{n}\sum_{i=1}^{n}(X_i - \overline{X})^2\right]$

$$= \frac{n}{n-1}E\left[\frac{1}{n}\sum_{i=1}^{n}(X_i - \overline{X})^2\right] = \frac{n}{n-1}\frac{n-1}{n}\sigma^2 = \sigma^2$$

Since $E[S^2] = \sigma^2$, S^2 is an unbiased estimate of σ^2.

The chi-square density function is the special case of a gamma density with parameters $\sigma = \dfrac{K}{2}$ and $\lambda = \dfrac{1}{2}$. Find the mean, variance, and moment generating function of a chi-square random variable.

SOLUTION:

Earlier for the gamma distribution we found

$$M_X(t) = \left(\frac{\lambda}{\lambda - t}\right)^{\alpha} \text{ for } t < \lambda, \ E[X] = \frac{\alpha}{\lambda}, \text{ and var } (X) = \frac{\alpha}{\lambda^2}.$$

Making the substitution $\sigma = \dfrac{K}{2}$ and $\lambda = \dfrac{1}{2}$ into the formulae for the gamma distribution, we see that the chi-square distribution has

$$M_X(t) = \left|\frac{\dfrac{1}{2}}{\dfrac{1}{2} - t}\right|^{\frac{K}{2}} = \left(\frac{1}{1 - 2t}\right)^{\frac{K}{2}}, \qquad t < \frac{1}{2},$$

$$E[X] = \frac{K/2}{1/2} = \frac{K}{2} \times \frac{2}{1} = K,$$

and

$$\text{var } (X) = \frac{\dfrac{K}{2}}{\left(\dfrac{1}{2}\right)^2} = \frac{K}{2} \times \frac{4}{1} = 2K.$$

If $S^2 = \frac{1}{n-1}\sum_{i=1}^{n}(X_i - \bar{X})^2$ is the unbiased sample variance of a random sample from a normal distribution with mean μ and variance σ^2, then show that

$$U = \frac{(n-1)S^2}{\sigma^2}$$

has a chi-square distribution with $n - 1$ degrees of freedom.

SOLUTION:

Since $S^2 = \frac{1}{n-1}\sum_{i=1}^{n}(X_i - \bar{X})^2$,

$$U = \frac{(n-1)S^2}{\sigma^2} = \frac{n-1\frac{1}{n-1}\sum(X_i - \bar{X})^2}{\sigma^2} = \frac{\sum(X_i - \bar{X})^2}{\sigma^2}.$$

Now add and subtract μ within the parentheses, yielding

$$U = \frac{\sum(X_i - \mu - \bar{X} + \mu)^2}{\sigma^2} = \frac{\sum[(X_i - \mu) - (\bar{X} - \mu)]^2}{\sigma^2}$$

$$= \sum\left(\frac{X_i - \mu}{\sigma} - \frac{\bar{X} - \mu}{\sigma}\right)^2 = \sum(Z_i - \bar{Z})^2,$$

where the Z_i are standard normal.

A manufacturer of clocks claims that a certain model will last five years on average with a standard deviation of 1.2 years. A random sample of six clocks lasted 6, 5.5, 4, 5.2, 5, and 4.3 years. Compute:

$$\frac{(n-1)S^2}{\sigma^2}$$

and use the chi-square tables to find the probability of a χ^2 value this high, given that the claim is true.

SOLUTION:

First we calculate the sample mean as

$$\bar{X} = \frac{\sum\limits_{i=1}^{6} X_i}{n} = \frac{6 + 5.5 + 4 + 5.2 + 5 + 4.3}{6} = \frac{30}{6} = 5. \text{ Then}$$

$$S^2 = \frac{1}{n-1}\sum\limits_{i=1}^{6}(X_i - \bar{X})^2 = \frac{1}{6-1}[(6-5)^2 + (5.5-5)^2 + (4-5)^2 + (5.2-5)^2$$

$$+ (4.3 - 5)^2]$$

$$= \frac{1}{5}(1^2 + (0.5)^2 + (-1)^2 + (0.2)^2 + 0^2 + (-0.7)^2)$$

$$= \frac{1}{5}(1 + 0.25 + 1 + 0.04 + 0.49) = \frac{1}{5} \times 2.78$$

$$= 0.556$$

The standard deviation, σ, is 1.2. Hence, $\sigma^2 = (1.2)^2 = 1.44$.
Finally,

$$U = \frac{(n-1)S^2}{\sigma^2} = \frac{(6-1)(0.556)}{1.44} = 1.931.$$

In this case U has a chi-square distribution with $n - 1 = 5$ degrees of freedom. On a chi-square table, look down the left side for the row with 5 degrees of freedom. The probabilities on the top row are $P(\chi^2_{(n-1)} \geq U)$. Looking across the row for 5 degrees of freedom, we see that the value for $P = 0.80$ is 2.343 and that for $P = 0.90$ is 1.610. To find $P\{\chi_5^2 \geq 1.931\}$, we use linear interpolation,

$$\frac{1.931 - 1.610}{2.343 - 1.610} = \frac{X - 0.90}{0.80 - 0.90}$$

Thus,
$$X = 0.90 + (0.80 - 0.90)\left(\frac{1.931 - 1.610}{2.343 - 1.610}\right)$$

$$= 0.90 - 0.1\left(\frac{0.321}{0.743}\right) = 0.90 - 0.1\,(0.432)$$

$$= 0.857$$

Hence, $P\{\chi_5^2 \geq 1.931\} = 0.857$.

Suppose a random sample of 10 observations is to be drawn, where X_1, X_2, ..., X_{10} are independent normally distributed random variables each with mean μ and variance σ^2. Find $P\{\sigma^2 \geq 0.5319S^2\}$, where

$$S^2 = \text{sample variance} = \frac{\sum_{i=1}^{10}(X_i - \overline{X})^2}{9} .$$

SOLUTION:

In this problem $S^2 = \dfrac{\sum_{i=1}^{10}(X_i - \overline{X})^2}{9}$ is a random variable. We must determine the distribution of S^2.

Let Z equal the standard normal variable. Define the random variable $\chi_1^2 = Z^2$. This new random variable is distributed with a chi-square distribution with one degree of freedom. An interesting property of χ^2 is that if $Y = \chi_1^2 + \chi_1^2$, then Y is also chi-square but with two degrees of freedom, $Y = \chi_2^2$. This property generalizes to

$$\chi_n^2 = \underbrace{\chi_1^2 + \chi_1^2 + ... + \chi_1^2}_{n \text{ terms}}$$

We wish to find

$$P = \{\sigma^2 \geq 0.5319S^2\} = P\left\{\frac{S^2}{\sigma^2} \leq \frac{1}{0.5319}\right\}$$

$$= P\left\{\frac{S^2}{\sigma^2} \leq 1.88\right\}.$$

What is the distribution of $\dfrac{S^2}{\sigma^2}$?

We know that

$$(n-1)\,S^2 = \sum_{i=1}^{10}(x_i - \overline{x})^2 \text{ and } \frac{(n-1)S^2}{\sigma^2} = \frac{\sum_{i=1}^{10}(x_i - \overline{x})^2}{\sigma^2} = \sum_{i=1}^{10}\left(\frac{x_i - \overline{x}}{\sigma}\right)^2 .$$

Intuitively, if we replace $\overline{x}$ by μ then

$$\frac{(n-1)S^2}{\sigma^2} = \sum_{i=1}^{10}\left(\frac{x_i - \mu}{\sigma}\right)$$

or

$$= \sum_{i=1}^{10} Z_i^2,$$

where Z is a standard normal random variable. Thus, $\dfrac{(n-1)S^2}{\sigma^2}$ will be a chi-square random variable with 10 degrees of freedom. However, we cannot replace $\bar{x}$ by μ without any justification. This substitution only provides motivation for the following result: $\dfrac{(n-1)S^2}{\sigma^2}$ is distributed as chi-square with $n-1$ degrees of freedom. We must now use the table of χ^2 – values with nine degrees of freedom to find

$$P\left\{\frac{9S^2}{\sigma^2} \le 9(1.88)\right\} = P\left\{\frac{9S^2}{\sigma^2} \le 16.92\right\}.$$

This equals $1 - 0.05 = 0.95$. Thus, $P\{\sigma^2 \ge 0.5319S^2\} = 0.95$.

● PROBLEM 10–20

Find the probability that X is greater than 3.28 if X has an F-distribution with 12 and eight degrees of freedom.

SOLUTION:

Look across the top of the cumulative F-table for 12, the degrees of freedom of the numerator. Now we look along the side for 8, the degrees of freedom of the denominator. Find the block that is in row 8 and column 12. In it the value 3.28 corresponds to the G-value 0.95 in the extreme left-hand column. This signifies $G(3.28) = P\{X < 3.28\} = 0.95$. Hence, $P\{X > 3.28\} = 1 - P\{X < 3.28\} = 1 - 0.95 = 0.05$.

Find the value $\xi_{0.05}$ such that for an F-distribution with 12 and eight degrees of freedom $P\{X < \xi_{0.05}\} = 0.05$.

SOLUTION:

This problem provides a real exercise in reading the F-table. Note the following. If X has an F-distribution with m and n degrees of freedom, then X is of the form

$$\frac{U/m}{V/n},$$

where U and V are chi-square random variables with m and n degrees of freedom, respectively. Then $\dfrac{1}{X}$ will be of the form

$$\frac{V/n}{U/m}$$

and will have an F-distribution with n and m degrees of freedom. This allows one to table the F-distribution for the upper tail only. For example, if the quantile $\xi_{0.95}$ is given for an F-distribution with m and n degrees of freedom, then the quantile $\xi'_{0.05}$ for an F-distribution with n and m degrees of freedom is given by $\dfrac{1}{\chi_{0.95}}$.

In general, if X has an F-distribution with m and n degrees of freedom, then the pth quantile of X, ξ_p, is the reciprocal of the $(1 - p)^{th}$ quantile of Y, ξ'_{1-p} of an F-distribution with n and m degrees of freedom, as the following shows:

$$p = P\{X \le \xi_p\} = P\left\{\frac{1}{X} \ge \frac{1}{\xi_p}\right\}$$

$$= P\left\{Y \ge \frac{1}{\xi_p}\right\} = 1 - P\left\{Y \le \frac{1}{\xi_p}\right\};$$

but

$$1 - p = P\{Y \le \xi'_{1-p}\}$$

$$= 1 - \left[1 - P\left\{Y \le \frac{1}{\xi_p}\right\}\right]$$

$$= P\left\{Y \le \frac{1}{\xi_p}\right\}.$$

Hence, $\dfrac{1}{\xi'_p} = \xi'_{1-p}$. Therefore,

$$\xi_{0.05}\,(12,\,8) = \frac{1}{\chi_{0.95}\,(8,\,12)} = \frac{1}{2.85} = 0.351.$$

The results of the last two problems are illustrated below.

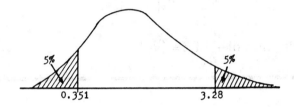

● **PROBLEM 10-22**

Find the tenth quantile point of an F-distribution with 15 and seven degrees of freedom.

SOLUTION:

We know that if the pth quantile ξ_p is given for an F-distribution with m and n degrees of freedom, then the quantile ξ'_{1-p} for an F-distribution with n and m degrees of freedom is given by $\dfrac{1}{\xi_p}$.

Following this, we see

$$\xi_{0.10}\,(15,\,7) = \frac{1}{\xi_{0.90}\,(7,\,15)} = \frac{1}{2.16} = 0.463.$$

297

Let X_1, X_2 be a random independent sample from $N(0, 1)$.

a) What is the distribution of $\dfrac{X_2 - X_1}{\sqrt{2}}$?

b) What is the distribution of $\dfrac{(X_1 + X_2)^2}{(X_2 - X_1)^2}$?

c) What is the distribution of $\dfrac{(X_1 + X_2)}{\sqrt{(X_2 - X_1)^2}}$?

d) What is the distribution of $\dfrac{1}{Z}$ if $Z = \dfrac{X_1^2}{X_2^2}$?

SOLUTION:

First notice that $X_1 + X_2$ is the sum of two independent normal random variables. Hence, it is normally distributed with mean $E[X_1 + X_2] = E[X_1] + E[X_2] = 0 + 0 = 0$, and $V(X_1 + X_2) = V(X_1) + V(X_2) = 1 + 1 = 2$, since X_1 and X_2 are independent.

Similarly, $X_2 - X_1$ will also be normally distributed with mean

$$E[X_2 - X_1] = E[X_2] - E[X_1] = 0 - 0 = 0,$$

and

$$V(X_2 - X_1) = V(X_2) + V(X_1) = 1 + 1 = 2.$$

(a) We have now $\dfrac{1}{\sqrt{2}}$ $N(0, 2)$. A constant times a normal distribution

will still be normally distributed. The new mean will be

$\dfrac{1}{\sqrt{2}} \times 0 = 0$, and the new variance will be

$$\left(\frac{1}{\sqrt{2}}\right)^2 (2) = 1.$$

The new distribution is $N(0, 1)$.

(b) We start with

$$\frac{(X_1 + X_2)^2}{(X_2 - X_1)^2}.$$

298

Multiply the numerator and denominator by $\dfrac{1}{2}$ to obtain

$$\frac{\dfrac{1}{2}(X_1 + X_2)^2}{\dfrac{1}{2}(X_2 - X_1)^2} = \frac{\left(\dfrac{X_1 + X_2}{\sqrt{2}}\right)^2}{\left(\dfrac{X_2 - X_1}{\sqrt{2}}\right)^2} \, .$$

From part (a) we know the denominator is $[N\,(0,\,1)]^2$. For similar reasons the numerator is also $[N\,(0,\,1)]^2$. But we know that a $[N\,(0,\,1)]^2$ is $\chi^2\,(1)$. We now have

$$\frac{\chi^2(1)}{\chi^2(1)} = \frac{\chi^2(1)/1}{\chi^2(1)/1} \, .$$

By definition this is an $F(1,\,1)$ random variable since the numerator and denominator were previously shown to be independent.

(c) We start with $\dfrac{(X_1 + X_2)}{\sqrt{(X_2 - X_1)^2}}$.

Multiply the numerator and denominator by $\dfrac{1}{\sqrt{2}}$ to obtain

$$\frac{\dfrac{1}{\sqrt{2}}(X_1 + X_2)}{\dfrac{1}{\sqrt{2}}\sqrt{(X_2 - X_1)^2}} = \frac{\dfrac{(X_1 + X_2)}{\sqrt{2}}}{\sqrt{\left(\dfrac{X_2 - X_1}{\sqrt{2}}\right)^2}} \, .$$

From previous experience $\dfrac{X_1 + X_2}{\sqrt{2}}$ and $\dfrac{X_2 - X_1}{\sqrt{2}}$ are both $N\,(0,\,1)$.

We now have

$$\frac{N\,(0,\,1)}{\sqrt{[N\,(0,\,1)]^2}} = \frac{N\,(0,\,1)}{\sqrt{\chi^2(1)}} \, ,$$

since $[N\,(0,\,1)]^2$ is $\chi^2(1)$,

$$= \frac{N\,(0,\,1)}{\sqrt{\dfrac{\chi^2(1)}{1}}} = t(1) \text{ by definition.}$$

d)   If $Z = \dfrac{X_1^{\,2}}{X_2^{\,2}}$, then $\dfrac{1}{Z} = \dfrac{X_2^{\,2}}{X_1^{\,2} \times X_1^{\,2}}$ and $X_2^{\,2}$ are both $[N\,(0,\,1)]^2$ and

thereby $\chi^2\,(1)$, $\dfrac{1}{Z}$ is therefore

$$\dfrac{\chi^2(1)}{\chi^2(1)} = \dfrac{\chi^2(1)/1}{\chi^2(1)/1}$$

which is $F(1,\,1)$ by definition since X_1 and X_2 are independent.

● **PROBLEM 10-24**

Let $X_1,\ \ldots,\ X_n$ be a random sample form $N\,(0,\,1)$. Define

$$\overline{X}_k = \dfrac{1}{k}\sum_1^k X_i \text{ and } \overline{X}_{n-k} = \dfrac{1}{n-k}\sum_{k+1}^n X_i\ .$$

(a) What is the distribution of $\dfrac{1}{2}(\overline{X}_k + \overline{X}_{n-k})$?

(b) What is the distribution of $k\overline{X}_k^{\,2} + (n-k)\overline{X}_{n-k}^2$?

(c) What is the distribution of $\dfrac{X_1^{\,2}}{X_2^{\,2}}$?

SOLUTION:

a)   Both $\overline{X}_k$ and $\overline{X}_{n-k}$ are sample means from a normal distribution. As such, they are normally distributed with means equal to the original distribution mean, 0. Their variances are

$$\dfrac{\sigma^2\ \text{orig.}}{\text{sample size}} = \dfrac{1}{k} \text{ and } \dfrac{1}{n-k} \text{ respectively.}$$

Now $\overline{X}_k + \overline{X}_{n-k}$ is normally distributed, being the sum of two normal distributions. By the linearity properties of expectation

$$E\,[\,\overline{X}_k + \overline{X}_{n-k}] = E\,[\overline{X}_k] + E\,[\overline{X}_{n-k}] = 0 + 0 = 0.$$

But $\overline{X}_k + \overline{X}_{n-k}$ are based on different observations; hence, they are independent. In light of this,

$$V(\overline{X}_k + \overline{X}_{n-k}) = V(\overline{X}_k) + V(\overline{X}_{n-k}) = \frac{1}{k} + \frac{1}{n-k} .$$

We now see $Y = \overline{X}_k + \overline{X}_{n-k}$ is distributed $N\left(0, \frac{1}{k}, \frac{1}{n-k}\right)$, so $\frac{1}{2}Y$ will still be normally distributed. By linearity properties

$$E\left[\frac{1}{2}Y\right] = \frac{1}{2}E[Y] = \frac{1}{2} \times 0 = 0.-$$

Since $V(aY) = a^2 V(Y)$, $V\left(\frac{1}{2}Y\right) = \frac{1}{4}VY = \frac{1}{4}\left(\frac{1}{k} + \frac{1}{n-k}\right) =$

$$\frac{1}{4k} + \frac{1}{4n-4k} .$$

Therefore, $\frac{1}{2}(\overline{X}_k + \overline{X}_{n-k})$ has a distribution which is

$$N\left(0, \frac{1}{4k} + \frac{1}{4n-4k}\right).$$

(b) Here we concern ourselves with $k\overline{X}_k^2 + (n-k)\overline{X}_{n-k}^2$. Note that $\overline{X}_k$ is distributed normally with mean 0 and variance $\frac{1}{k}$. Now $\sqrt{k}\,\overline{X}_k$ will still be normally distributed with mean zero but the variance will be 1.

Since 1 $V(aX) = a^2 V(X)$; $V(\sqrt{k}\,\overline{X}_k) = k V(\overline{X}_k) = k\frac{1}{k} = 1$, $\sqrt{k}\,\overline{X}_k$ is distributed $N(0, 1)$. An identical argument applies to $\sqrt{n-k}\,\overline{X}_{n-k}$. Note that $k\overline{X}_k^2 + (n-k)\overline{X}_{n-k}^2 = (\sqrt{k}\,\overline{X}_k)^2$ $= (\sqrt{n-k}\,\overline{X}_{n-k})^2$, which is distributed as $[N(0, 1)]^2 + [N(0, 1)]^2$. Since $[N(0, 1)]^2$ is χ_1^2, we have $\chi_1^2 + \chi_1^2$. We know that $\chi_m^2 + \chi_n^2 = \chi_{m+n}^2$, so our final answer is $\chi_{1+1}^2 + \chi_2^2$.

(c) Since both X_1 and X_2 are standard normal random variables, $\dfrac{X_1^2}{X_2^2}$

is the quotient of the squares of two standard normal quantities. Equivalently, it is the quotient of two chi-square random variables, each with one degree of freedom. But

$$\frac{\chi_1^2}{\chi_1^2} = \frac{\chi_1^2/1}{\chi_1^2/1}$$

which by definition is distributed $F(1, 1)$, since the numerator and denominator are independent of each other.

● PROBLEM 10–25

Let $X_1, ..., X_n$ be a random sample from $N(\mu, \sigma^2)$. Define

$$\bar{X}_k = \frac{1}{k}\sum_1^k X_i,$$

$$\bar{X}_{n-k} = \frac{1}{n-k}\sum_{k+1}^n X_i,$$

$$\bar{X} = \frac{1}{n}\sum_1^n X_i,$$

$$S_k^2 = \frac{1}{n-k}\sum_1^k (X_i - \bar{X}_k)^2,$$

$$S_{n-k}^2 = \frac{1}{n-k-1}\sum_{k+1}^n (X_i - \bar{X}_{n-k})^2, \text{ and}$$

$$S^2 = \frac{1}{n-1}\sum_1^n (X_i - \bar{X})^2.$$

(a) What is the distribution of $\sigma^{-2}[(k-1)S_k^2 + (n-k-1)S_{n-k}^2]$?

(b) What is the distribution of $\frac{1}{2}(\bar{X}_k + \bar{X}_{n-k})$?

(c) What is the distribution of $\sigma^{-2}(X_i - \mu)^2$?

(d) What is the distribution of $\dfrac{S_k^2}{S_{n-k}^2}$?

302

SOLUTION:

(a)   We are concerned with

$$\frac{(k-1)S_k^2}{\sigma^2} + \frac{(n-k-1)S_{n-k}^2}{\sigma^2}.$$

From a previous problem and the general theory, we know that

$\dfrac{(n-1)S^2}{\sigma^2}$ has a chi-square distribution with $n-1$ degrees of freedom. Applying this to our situation

$$\frac{(k-1)S_k^2}{\sigma^2} \quad \text{and} \quad \frac{(n-k-1)S_{n-k}^2}{\sigma^2}$$

are chi-square distributed with $k-1$ and $n-k-1$ degrees of freedom respectively.

Since chi-square degrees of freedom are additive, our answer is

$$\chi_{(k-1)+(n-k-1)}^2 = \chi_{n-2}^2.$$

(b)   Since $\bar{X}_k$ and $\bar{X}_{n-k}$ are sample means taken from a normal distribution, they will be normally distributed with mean equal to the original population mean μ. The variances are found by dividing the population variance by the sample sizes. We obtain

$$\frac{\sigma^2}{k} \quad \text{and} \quad \frac{\sigma^2}{n-k}.$$

A linear combination of normal distributions, such as $\frac{1}{2}(\bar{X}_k + \bar{X}_{n-k})$, will be normally distributed. By the linearity properties of expectation,

$$E\left[\frac{1}{2}(\bar{X}_k + \bar{X}_{n-k})\right] = \frac{1}{2}\left(E[\bar{X}_k] + E[\bar{X}_{n-k}]\right) = \frac{1}{2}2\mu = \mu.$$

Since $\bar{X}_k$ and $\bar{X}_{n-k}$ are formed from different observations, they will be independent. The formula var $(aX + bY) = a^2$ var $(X) + b^2$ var (Y) will apply. In our example,

$$V\left[\frac{1}{2}(\bar{X}_k + \bar{X}_{n-k})\right] = V\left(\frac{1}{2}\bar{X}_k + \frac{1}{2}\bar{X}_{n-k}\right)$$

$$= \frac{1}{4}V(\bar{X}_k) + \frac{1}{4}V(\bar{X}_{n-k})$$

$$= \frac{1}{4}\frac{\sigma^2}{k} + \frac{1}{4}\frac{\sigma^2}{n-k} = \frac{\sigma^2}{4k} + \frac{\sigma^2}{4n-4k} .$$

Our final distribution is

$$N\left(\mu, \frac{\sigma^2}{4k} + \frac{\sigma^2}{4n-4k}\right).$$

(c) Since X_i is normally distributed with mean μ and variance σ^2,

$$\frac{X_i - \mu}{\sigma}$$

is distributed $N(0, 1)$. Note the following:

$$\sigma^{-2}(X_i - \mu)^2 = \left(\frac{X_i - \mu}{\sigma}\right)^2 \sim [N(0, 1)]^2$$

and we know that the square of a standard normal random variable follows a chi-square distribution with one degree of freedom.

(d) We will manipulate the quantity $\dfrac{S_k^2}{S_{n-k}^2}$. First divide the numerator and denominator by σ^2,

$$\frac{S_k^2/\sigma^2}{S_{n-k}^2/\sigma^2} .$$

Now multiply the numerator by $\dfrac{k-1}{k-1}$ and the denominator by

$\dfrac{n-k-1}{n-k-1}$, resulting in

$$\frac{\dfrac{1}{k-1}\left(\dfrac{(k-1)S_k^2}{\sigma^2}\right)}{\dfrac{1}{n-k-1}\left(\dfrac{(n-k-1)S_{n-k}^2}{\sigma^2}\right)} .$$

From previous work, we recognize the quantities in the parentheses as chi-square random variables. We have

$$\frac{\chi_{k-1}^2 / k-1}{\chi_{n-k-1}^2 / n-k-1} .$$

By definition this ratio has a distribution which is $F(k - 1, n - k - 1)$, since the numerator and denominator are independent chi-square random variables.

ORDER STATISTICS

Let $Y_1 \le Y_2 \le \ldots \le Y_n$ represent the order statistics of the sample $\{X_1, \ldots, X_n\}$ from a cumulative distribution function F. Find the marginal cumulative distribution function of Y_i, $i = 1, 2, \ldots, n$.

SOLUTION:

For any fixed y, let $Z_i = 1$ if X_i is in the interval $(-\infty, y]$ and 0 if not. The sum $\sum\limits_{i=1}^{n} Z_i$ will then be the number of the X_i that are less than or equal to y. Note that $F(y)$ is the constant probability that $X_i \le y$, and there are n Bernoulli "trials" to see whether $X_i \le y$ or not.

From this description, we see that $\sum\limits_{i=1}^{n} Z_i$ has a binomial distribution with parameters n and $F(y)$.

We are looking for

$$F_{yk}(y) = P\{y_k \le y\} = P\left[\sum Z_i \ge k\right]$$

$$= \sum_{j=k}^{n} \binom{n}{j} [F(y)]^j [1 - F(y)]^{n-j}$$

The key step in this problem is the equivalence of the two events $\{Y_k \le y\}$ and $\{\Sigma Z_i \ge k\}$. If the kth order statistic is less than or equal to y, then surely the number of X_i less than or equal to y is greater than or equal to k. The converse holds as well.

Let x be a random variable with cumulative distribution function $F(y) = y^2$ for $0 \le y \le 2$. Then find the cumulative distribution for the twelfth order statistic in a sample of 13.

SOLUTION:

We know that

$$F_{Y_\alpha}(y) = \sum_{j=a}^{n} \binom{n}{j} [F(y)]^j [1 - F(y)]^{n-j}.$$

Therefore,

$$F_{Y_{12}}(y) = \sum_{j=12}^{13} \binom{13}{j} (y^2)^j (1 - y^2)^{n-j}$$

$$= \binom{13}{12} (y^2)^{12} (1 - y^2)^{13-12} + \binom{13}{13} (y^2)^{13} (1 - y)^{13-13}$$

$$= 13y^{24} (1 - y^2)^1 + y^{26} = 13y^{24} - 13y^{26} + y^{26}$$

$$= 13y^{24} - 12y^{26}$$

SHORT ANSWER QUESTIONS FOR REVIEW

Choose the correct answer.

1. If a set of random variables is independent and each has a finite variance (and therefore a finite mean), then the Z-score of the sample mean will tend towards a normal distribution with mean 0 and variance (a) 0. (b) 1. (c) 2. (d) 3.

2. The probability that a random variable will be within two standard deviations of its mean, given that its standard deviation is 1, is at least (a) 0.00. (b) 0.68. (c) 0.75. (d) 0.95.

3. The probability that a normal random variable will be within two standard deviations of its mean, given that its standard deviation is 1, is at least (a) 0.00. (b) 0.68. (c) 0.75. (d) 0.95.

4. A random sample size of 25 is taken from a distribution with mean 5 and variance 25. The probability, according to the Central Limit Theorem, that the sample mean exceeds 6 is (a) 0.16. (b) 0.34. (c) 0.68. (d) 0.84.

5. If X and Y are independent, and each has a continuous uniform distribution with range $[0, 1]$, then the probability that the $Z = \max(X + Y) > 0.5$ is (a) 0.25. (b) 0.50. (c) 0.75. (d) 1.00.

6. The distribution of the square of a standard normal random variable is (a) normal. (b) chi-square. (c) t. (d) F.

Fill in the blanks.

7. If X and Y are independent and each has a standard normal distribution, then the distribution of $Z = X^2 + Y^2$ is _____ with _____ degrees of freedom.

8. If X and Y are independent and each has a uniform distribution with range $[0, 2]$, then the probability that $Z = \min(XY)$ exceeds 0.5 is _____ .

9. If X has a chi-square distribution with two degrees of freedom and Y has a chi-square distribution with three degrees of freedom, then the

distribution of $Z = \dfrac{X/2}{Y/3}$, assuming that X and Y are independent, is

_____ with degrees of freedom in the numerator equal to _____ and the degrees of freedom in the denominator equal to _____ .

10. If X, Y, and Z are uniformly distributed on $[2, 6]$ and are independent, then the probability that $W = \max (X, Y, Z)$ exceeds 4 is _____ .

11. A random sample of size n from a population with mean 0 gives X as the sample mean and s as the sample standard deviation. The distribution of $\dfrac{X}{s/n^{0.5}}$ is _____ with _____ degrees of freedom.

Determine whether the following statements are true or false.

12. The Weak Law of Large Numbers places a lower bound on the probability that a random variable will differ from its mean by at least a pre-specified amount.

13. The Weak Law of Large Numbers applies only to normal random variables.

14. The Central Limit Theorem gives a lower probability of a random variable differing from its mean by at least a pre-specified amount than that of the Weak Law of Large Numbers.

15. The t-distribution gets closer and closer to the standard normal distribution as the degrees of freedom increase.

16. The ratio of one chi-square random variable to another has an F-distribution as long as the two random variables are independent.

17. The sample mean will always tend towards the normal distribution as the sample size on which the mean is based increases.

ANSWER KEY

1. b

2. c

3. d

4. a

5. c

6. b

7. chi-square, 2

8. $\dfrac{9}{16}$

9. F, 2, 3

10. $\dfrac{7}{8}$

11. t, $(n-1)$

12. False

13. False

14. True

15. True

16. False

17. False

INDEX

Numbers on this page refer to PROBLEM NUMBERS, not page numbers.

Numbers on this page refer to PROBLEM NUMBERS, not page numbers.

APPENDIX

DECIMAL EQUIVALENTS OF FRACTIONS
OF AN INCH

1/64 = 0.015 625	11/32 22/64 = 0.343 75	43/64 = 0.671 875
1/32 2/64 = .031 25	23/64 = .359 375	11/16 22/32 44/64 = .687 5
3/64 = .046 875	3/8 12/32 24/64 = .375	45/64 = .703 125
1/16 2/32 4/64 = .062 5	25/64 = .390 625	23/32 46/64 = .718 75
5/64 = .078 125	13/32 26/64 = .406 25	47/64 = .734 375
3/32 6/64 = .093 75	27/64 = .421 875	3/4 24/32 48/64 = .75
7/64 = .109 375	7/16 14/32 28/64 = .437 5	49/64 = .765 625
1/8 4/32 8/64 = .125	29/64 = .453 125	25/32 50/64 = .781 25
9/64 = .140 625	15/32 30/64 = .468 75	51/64 = .796 875
5/32 10/64 = .156 25	31/64 = .484 375	13/16 26/32 52/64 = .812 5
11/64 = .171 875	1/2 16/32 32/64 = .50	53/64 = .828 125
3/16 6/32 12/64 = .187 5	33/64 = .515 625	27/32 54/64 = .843 75
13/64 = .203 125	17/32 34/64 = .531 25	55/64 = .859 375
7/32 14/64 = .218 75	35/64 = .546 875	7/8 28/32 56/64 = .875
15/64 = .234 375	9/16 18/32 36/64 = .562 5	57/64 = .890 625
1/4 8/32 16/64 = .25	37/64 = .578 125	29/32 58/64 = .906 25
17/64 = .265 625	19/32 38/64 = .593 75	59/64 = .921 875
9/32 18/64 = .281 25	39/64 = .609 375	15/16 30/32 60/64 = .937 5
19/64 = .296 875	5/8 20/32 40/64 = .625	61/64 = .953 125
5/16 10/32 20/64 = .312 5	41/64 = .640 625	31/32 62/64 = .968 75
21/64 = .328 125	21/32 42/64 = .656 25	63/64 = .984 375

UNIT CONVERSION FACTORS

I. The Metric System of Measurement

A. SI base units

The SI is constructed from seven base units for independent quantities plus two supplementary units for plane angle and solid angle.

Quantity	Name	Symbol
SI base units:		
length	meter	m
mass	kilogram	kg
time	second	s
electric current	ampere	A
thermodynamic temperature	kelvin	K
amount of substance	mole	mol
luminous intensity	candela	cd
SI supplementary units:		
plane angle	radian	rad
solid angle	steradian	sr

B. SI derived units

Quantity	SI Unit Name	Symbol	Expression in terms of other units
frequency	hertz	Hz	$1/s$
force	newton	N	$kg \cdot m/s^2$
pressure, stress	pascal	Pa	N/m^2
energy, work, quantity of heat	joule	J	$N \cdot m$
power, radiant flux	watt	W	J/s
quantity of electricity, electric charge	coulomb	C	$A \cdot s$
electric potential, potential difference, electromotive force	volt	V	W/A
capacitance	farad	F	C/V
electric resistance	ohm	Ω	V/A
conductance	siemens	S	A/V
magnetic flux	weber	Wb	$V \cdot s$
magnetic flux density	tesla	T	Wb/m^2
inductance	henry	H	Wb/A
luminous flux	lumen	lm	$cd \cdot sr$
illuminance	lux	lx	lm/m^2
activity (of ionizing radiation source)	becquerel	Bq	$1/s$
absorbed dose[a]	gray	Gy	J/kg

[a] Absorbed dose in rads (symbol rd) is the most often utilized quantity. In this handbook rad is also used as a unit symbol, following common usage (10^{-2} Gy = 1 rad). Note that rad is the accepted SI unit symbol for plane angle.

C. Multiplier prefixes for SI units

For use with SI units there is a set of 16 prefixes to form multiples and submultiples of the units. It is important to note that the kilogram is the only SI base unit with a prefix. Because double prefixes are not to be used, the prefixes, in the case of mass, are to be used with gram (symbol g) and not with kilogram (symbol kg).

SI prefixes

Factor	Prefix	Symbol
10^{18}	exa	E
10^{15}	peta	P
10^{12}	tera	T
10^{9}	giga	G
10^{6}	mega	M
10^{3}	kilo	k
10^{2}	hecto	h
10^{1}	deka	da
10^{-1}	deci	d
10^{-2}	centi	c
10^{-3}	milli	m
10^{-6}	micro	μ
10^{-9}	nano	n
10^{-12}	pico	p
10^{-15}	femto	f
10^{-18}	atto	a

A. Length

	cm	m	km	in	ft	mi
1 centimeter =	1	10^{-2}	10^{-5}	0.3937	3.281×10^{-2}	6.214×10^{-6}
1 METER =	100	1	10^{-3}	39.3	3.281	6.214×10^{-4}
1 kilometer =	10^{5}	1000	1	3.937×10^{4}	3281	0.6214
1 inch =	2.540	2.540×10^{-2}	2.540×10^{-5}	1	8.333×10^{-2}	1.578×10^{-5}
1 foot =	30.48	0.3048	3.048×10^{-4}	12	1	1.894×10^{-4}
1 mile =	1.609×10^{5}	1609	1.609	6.336×10^{4}	5280	1

1 angstrom = 10^{-10} m
1 nautical mile = 1852 m
= 1.151 miles = 6076 ft

1 light year = 9.4600×10^{12} km
1 parsec = 3.084×10^{13} km
1 fathom = 6 ft

1 yard = 3 ft
1 rod = 16.5 ft
1 mil = 10^{-3} in

PHYSICAL CONSTANTS AND CONVERSION FACTORS

Length Conversions

Unit	Symbol (or Abbreviation)	Relationship		Conversion to Meter (m)
Fermi	—	—		10^{-15}
Angstrom	Å	—		10^{-10}
Micron	μm	10^{4} Å	= 1 μm	10^{-6}
Inch	in.	2.54 cm	= 1 in.	0.0254*
Foot	ft	12 in.	= 1 ft	0.3048*
Yard	yd	3 ft (36 in.)	= 1 yd	0.9144*
Fathom	fath	2 yd (6 ft.)	= 1 fath	1.8288*
Link	—	7.92 in.	= 1 link	0.201168*
Rod	—	25 link (5.5 yd)	= 1 rod	5.0292
Chain	—	4 rod (22 yd)	= 1 chain	20.1168*
Furlong	fur	10 chain (220 yd)	= 1 fur	201.168*
Statute mile	mi	8 fur (1760 yd)	= 1 mi	1609.344
Nautical mile	nmi	1.15078 mi	= 1 nmi	1852.0*
Astronomical unit	AU	8.07775×10^{7} nmi	= 1 AU	1.49600×10^{11}
Light year	light yr	6.3239×10^{4} AU	= 1 light yr	9.46055×10^{15}
Parsec	pc	3.2562 light yr	= 1 pc	3.0857×10^{16}

*Defined value (1 in. = 2.54 cm exactly).

Area Conversions

Unit	Symbol	Relationship	Conversion to Square Meter (m^2)*
Barn	–	–	1.0×10^{-28}
Are	–	–	1.0×10^2
Hectare	–	–	1.0×10^4
Square inch	in.^{2}	–	6.4516×10^{-4}
Square foot	ft^2	144 in.^{2} = 1 ft^2	9.290304×10^{-2}
Square yard	yd^2	9 ft^2 = 1 yd^2	8.3612736×10^{-1}
Acre	–	43,560 ft^2 = 1 acre	4.0468564224×10^3
Square statute mile	mi^2	640 acre = 1 mi^2	$2.589988110336 \times 10^6$
Section	–	1 mi^2 = 1 section	$2.589988110336 \times 10^6$
Township	–	36 section = 1 township	9.3239572×10^7

*Defined values.

Volume Conversions

Unit	Symbol	Relationship	Conversion to Cubic Meter (m^3)
Cubic centimeter	cm^3	–	10^{-6}
Liter	l	10^3 cm^3 = 1 l	10^{-3}
Cubic inch	in.^{3}	1.6387064×10 cm^3 = 1 in.^{3}	1.6387064×10^{-5}*
Fluid ounce	fl oz	1.80469 in.^{3} = 1 fl oz	2.9573530×10^{-5}
Pint (liquid)	pt	16 fl oz = 1 pt	$4.73176473 \times 10^{-4}$*
Quart (liquid)	qt	2 pt = 1 qt	$9.46352946 \times 10^{-4}$*
Gallon (liquid)	gal	4 qt = 1 gal	$3.785411784 \times 10^{-3}$*
Cubic foot	ft^3	7.481 gal = 1 ft^3	$2.8316846592 \times 10^{-2}$*
Cubic yard	yd^3	27 ft^3 = 1 yd^3	$7.6455485844 \times 10^{-1}$*
Acre foot	–	–	1.2334818×10^3

*Defined values.

Angle Conversions

The radian, rad, is the basic unit of a plane angle. The steradian, sr, is the base unit of a solid angle.

Unit	Symbol	Relationship	Conversion to Radian (rad)
Milliradian	mrad	–	10^{-3}
Second	sec	–	$4.848136811 \times 10^{-6}$
Minute	min	60 sec = 1 min	$2.908882087 \times 10^{-4}$
Degree	° or deg	60 min = 1 deg	$1.745329252 \times 10^{-2}$
Quadrant	–	90 deg = 1 quadrant	1.570796327
Centesimal second	centesimal sec	10^{-6} quadrant = 1 centesimal sec	$1.570796327 \times 10^{-6}$
Centesimal minute	centesimal min	10^{-4} quadrant = 1 centesimal min	$1.570796327 \times 10^{-4}$
Grad	–	10^{-2} quadrant = 1 grad	$1.570796327 \times 10^{-2}$
Circumference	–	4 quadrant = 2π rad = 1 circumference	6.283185308
Mil (military)	–	1/6400 circumference = 1 mil	$9.817477044 \times 10^{-4}$

53479	81115	98036	12217	59526	40238	40577	39351	43211	69255
97344	70328	58116	91964	26240	44643	83287	97391	92823	77578
66023	38277	74523	71118	84892	13956	98899	92315	65783	59640
99776	75723	03172	43112	83086	81982	14538	26162	24899	20551
30176	48979	92153	38416	42436	26636	83903	44722	69210	69117
81874	83339	14988	99937	13213	30177	47967	93793	86693	98854
19839	90630	71863	95053	55532	60908	84108	55342	48479	63799
09337	33435	53869	52769	18801	25820	96198	66518	78314	97013
31151	58295	40823	41330	21093	93882	49192	44876	47185	81425
67619	52515	03037	81699	17106	64982	60834	85319	47814	08075
61946	48790	11602	83043	22257	11832	04344	95541	20366	55937
04811	64892	96346	79065	26999	43967	63485	93572	80753	96582
05763	39601	56140	25513	86151	78657	02184	29715	04334	15678
73260	56877	40794	13948	96289	90185	47111	66807	61849	44686
54909	09976	76580	02645	35795	44537	64428	35441	28318	99001
42583	36335	60068	04044	29678	16342	48592	25547	63177	75225
27266	27403	97520	23334	36453	33699	23672	45884	41515	04756
49843	11442	66682	36055	32002	78600	36924	59962	68191	62580
29316	40460	27076	69232	51423	58515	49920	03901	26597	33068
30463	27856	67798	16837	74273	05793	02900	63498	00782	35097
28708	84088	65535	44258	33869	82530	98399	26387	02836	36838
13183	50652	94872	28257	78547	55286	33591	61965	51723	14211
60796	76639	30157	40295	99476	28334	15368	42481	60312	42770
13486	46918	64683	07411	77842	01908	47796	65796	44230	77230
34914	94502	39374	34185	57500	22514	04060	94511	44612	10485
28105	04814	85170	86490	35695	03483	57315	63174	71902	71182
59231	45028	01173	08848	81925	71494	95401	34049	04851	65914
87437	82758	71093	36833	53582	25986	46005	42840	81683	21459
29046	01301	55343	65732	78714	43644	46248	53205	94868	48711
62035	71886	94506	15263	61435	10369	42054	68257	14385	79436
38856	80048	59973	73368	52876	47673	41020	82295	26430	87377
40666	43328	87379	86418	95841	25590	54137	94182	42308	07361
40588	90087	37729	08667	37256	20317	53316	50982	32900	32097
78237	86556	50276	20431	00243	02303	71029	49932	23245	00862
98247	67474	71455	69540	01169	03320	67017	92543	97977	52728
69977	78558	65430	32627	28312	61815	14598	79728	55699	91348
39843	23074	40814	03713	21891	96353	96806	24595	26203	26009
62880	87277	99895	99965	34374	42556	11679	99605	98011	48867
56138	64927	29454	52967	86624	62422	30163	76181	95317	39264
90804	56026	48994	64569	67465	60180	12972	03848	62582	93855
09665	44672	74762	33357	67301	80546	97659	11348	78771	45011
34756	50403	76634	12767	32220	34545	18100	53513	14521	72120
12157	73327	74196	26668	78087	53636	52304	00007	05708	63538
69384	07734	94451	76428	16121	09300	67417	68587	87932	38840
93358	64565	43766	45041	44930	69970	16964	08277	67752	60292
38879	35544	99563	85404	04913	62547	78406	01017	86187	22072
58314	60298	72394	69668	12474	93059	02053	29807	63645	12792
83568	10227	99471	74729	22075	10233	21575	20325	21317	57124
28067	91152	40568	33705	64510	07067	64374	26336	79652	31140
05730	75557	93161	80921	55873	54103	34801	83157	04534	81368

2500 FIVE DIGIT RANDOM NUMBERS

26687	74223	43546	45699	94469	82125	37370	23966	68926	37664
60675	75169	24510	15100	02011	14375	65187	10630	64421	66745
45418	98635	83123	98558	09953	60255	42071	40930	97992	93085
69872	48026	89755	28470	44130	59979	91063	28766	85962	77173
03765	86366	99539	44183	23886	89977	11964	51581	18033	56239
84686	57636	32326	19867	71345	42002	96997	84379	27991	21459
91512	49670	32556	85189	28023	88151	62896	95498	29423	38138
10737	49307	18307	22246	22461	10003	93157	66984	44919	30467
54870	19676	58367	20905	38324	00026	98440	37427	22896	37637
48967	49579	65369	74305	62085	39297	10309	23173	74212	32272
91430	79112	03685	05411	23027	54735	91550	06250	18705	18909
92564	29567	47476	62804	73428	04535	86395	12162	59647	97726
41734	12199	77441	92415	63542	42115	84972	12454	33133	48467
25251	78110	54178	78241	09226	87529	35376	90690	54178	08561
91657	11563	66036	28523	83705	09956	76610	88116	78351	50877
00149	84745	63222	50533	50159	60433	04822	49577	89049	16162
53250	73200	84066	59620	61009	38542	05758	06178	80193	26466
25587	17481	56716	49749	70733	32733	60365	14108	52573	39391
01176	12182	06882	27562	75456	54261	38564	89054	96911	88906
83531	15544	40834	20296	88576	47815	96540	79462	78666	25353
19902	98866	32805	61091	91587	30340	84909	64047	67750	87638
96516	78705	25556	35181	29064	49005	29843	68949	50506	45862
99417	56171	19848	24352	51844	03791	72127	57958	08366	43190
77699	57853	93213	27342	28906	31052	65815	21637	49385	75406
32245	83794	99528	05150	27246	48263	62156	62469	97048	16511
12874	72753	66469	13782	64330	00056	73324	03920	13193	19466
63899	41910	45484	55461	66518	82486	74694	07865	09724	76490
16255	43271	26540	41298	35095	32170	70625	66407	01050	44225
75553	30207	41814	74985	40223	91223	64238	73012	83100	92041
41772	18441	34685	13892	38843	69007	10362	84125	08814	66785
09270	01245	81765	06809	10561	10080	17482	05471	82273	06902
85058	17815	71551	36356	97519	54144	51132	83169	27373	68609
80222	87572	62758	14858	36350	23304	70453	21065	63812	29860
83901	88028	56743	25598	79349	47880	77912	52020	84305	02897
36303	57833	77622	02238	53285	77316	40106	38456	92214	54278
91543	63886	60539	96334	20804	72692	08944	02870	74892	22598
14415	33816	78231	87674	96473	44451	25098	29296	50679	07798
82465	07781	09938	66874	72128	99685	84329	14530	08410	45953
27306	39843	05634	96368	72022	01278	92830	40094	31776	41822
91960	82766	02331	08797	33858	21847	17391	53755	58079	48498
59284	96108	91610	07483	37943	96832	15444	12091	36690	58317
10428	96003	71223	21352	78685	55964	35510	94805	23422	04492
65527	41039	79574	05105	59588	02115	33446	56780	18402	36279
59688	43078	93275	31978	08768	84805	50661	18523	83235	50602
44452	10188	43565	46531	93023	07618	12910	60934	53403	18401
87275	82013	59804	78595	60553	14038	12096	95472	42736	08573
94155	93110	49964	27753	85090	77677	69303	66323	77811	22791
26488	76394	91282	03419	68758	89575	66469	97835	66681	03171
37073	34547	88296	68638	12976	50896	10023	27220	05785	77538
83835	89575	55956	93957	30361	47679	83001	35056	07103	63072

2500 FIVE DIGIT RANDOM NUMBERS

```
55034  81217  90564  81943  11241  84512  12288  89862  00760  76159
25521  99536  43233  48786  49221  06960  31564  21458  88199  06312
85421  72744  97242  66383  00132  05661  96442  37388  57671  27916
61219  48390  47344  30413  39392  91365  56203  79204  05330  31196
20230  03147  58854  11650  28415  12821  58931  30508  65989  26675

95776  83206  56144  55953  89787  64426  08448  45707  80364  60262
07603  17344  01148  83300  96955  65027  31713  89013  79557  49755
00645  17459  78742  39005  36027  98807  72666  54484  68262  38827
62950  83162  61504  31557  80590  47893  72360  72720  08396  33674
79350  10276  81933  26347  08068  67816  06659  87917  74166  85519

48339  69834  59047  82175  92010  58446  69591  56205  95700  86211
05842  08439  79836  50957  32059  32910  15842  13918  41365  80115
25855  02209  07307  59942  71389  76159  11263  38787  61541  22606
25272  16152  82323  70718  98081  38631  91956  49909  76253  33970
73003  29058  17605  49298  47675  90445  68919  05676  23823  84892

81310  94430  22663  06584  38142  00146  17496  51115  61458  65790
10024  44713  59832  80721  63711  67882  25100  45345  55743  67618
84671  52806  89124  37691  20897  82339  22627  06142  05773  03547
29296  58162  21858  33732  94056  88806  54603  00384  66340  69232
51771  94074  70630  41286  90583  87680  13961  55627  23670  35109

42166  56251  60770  51672  36031  77273  85218  14812  90758  23677
78355  67041  22492  51522  31164  30450  27600  44428  96380  26772
09552  51347  33864  89018  73418  81538  77399  30448  97740  18158
15771  63127  34847  05660  06156  48970  55699  61818  91763  20821
13231  99058  93754  36730  44286  44326  15729  37500  47269  13333

50583  03570  38472  73236  67613  72780  78174  18718  99092  64114
99485  57330  10634  74905  90671  19643  69903  60950  17968  37217
54676  39524  73785  48864  69835  62798  65205  69187  05572  74741
99343  71549  10248  76036  31702  76868  88909  69574  27642  00336
35492  40231  34868  55356  12847  68093  52643  32732  67016  46784

98170  25384  03841  23920  47954  10359  70114  11177  63298  99903
02670  86155  56860  02592  01646  42200  79950  37764  82341  71952
36934  42879  81637  79952  07066  41625  96804  92388  88860  68580
56851  12778  24309  73660  84264  24668  16686  02239  66022  64133
05464  28892  14271  23778  88599  17081  33884  88783  39015  57118

15025  20237  63386  71122  06620  07415  94982  32324  79427  70387
95610  08030  81469  91066  88857  56583  01224  28097  19726  71465
09026  40378  05731  55128  74298  49196  31669  42605  30368  96424
81431  99955  52462  67667  97322  69808  21240  65921  12629  92896
21431  59335  58627  94822  65484  09641  41018  85100  16110  32077

95832  76145  11636  80284  17787  97934  12822  73890  66009  27521
99813  44631  43746  99790  86823  12114  31706  05024  28156  04202
77210  31148  50543  11603  50934  02498  09184  95875  85840  71954
13268  02609  79833  66058  80277  08533  28676  37532  70535  82356
44285  71735  26620  54691  14909  52132  81110  74548  78853  31996

70526  45953  79637  57374  05053  31965  33376  13232  85666  86615
88386  11222  25080  71462  09818  46001  19065  68981  18310  74178
83161  73994  17209  79441  64091  49790  11936  44864  86978  34538
50214  71721  33851  45144  05696  29935  12823  01594  08453  52825
97689  29341  67747  80643  13620  23943  49396  83686  37302  95350
```

318

2500 FIVE DIGIT RANDOM NUMBERS

12367	23891	31506	90721	18710	89140	58595	99425	22840	08267
38890	30239	34237	22578	74420	22734	26930	40604	10782	80128
80788	55410	39770	93317	18270	21141	52085	78093	85638	81140
02395	77585	08854	23562	33544	45796	10976	44721	24781	09690
73720	70184	69112	71887	80140	72876	38984	23409	63957	44751
61383	17222	55234	18963	39006	93504	18273	49815	52802	69675
39161	44282	14975	97498	25973	33605	60141	30030	77677	49294
80907	74484	39884	19885	37311	04209	49675	39596	01052	43999
09052	65670	63660	34035	06578	87837	28125	48883	50482	55735
33425	24226	32043	60082	20418	85047	53570	32554	64099	52326
72651	69474	73648	71530	55454	19576	15552	20577	12124	50038
04142	32092	83586	61825	35482	32736	63403	91499	37196	02762
85226	14193	52213	60746	24414	57858	31884	51266	82293	73553
54888	03579	91674	59502	08619	33790	29011	85193	62262	28684
33258	51516	82032	45233	39351	33229	59464	65545	76809	16982
75973	15957	32405	82081	02214	57143	33526	47194	94526	73253
90638	75314	35381	34451	49246	11465	25102	71489	89883	99708
65061	15498	93348	33566	19427	66826	03044	97361	08159	47485
64420	07427	82233	97812	39572	07766	65844	29980	15533	90114
27175	17389	76963	75117	45580	99904	47160	55364	25666	25405
32215	30094	87276	56896	15625	32594	80663	08082	19422	80717
54209	58043	72350	89828	02706	16815	89985	37380	44032	59366
59286	66964	84843	71549	67553	33867	83011	66213	69372	23903
83872	58167	01221	95558	22196	65905	38785	01355	47489	28170
83310	57080	03366	80017	39601	40698	56434	64055	02495	50880
64545	29500	13351	78647	92628	19354	60479	57338	52133	07114
39269	00076	55489	01524	76568	22571	20328	84623	30188	43904
29763	05675	28193	65514	11954	78599	63902	21346	19219	90286
06310	02998	01463	27738	90288	17697	64511	39552	34694	03211
97541	47607	57655	59102	21851	44446	07976	54295	84671	78755
82968	85717	11619	97721	53513	53781	98941	38401	70939	11319
76878	34727	12524	90642	16921	13669	17420	84483	68309	85241
87394	78884	87237	92086	95633	66841	22906	64989	86952	54700
74040	12731	59616	33697	12592	44891	67982	72972	89795	10587
47896	41413	66431	70046	50793	45920	96564	67958	56369	44725
87778	71697	64148	54363	92114	34037	59061	62051	62049	33526
96977	63143	72219	80040	11990	47698	95621	72990	29047	85893
43820	13285	77811	81697	29937	70750	02029	32377	00556	86687
57203	83960	40096	39234	65953	59911	91411	55573	88427	45573
49065	72171	80939	06017	90323	63687	07932	99587	49014	26452
94250	84270	95798	13477	80139	26335	55169	73417	40766	45170
68148	81382	82383	18674	40453	92828	30042	37412	43423	45138
12208	97809	33619	28868	41646	16734	88860	32636	41985	84615
88317	89705	26119	12416	19438	65665	60989	59766	11418	18250
56728	80359	29613	63052	15251	44684	64681	42354	51029	77680
07138	12320	01073	19304	87042	58920	28454	81069	93978	66659
21188	64554	55618	36088	24331	84390	16022	12200	77559	75661
02154	12250	88738	43917	03655	21099	60805	63246	26842	35816
90953	85238	32771	07305	36181	47420	19681	33184	41386	03249
80103	91308	12858	41293	00325	15013	19579	91132	12720	92603

2500 FIVE DIGIT RANDOM NUMBERS

92630	78240	19267	95457	53497	23894	37708	79862	76471	66418
79445	78735	71549	44843	26104	67318	00701	34986	66751	99723
59654	71966	27386	50004	05358	94031	29281	18544	52429	06080
31524	49587	76612	39789	13537	48086	59483	60680	84675	53014
06348	76938	90379	51392	55887	71015	09209	79157	24440	30244
28703	51709	94456	48396	73780	06436	86641	69239	57662	80181
68108	89266	94730	95761	75023	48464	65544	96583	18911	16391
99938	90704	93621	66330	33393	95261	95349	51769	91616	33238
91543	73196	34449	63513	83834	99411	58826	40456	69268	48562
42103	02781	73920	56297	72678	12249	25270	36678	21313	75767
17138	27584	25296	28387	51350	61664	37893	05363	44143	42677
28297	14280	54524	21618	95320	38174	60579	08089	94999	78460
09331	56712	51333	06289	75345	08811	82711	57392	25252	30333
31295	04204	93712	51287	05754	79396	87399	51773	33075	97061
36146	15560	27592	42089	99281	59640	15221	96079	09961	05371
29553	18432	13630	05529	02791	81017	49027	79031	50912	09399
23501	22642	63081	08191	89420	67800	55137	54707	32945	64522
57888	85846	67967	07835	11314	01545	48535	17142	08552	67457
55336	71264	88472	04334	63919	36394	11196	92470	70543	29776
10087	10072	55980	64688	68239	20461	89381	93809	00796	95945
34101	81277	66090	88872	37818	72142	67140	50785	21380	16703
53362	44940	60430	22834	14130	96593	23298	56203	92671	15925
82975	66158	84731	19436	55790	69229	28661	13675	99318	76873
54827	84673	22898	08094	14326	87038	42892	21127	30712	48489
25464	59098	27436	89421	80754	89924	19097	67737	80368	08795
67609	60214	41475	84950	40133	02546	09570	45682	50165	15609
44921	70924	61295	51137	47596	86735	35561	76649	18217	63446
33170	30972	98130	95828	49786	13301	36081	80761	33985	68621
84687	85445	06208	17654	51333	02878	35010	67578	61574	20749
71886	56450	36567	09395	96951	35507	17555	35212	69106	01679
00475	02224	74722	14721	40215	21351	08596	45625	83981	63748
25993	38881	68361	59560	41274	69742	40703	37993	03435	18873
92882	53178	99195	93803	56985	53089	15305	50522	55900	43026
25138	26810	07093	15677	60688	04410	24505	37890	67186	62829
84631	71882	12991	83028	82484	90339	91950	74579	03539	90122
34003	92326	12793	61453	48121	74271	28363	66561	75220	35908
53775	45749	05734	86169	42762	70175	97310	73894	88606	19994
59316	97885	72807	54966	60859	11932	35265	71601	55577	67715
20479	66557	50705	26999	09854	52591	14063	30214	19890	19292
86180	84931	25455	26044	02227	52015	21820	50599	51671	65411
21451	68001	72710	40261	61281	13172	63819	48970	51732	54113
98062	68375	80089	24135	72355	95428	11808	29740	81644	86610
01788	64429	14430	94575	75153	94576	61393	96192	03227	32258
62465	04841	43272	68702	01274	05437	22953	18946	99053	41690
94324	31089	84159	92933	99989	89500	91586	02802	69471	68274
05797	43984	21575	09908	70221	19791	51578	36432	33494	79888
10395	14289	52185	09721	25789	38562	54794	04897	59012	89251
35177	56986	25549	59730	64718	52630	31100	62384	49483	11409
25633	89619	75882	98256	02126	72099	57183	55887	09320	73463
16464	48280	94254	45777	45150	68865	11382	11782	22695	41988

The High School Tutors

  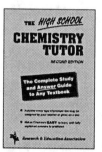  

The **HIGH SCHOOL TUTORS** series is based on the same principle as the more comprehensive **PROBLEM SOLVERS**, but is specifically designed to meet the needs of high school students. REA has recently revised all the books in this series to include expanded review sections, new material, and newly-designed covers. This makes the books even more effective in helping students to cope with these difficult high school subjects.

If you would like more information about any of these books,
complete the coupon below and return it to us or go to your local bookstore.

RESEARCH & EDUCATION ASSOCIATION
61 Ethel Road W. • Piscataway, New Jersey 08854
Phone: (908) 819-8880

Please send me more information about your High School Tutor books.

Name _____

Address _____

City _____ State _____ Zip _____

"The ESSENTIALS" of Math & Science

Each book in the ESSENTIALS series offers all essential information of the field it covers. It summarizes what every textbook in the particular field must include, and is designed to help students in preparing for exams and doing homework. The ESSENTIALS are excellent supplements to any class text.

The ESSENTIALS are complete and concise with quick access to needed information. They serve as a handy reference source at all times. The ESSENTIALS are prepared with REA's customary concern for high professional quality and student needs.

Available in the following titles:

Advanced Calculus I & II
Algebra & Trigonometry I & II
Anatomy & Physiology
Anthropology
Astronomy
Automatic Control Systems /
   Robotics I & II
Biology I & II
Boolean Algebra
Calculus I, II & III
Chemistry
Complex Variables I & II
Data Structures I & II
Differential Equations I & II
Electric Circuits I & II
Electromagnetics I & II

Electronics I & II
Electronic
   Communications I & II
Finite & Discrete Math
Fluid Mechanics /
   Dynamics I & II
Fourier Analysis
Geometry I & II
Group Theory I & II
Heat Transfer I & II
LaPlace Transforms
Linear Algebra
Math for Engineers I & II
Mechanics I, II & III
Microbiology
Modern Algebra

Numerical Analysis I & II
Organic Chemistry I & II
Physical Chemistry I & II
Physics I & II
Pre-Calculus
Probability
Psychology I & II
Real Variables
Set Theory
Statistics I & II
Strength of Materials &
   Mechanics of Solids I & II
Thermodynamics I & II
Topology
Transport Phenomena I & II
Vector Analysis

If you would like more information about any of these books,
complete the coupon below and return it to us or go to your local bookstore.

RESEARCH & EDUCATION ASSOCIATION
61 Ethel Road W. • Piscataway, New Jersey 08854
Phone: (908) 819-8880

Please send me more information about your Math & Science Essentials Books

Name _____

Address _____

City _____ State _____ Zip _____

REA's **Problem Solvers**

The "PROBLEM SOLVERS" are comprehensive supplemental text-books designed to save time in finding solutions to problems. Each "PROBLEM SOLVER" is the first of its kind ever produced in its field. It is the product of a massive effort to illustrate almost any imaginable problem in exceptional depth, detail, and clarity. Each problem is worked out in detail with a step-by-step solution, and the problems are arranged in order of complexity from elementary to advanced. Each book is fully indexed for locating problems rapidly.

ACCOUNTING
ADVANCED CALCULUS
ALGEBRA & TRIGONOMETRY
AUTOMATIC CONTROL
   SYSTEMS/ROBOTICS
BIOLOGY
BUSINESS, ACCOUNTING, & FINANCE
CALCULUS
CHEMISTRY
COMPLEX VARIABLES
COMPUTER SCIENCE
DIFFERENTIAL EQUATIONS
ECONOMICS
ELECTRICAL MACHINES
ELECTRIC CIRCUITS
ELECTROMAGNETICS
ELECTRONIC COMMUNICATIONS
ELECTRONICS
FINITE & DISCRETE MATH
FLUID MECHANICS/DYNAMICS
GENETICS
GEOMETRY

HEAT TRANSFER
LINEAR ALGEBRA
MACHINE DESIGN
MATHEMATICS for ENGINEERS
MECHANICS
NUMERICAL ANALYSIS
OPERATIONS RESEARCH
OPTICS
ORGANIC CHEMISTRY
PHYSICAL CHEMISTRY
PHYSICS
PRE-CALCULUS
PROBABILITY
PSYCHOLOGY
STATISTICS
STRENGTH OF MATERIALS &
   MECHANICS OF SOLIDS
TECHNICAL DESIGN GRAPHICS
THERMODYNAMICS
TOPOLOGY
TRANSPORT PHENOMENA
VECTOR ANALYSIS

If you would like more information about any of these books,
complete the coupon below and return it to us or visit your local bookstore.

RESEARCH & EDUCATION ASSOCIATION
61 Ethel Road W. • Piscataway, New Jersey 08854
Phone: (908) 819-8880

Please send me more information about your Problem Solver Books

Name _____

Address _____

City _____ State _____ Zip _____

MAXnotes®

REA's Literature Study Guides

MAXnotes® are student-friendly. They offer a fresh look at masterpieces of literature, presented in a lively and interesting fashion. **MAXnotes®** offer the essentials of what you should know about the work, including outlines, explanations and discussions of the plot, character lists, analyses, and historical context. **MAXnotes®** are designed to help you think independently about literary works by raising various issues and thought-provoking ideas and questions. Written by literary experts who currently teach the subject, **MAXnotes®** enhance your understanding and enjoyment of the work.

Available **MAXnotes®** include the following:

Absalom, Absalom!
The Aeneid of Virgil
Animal Farm
Antony and Cleopatra
As I Lay Dying
As You Like It
The Autobiography of
    Malcolm X
The Awakening
Beloved
Beowulf
Billy Budd
The Bluest Eye, A Novel
Brave New World
The Canterbury Tales
The Catcher in the Rye
The Color Purple
The Crucible
Death in Venice
Death of a Salesman
The Divine Comedy I: Inferno
Dubliners
Emma
Euripedes' Electra & Medea
Frankenstein
Gone with the Wind
The Grapes of Wrath
Great Expectations
The Great Gatsby
Gulliver's Travels
Hamlet
Hard Times

Heart of Darkness
Henry IV, Part I
Henry V
The House on Mango Street
Huckleberry Finn
I Know Why the Caged
    Bird Sings
The Iliad
Invisible Man
Jane Eyre
Jazz
The Joy Luck Club
Jude the Obscure
Julius Caesar
King Lear
Les Misérables
Lord of the Flies
Macbeth
The Merchant of Venice
The Metamorphoses of Ovid
The Metamorphosis
Middlemarch
A Midsummer Night's Dream
Moby-Dick
Moll Flanders
Mrs. Dalloway
Much Ado About Nothing
My Antonia
Native Son
1984
The Odyssey
Oedipus Trilogy

Of Mice and Men
On the Road
Othello
Paradise Lost
A Passage to India
Plato's Republic
Portrait of a Lady
A Portrait of the Artist
    as a Young Man
Pride and Prejudice
A Raisin in the Sun
Richard II
Romeo and Juliet
The Scarlet Letter
Sir Gawain and the
    Green Knight
Slaughterhouse-Five
Song of Solomon
The Sound and the Fury
The Stranger
The Sun Also Rises
A Tale of Two Cities
Taming of the Shrew
The Tempest
Tess of the D'Urbervilles
Their Eyes Were Watching God
To Kill a Mockingbird
To the Lighthouse
Twelfth Night
Uncle Tom's Cabin
Waiting for Godot
Wuthering Heights

RESEARCH & EDUCATION ASSOCIATION
61 Ethel Road W. • Piscataway, New Jersey 08854
Phone: (908) 819-8880

Please send me more information about MAXnotes®.

Name _____

Address _____

City _____ State _____ Zip _____